Saving Buddhism

Southeast Asia

POLITICS, MEANING, AND MEMORY

David Chandler and Rita Smith Kipp

SERIES EDITORS

Saving Buddhism

The Impermanence of Religion

in Colonial Burma

ALICIA TURNER

UNIVERSITY OF HAWAI'I PRESS   *Honolulu*

Paperback Edition 2017

Printed in the United States of America

22 21 20 19 18 17   6 5 4 3 2 1

Library of Congress Cataloging-in-Publication Data
Turner, Alicia Marie, author.
    Saving Buddhism : the impermanence of religion in colonial Burma / Alicia Turner.
        pages   cm
    Includes bibliographical references and index.
    ISBN 978-0-8248-3937-6 (alk. paper)
        1. Buddhism and politics—Burma—History—19th century.   2. Buddhism and politics—Burma—
History—20th century.   3. Burma—Politics and government—1824–1948.   4. Group identity—
Burma—History.   I. Title.
    BQ436.T87   2014
    294.309591—dc23

                                                                    2014021614

ISBN 978-0-8248-7286-1 (pbk.)

An earlier version of a portion of Chapter 3 appeared as Alicia Turner, "Religion Making and Its
Failures: Turning Monasteries into Schools and Buddhism into a Religion in Colonial Burma,"
chapter 11 of *Secularism and Religion Making* (pp. 226–42), edited by Markus Dressler and
Arvind Mandair (2011). By permission of Oxford University Press.

University of Hawai'i Press books are printed on acid-free paper and meet the guidelines for
permanence and durability of the Council on Library Resources.

Series design by Rich Hendel

CONTENTS

ACKNOWLEDGMENTS

Many people aided me in my obsessions with the records of Buddhist lay associations, colonial newspapers, and subscription lists that lie at the heart of this book. Their indulgence and their growing interest made the project possible, and it is a debt that I will never be able to fully repay. All of these interactions offered further inspiration as well: as I described my research and the sources I sought, I would hear a frequent refrain that, while what I was working on was very interesting, it wasn't *really* Buddhism. My research did not involve meditation, philosophy, monastic history, or even daily Buddhist practice that these friends in Myanmar and some colleagues and students in North America considered to constitute *real* Buddhism. In hearing this response so often I became convinced that there was something interesting and important in the practical work of defining Buddhism—in colonial Burma as much as today. This, together with an insight that the questions about the category of religion that are currently debated by scholars are not so different from what was being worked out on the ground by Burmese and British at the turn of the twentieth century, set this book project in motion.

I want to express my gratitude to all those listed here and others too numerous to mention. U Maung Maung Thein and Ko Nyi Nyi Aung, who at the time of my research were both at the Microfilm Department of Universities Central Library, Yangon University, deserve my first thanks because they helped me find and examine the masses of Buddhist journals and newspapers that are at the core of this book. I will always be in their debt, not just for their expertise as librarians and patience as teachers, but for their friendship and the hours of laughter spent at the tea shop.

Many other individuals and institutions in Myanmar graciously gave me access to their precious research materials. My thanks to the staff of Universities Central Library, Universities Historical Research Centre, the National Archives of Myanmar, the Library of Archives of Buddhism at the Shwedagon Pagoda, and the Library of the Ministry of Religious Affairs at the Kaba Aye Pagoda. Dr. Myo Myint, U Thaw Kaung, Dr. Thant Thaw Kaung, Daw Tin Phone Nwe, Sitagu Sayadaw, U Aung Myo, Ludu Daw Ahmar and her family, and U Maung Maung Gyi were more than generous with their knowledge and assistance with research in Myanmar.

The booksellers of Pansodan Street helped in a pinch with an ability to find the most obscure materials. Numerous Buddhist associations and individuals generously allowed me access to their records and private libraries. Beyond Myanmar, the India Records Office of the British Library and the collections of Northern Illinois University, the University of Chicago, and Cornell University libraries were vital to my research. I owe particular thanks to the staff of York University Library's Interlibrary Loan Department, who were not only willing to learn about Burmese colonial sources, but were unrelenting in finding copies from libraries around the world.

My research was funded by a Fulbright-Hays Fellowship from the U.S. Department of Education, the Divinity School and the Committee on Southern Asian Studies at the University of Chicago, York University Internal Research Grants, and the Canadian Social Sciences and Humanities Research Council Small Grants. I would like to offer my thanks for the financial support offered by these institutions. I presented portions of the chapters at Cornell University, Harvard University, McMaster University, the University of Toronto, Kalamazoo College, and to a particularly engaging group of graduate students at the University of California, Berkeley. The feedback from these audiences and their insightful questions made the book richer. I originally presented portions of Chapter 3 at a conference organized on "The Politics of Religion-Making" and this earlier version subsequently appeared as "Religion Making and Its Failures: Turning Monasteries into Schools and Buddhism into a Religion in Colonial Burma" in *Secularism and Religion Making,* ed. Markus Dressler and Arvind Mandair (New York: Oxford University Press, 2011), 226–42. The insights from the conference participants came to shape my thinking in key ways. I would like to thank the organizers and Oxford University Press for allowing me to reuse the material.

Starting from my time in Yangon, a collection of intellectuals and scholars grew to form an invaluable cadre of colleagues and friends who have made Burma studies such a welcoming home. Nance Cunningham and Aung Soe Min are organic intellectuals and facilitators of the highest caliber, offering hours of fascinating conversation and advice on the logistics of research in Burma that made my work possible and my time there much richer. They opened up not just their home and their informal intellectual salon, but also their amazing personal collection of old books and journals. Aurore Candier and I sat side by side at microfilm readers in 2005, sharing the joys and troubles of research. Francois Tanturnier shared not just his friendship on three continents but his flat in Yangon and the aid of the Inya Institute. Erik Braun offered long and fruitful discussions about Buddhism in colonial Burma and shared his own research. Patrick Pranke has patiently led me through the implications of royal and monastic debates at the turn of the nineteenth century and shared the wealth of his insights into Burmese Buddhist history. Alexey Kirichenko offered not only careful commentary on earlier drafts and his unsurpassed knowledge of precolonial Burmese sources but an ongoing animated conversation about the study of Burmese history. Michael Charney, Atsuko Naono, Ian Brown, Chie Ikeya, Christian Lammerts, Christoph Emmrich, Patrick McCormick, Niklas Foxeus, and Charlie Carstens all offered support and friendship that aided the project in numerous ways. Maung Zeyya's work and discussions helped me to understand the figures at work in this book and their interactions. Bo Bo Lasin has become an invaluable ally for locating and interpreting Burmese sources from almost any period and helped me find and translate hidden gems in early Burmese newspapers. Chris Clark did wonderful work transliterating and proofing bibliographic entries.

Thomas Patton was not just a champion of this book in its early drafts, but offered wonderful feedback on chapters. Lilian Handlin offered a careful read of the manuscript and many long hours of witty conversation. Together these two gave perhaps the most generous help with completing the manuscript—they took over duties at *The Journal of Burma Studies* at a key juncture to let me write, safe in the knowledge that the *Journal* was in good hands. Together with Catherine Raymond and Beth Bjorneby of the Center for Burma Studies, they have provided invaluable support to my research and the work of forwarding Burma studies as a field.

Penny Edwards provided both inspiration and encouragement at a critical juncture that helped me develop my claims with confidence and move the project forward to publication. Anne Hansen's careful and generous reading helped me to clarify the argument and make it a much more accessible book. My thanks as well to Justin McDaniel, Anne Blackburn, Patrick Pranke, and Maitrii Aung-Thwin for their insightful and encouraging feedback on the manuscript at a late stage. Laurence Cox and Brian Bocking have both been encouraging and endlessly patient with the time this book has taken from our collaborative endeavors. Starting from our days in Chicago, Erik Davis and Thomas Borchert have become close and trusted colleagues—always willing to let me try out an argument and offering critical feedback. My thanks go to both of them for the wonderful ongoing conversations.

My colleagues at York University offered boundless support—my thanks to Patrick Taylor, Becky Lee, Amila Buturovic, Selma Zecevic, Susan

Henders, and Alicia Filipowich. Thomas Cohen gave me many long hours of his careful eye, reading each of the chapters and offering detailed suggestions on writing and argumentation. Much of the clarity and some of the witty turns of phrase in these pages are the result of his patience and generosity. Sarah Blake not only read the chapters and offered suggestions, but provided the sanity of friendship and counsel from a fellow traveler on the tenure track.

I have had the privilege of wonderful mentors and teachers over the years. U Saw Tun was my first Burmese teacher and remains a source I turn to for advice. Daw Than Than Win taught me the joys of Burmese language and proved that laughter is often the best pedagogical approach. John Okell not only taught me about Burmese language and culture, he and Sue Okell opened their home to Michelle and me to make my research in London possible and became cherished friends. Carol Anderson, who first inspired my interest in a critical study of Buddhism, and Annie McCombs have offered generous advice over the years as mentors and friends.

Bruce Lincoln's critical eye for religious discourses and his own scholarship are a continuing inspiration. His incisive questions at crucial junctures helped me improve my own thinking and the argument presented here. Steven Collins remains a valued guide and mentor, keeping me honest by asking tough questions of my evidence and providing a model of the best in scholarship on Buddhism.

I want to thank, as well, David Chandler and Rita Smith Kipp, the series editors, for their support for the book, and Pamela Kelley from University of Hawai'i Press for her expert editorial hand. Virginia Perrin and John Donohue served as expert copyeditors, an art too long underappreciated for its power to transform a manuscript full of infelicities and inconsistencies into a polished publication. It goes without saying that any mistakes in this book are my own and likely the result of not sufficiently heeding the counsel of all of those mentioned above.

Finally, in countless ways, this book would not have been possible without the endless support of my family. My mother, Molly Turner, always appeared with pragmatic support and chocolate to make the writing easier, as well as boundless love, joy, and wise words. My father, Arthur Turner, joined me in London during my research to offer a needed break and offered practical help with computers and cameras. He and his wife, Johncie, together offered encouragement in the later stages. My brother, Geoff Turner, was a constant source of camaraderie and support, ranging from technical help digitizing books to making sure my house did not fall down around me. My stepsons, Chad (and his wife Mariah), Kyle, and Brent Hubert generously made me part of their lives and reminded me that there is a world outside of old books and newspapers. My partner, Michelle Hubert, has been throughout my greatest encouragement and best friend. Words can never express my gratitude to her for her love, support, and endurance.

NOTE ON TRANSLITERATION

Throughout this book I have used the colonial-era transcriptions of Burmese names and terms that reflect the most common usage of that time. This includes the name "Burma" to refer to the colonial province.[1] Despite multiple attempts at standardization, much Burmese transcription was done on an ad hoc basis in the colonial period.[2] For consistency, I have used the most common forms of the time for personal and place names, names of organizations, and key terms. In some cases this means I have used the less linguistically precise but more common transcriptions, such as "sayadaw" rather than "hsayadaw." In cases where multiple transcriptions of the same name or term were in use, I list the alternatives in the footnotes.

In the endnote citations and bibliographic entries, I have used the Okell method of transliteration that preserves the spelling and tonal marks of Burmese script for the titles of articles, books, journals, and publishers.[3] The transcriptions of the titles of works referred to in the body of the book are included in brackets in these citations. For ease of reference, if the author of the cited text is mentioned in the prose with a standard roman rendering, this transcription of the name appears in the bibliography.

Passages in Pali are transliterated according to Pali Text Society conventions. However, individual terms originating in Pali and adopted into Burmese names appear in Burmese form. Thus, I have opted for the Pali "*sāsana*" when discussing the general concept, but the Burmese "thathana" when referring to particular Burmese organizations and names, unless the original transcribed it otherwise (i.e., Buddha Thathana Noggaha Anglo-vernacular School, but the Sasanadara Society).

1

Introduction

In the decades after the fall of the monarchy to the British in 1885, Burmese felt the ground shifting under their feet. Everywhere they turned, their colonial condition seemed to be characterized by decline. Knowledge of the Buddha's teachings was slipping away before their eyes. Boys no longer learned the basics. They abandoned studying in the monasteries to attend government schools in hopes of a lucrative career as a clerk. The monks no longer held the same respect. Some were lax in their practices, but the authority of even the most esteemed appeared to wane in the face of a new set of experts: those trained in the bureaucratic sciences of colonial rule. Precepts that had guided moral life were ignored. Burmese were drinking and gambling, precipitating a crisis of morals. Dress, comportment, manners, respect for elders—examined in the light of this moment, all offered up evidence to confirm the uneasy feeling that their world was sliding into decay.

British colonial rule had come in three stages over the past six decades, taking over territories in the extreme southeast and southwest in 1826 and the southern half to create British Lower Burma in 1852. The loss of the Buddhist monarchy in Mandalay in 1885, however, marked an epochal change, ending the lineage of royal Buddhist patronage and creating new fears for the future of Buddhism. All of Burma now became part of British India, under imperial rule from a Christian queen far away.

Burmese Buddhists read the political and social changes between 1890 and 1920 as signs that the Buddha's *sāsana* was deteriorating. The *sāsana* is the life of the Buddha's teachings after he is gone; it is the condition of possibility for making merit and liberation. Like everything else in the Buddhist worldview, the teachings themselves are impermanent. The *sāsana* is in inevitable decline from the moment of the Buddha's enlightenment, eventually disappearing completely in preparation for the next Buddha. The dramatic changes of the late nineteenth century made sense in the longer arc of the *sāsana* in decline. At the same time however, local histories have long asserted that the *sāsana* is subject to temporary protection and flourishing in places of active patronage and support. In this sense, the signs of decline highlighted points of intervention where Buddhists could band together to slow its deterioration. Burmese reimagined themselves as protectors of Buddhism and organized to preserve the *sāsana*. They set out to save Buddhism, but brought about much more: Burmese Buddhists took advantage of the indeterminacy of the moment to challenge the colonial frameworks that were coming to shape their world.

Although insurgencies against the British had mobilized disparate groups on the fringes, this movement was the first to organize masses throughout Burma. The need to stem the decline of Buddhism brought waves of Buddhist publishing, preaching, and organizing, and led Buddhist laypeople in towns across Burma to found hundreds of associations. From drives for vegetarianism and campaigns to curtail lavish spending on rituals to efforts to teach morals to schoolboys and prisoners, Buddhist associations rallied the Burmese to address the problems they read in their colonial condition. They carried out programs for educational, moral, and religious reform with the idea that a renewed enthusiasm and devotion among Buddhists could counter the erosion of the Buddha's *sāsana*. New Buddhist organizations gathered thousands into their projects to found schools, publish journals, and sponsor examinations. Coming together in this mission to preserve the *sāsana* engendered a sense of common purpose and belonging.

In the wake of the loss of the monarchy and the declining authority of the sangha, Buddhist laypeople responded to the new colonial configurations with Buddhist innovations. They embraced new technologies to achieve old ends, negotiating categories set in flux by colonial disjunctures. The emerging colonial frameworks meant that Buddhists had to bend old ideas to new purposes. In effect, these associations and their project of preserving the Buddha's *sāsana* reimagined Burmese identity. Out of the dissonance between goals of the colonial state and the Buddhist worldview that gave meaning to their efforts, they forged powerful new modes of mobilization and identity. The voluntary association, with membership dues, subscription journals, and an army of vice-presidents and recording secretaries, became a technology for rethinking identity and the relation of Buddhist laypeople to the problems in their world. The associations offered something more than simply bureaucratic structure. Their efforts forged a "moral community" out of a collective ethical project that oriented Burmese in Buddhist history and defined the importance of their actions in a changing world.

This book explores how a Buddhist framework for understanding the colonial condition enabled Burmese Buddhists in the decades surrounding the turn of the twentieth century to contest colonial categories that impinged on their lives and, ultimately, to renegotiate the terms of colonialism. It details the local conflicts and confrontations in which Burmese chose to engage and analyzes the ways in which these Buddhist bricoleurs brought together divergent aspects of Buddhist discourse and colonial innovations to create new means of understanding themselves individually and collectively. The Buddhist lay associations in Burma from 1890 to 1920, their campaigns for Buddhist education and moral reform, and their conflicts with the colonial state reveal the shifting nature of three formative discourses in this period: the concept of *sāsana,* collective belonging organized through moral community, and the category of religion. The layers of Buddhist history that emerge challenge us to see multiple modes of identity in colonial modernity and offer insights into the instabilities of categories we, as scholars, take for granted.

A slippage in translation, at times a powerful misreading—between Burmese *sāsana* and English religion or between the goals of the colonial state and the need to preserve the Buddha's teachings—animated the changes of this period and created spaces for adaptation and innovation. In the process, Burmese brought together as a moral community in the indeterminacy of the colonial moment came to subtly transform their world. Yet, the problems of translation between conceptual frameworks that produced hybrids in colonial Burma pose an equal challenge for understanding the changes that occurred. The transformations at work will not easily fit into a framework of analysis that seeks to explain the world in terms of nation, the role of religion in colonialism, or the creation of a modern Buddhism, without obscuring the multiplicity and depth of the Buddhist discourses at work.

In exploring the development of moral community, this book seeks to open up the concept of identity, moving the focus beyond the nation. Buddhist organizing in colonial Southeast Asian contexts has too often been read to shed light on the early history of nationalism, with scholars repeating mid-twentieth-century nationalists' claims that these movements were simply an outlet for political expression repressed by the colonial state. Such studies trace the roots of Buddhist identity in the colonial period in order to understand the role of Buddhist nationalism in contemporary political repression or ethnic conflict. Instead, I seek to take seriously the ways in which Buddhist discourse shaped a sense of collective belonging distinct from nation.

For all it has been critiqued as a mode of imagining in Southeast Asian studies, the story of the nation or the unfolding of a singular vision of modernity has come to reside not only in the nationalist texts we study, but in many assumptions that frame scholarly readings of this period. Too often, as Prasenjit Duara has warned, we accept the nation as the subject of our histories, or similarly assign to Buddhism or religion an analytical coherence disconsonant with the historical materials we seek to understand.[1] Concepts of nation, modernity, and even religion prove ineffective as analytical lenses because, as we forget, they were themselves active points of contention at the time, places where various forms of colonial politics were worked out. These frameworks obscure the multiple and complex forms of identity at work. As much as the unconscious assumption of these categories blinds research to multiple discourses of identity historically, it works to silence alternative voices in the present.

Understanding Burmese colonial history demands a more challenging frame of reference that broadens the analysis. Shifting the focus onto the dynamics of *sāsana* as a manner of seeing the world reveals the diverse modes of belonging at work in colonial Burma and offers insights into our own analytical categories. The worldview and inner workings of *sāsana* stand as one alternative framework that oriented Burmese in the colonial world. In this light, the nation was not an inevitable outcome of these confrontations, nor did colonialism and modernity exert singular or absolute agency. Burmese history, it turns out, was more complex; groups of Burmese collectively constituted themselves and their world in multiple ways. The moral community that the concern for the *sāsana* forged grew from distinct metaphysics and sets of goals. Focusing on its logic reveals modes of mobilization and collective belonging that continue to operate in Burmese life, seen momentously in the streets during the 2007 Saffron Revolution, and more recently in the devastating anti-Muslim campaigns. Just as importantly, shifting our focus in this way reveals the indeterminacy of our own categories. Concepts that we take for granted were fluid, undergoing a process of definition and redefinition through the colonial encounter.

An approach that seeks to explore these alternative forms must be sensitive to where the discourses of identity diverge from the worldview of nation or modernity to operate on other internal dynamics. To comprehend these other trajectories requires an ability to think in other frames of reference, ones that may challenge and broaden our analysis. I seek to explore the worldview and inner workings of the discourse of *sāsana* as one alternative to the logics of nationalism and colonial modernity. There were certainly others. To be attentive to the workings of *sāsana* as a mode of seeing the world particularizes the universalist narratives of nation and fixed concepts of colonial modernity, allowing us to look at the diversity of human modes of identity and belonging. Understanding the Buddhist movements in their terms and internal logic offers an opportunity to see the confrontations and transformations of the colonial period in a way that does not render the nation as the only or the inevitable outcome and does not cede agency to a singular and external force of colonialism or modernity. It allows for a different purchase on Burmese history that offers a more complex understanding of how groups of Burmese have collectively constituted themselves and their world.

THREE DISCOURSES

This book traces three discourses set in motion by the colonial encounter: the evolving understanding of *sāsana* as an orienting framework for change, the adaptive modes of identity made possible in the moral community, and the ongoing definition of religion as a site of conflict and negotiation of autonomy. The colonial encounter led Buddhists to reshape how they understood *sāsana,* how they understood themselves, and how they understood the idea of religion and its place in society. The dynamics of the colonial period become apparent by observing the flux of these three discourses. The work of fashioning each of these sets of ideas animated the interactions and clashes across the colonial divide and produced the conditions for twentieth-century developments. This book charts the flows in each of these three discourses set in motion by the colonial encounter as Buddhists came to reshape their world.

Sāsana

The work of the Buddhist movements in colonial Burma reveals a concept of *sāsana* that was both dynamic and multivalent. To focus on *sāsana* as key for this period puts the emphasis on long-standing local discourses. The Buddhist lay associations and their movements were an instance of *sāsana* reform, that is, part of a process of continual redefinition of what it meant to be Buddhist driven by the discourse of the decline of *sāsana*. The discourse of the decline and the possibility of preservation offered a means for lay Buddhists to make intelligible the changes brought by colonial rule and allowed them to actively intervene. In this sense, *sāsana* was both the means and the product of a continuing process of reform and reimagining.

The concept of *sāsana* served as much as a resource for innovation as an orienting frame. The changes of this period were part of a longer history of reform in Southeast Asian Buddhism—a process of continual redefinition carried out in royal and monastic initiatives. Studies of *sāsana* reform in the seventeenth and eighteenth centuries in Southeast Asia and Sri Lanka have demonstrated how new textual genres, reading practices, and sangha organization drove new inflections of orthodoxy. Anne Blackburn's work on Sri Lankan textual communities is key to this analysis, joined by critical studies of the creation of the Thudhamma lineage in Burma and the Thammayut in Siam.[2] Out of these studies of reform, scholars have come to understand Buddhist discourses not as means to produce or reproduce tradition, but as living and continually redefined orthodoxies. *Sāsana* reform continued into the colonial period in Burma, taking on the technologies of voluntary subscription associations, printed texts, and the creation of schools to achieve parallel goals. Placed in the context of previous reforms, the Buddhist lay movements were part of the continuing transformation of tradition. A continuity of change comes to the fore, revealing a tradition of reform that developed Buddhist discourses as engines of dynamic adaptation. The colonial discourse of the decline of the *sāsana* in Burma and a moral community forged for its protection was one instance of this tradition of reform. Bridging the histories of earlier monastic and royal reforms and the diversity of contemporary Buddhist modernities, the work of the lay Buddhist associations at the turn of the twentieth century came to realign the meaning of *sāsana* even as the need for its preservation mobilized the moral community.

A previous generation of scholarship approached colonialism as a disruption in Buddhist history, proposing a model of Protestant Buddhism that interpreted colonialism as a break in a posited static Buddhist tradition.[3] Blackburn has critiqued this approach, warning that it "appropriated tropes such as decline and revival . . . coming to see these as straight forward descriptions of recurrent trends in Buddhist societies" rather than conventions of representation that were used to promote specific kinds of change.[4] By reproducing these tropes as a description of Buddhist history, rather than active rhetorical strategies, studies of Protestant Buddhism were unable to account for the dynamic continuities and changes at work. Likewise, Blackburn is critical of approaches to Buddhism and colonialism that "assume that the weight of British colonial domination, with its forms of knowledge and technologies, ruptured long-standing social logics, power relations and sources of intellectual and psychological comfort and stability."[5] This book's focus on local discourse and categories for understanding change offers an ability to see Burmese agency distinct from its relation to colonial power. Many of the challenges facing Burmese in this period were not external confrontations with colonial power, but instead challenges internal to the Buddhist community and negotiations of existing social and political relations. Colonialism is ever present in this moment, inflecting the questions and changes, but Buddhists' positions were formulated in relation to a combination of long-standing local dynamics and new colonial conditions. Starting from an analysis of narratives of the decline of *sāsana* in Burmese history, this book builds a foundation in this longer local logic to understand the interactions of the colonial period.

Identity

In a similar way, this study is not framed by the question of Buddhism's relation to modernity. As Thomas Borchert explains, modern Buddhism, assumed to have its origins in the changes of this period, has long been understood to be characterized by a number of specific trends: focus on scriptural text, "rationalization of cosmology and superstition," increased authority of the laity, and new roles for women. Borchert, noting how limited these cases are in describing the breadth of twentieth-century Buddhism, suggests instead that it is not simply the particular "practices or discourses that are new as a result of modernity that we must pay attention to, but also the ways in which being human and being a member of a particular community have changed within an altered set of social conditions (conditions in which modernity provides the vocabulary of legitimacy)."[6] In a similar sense, Anne Hansen has argued that at the core, Buddhist changes in colonial Cambodia were changes in subjectivity and ethics.[7] This broader focus on changes in human subjectivity and collective belonging has much more relevance for the history of Buddhist movements in Burma at the turn of the twentieth century. Transformations in the ways members of the Buddhist associations understood themselves to be Burmese and to be Buddhist were particularly powerful. Their efforts to preserve the *sāsana* came to reshape the concept itself and its framework, offering them new understandings of themselves.

Some of the best and most innovative work in Southeast Asian studies has focused on techniques and technologies for the production of identity. Drawing from roots in Benedict Anderson's analysis of the imagined community, Southeast Asianists have offered insights into the construction of identity out of the interactions of the colonial period.[8] Penny Edwards' work on the development of ideas of Khmer nation and culture, and Thongchai Winichakul's analysis of the developing geo-body of Siam, explore how colonial interaction provided a means of national imagining.[9] They offer genealogies of Khmer and Thai ideas of nation and the colonial technologies that facilitated them. Such studies illuminate the flow of ideas between metropole and colony that made new modes of identity possible out of the intertwined dynamics of colonialism and nationalism. These are astute explorations of the technologies of constituting collective identities out of hybrid colonial projects. This book joins this conversation but seeks to build on their insights in a slightly different vein. Where those studies focus on innovations in the invention of tradition to understand the development of ideas of nation as the dominant discourse of twentieth-century Southeast Asia, the present study explores the transformations of identity as imagined through an older, long-standing discourse of belonging.

As Stephen Berkwitz has described for Sri Lanka, the idea of moral community as a means of constructing Buddhist collective belonging dates back to medieval Pali literature. The moral community allowed Buddhists to envision themselves as beneficiaries of those who had preserved Buddhism in the past and to feel an obligation to continue their work. He explains how a Buddhist *vaṃsa* narrative encouraged listeners to appreciate how the benefits and possibilities of the Buddha's *sāsana* they enjoyed were the result of the sacrifices and devotion of previous generations. The text worked to inculcate a sense of gratitude to those who came before that constructed Buddhists as collective heirs of the past work to promote the *sāsana* and created an obligation to continue the effort for future generations. "By instilling a sense of oneself as a beneficiary of the Buddha's acts, the Sinhala ... work to fashion grateful devotees who understand that helping others and acknowledging the help one has received constitute ethical obligations."[10] If knowledge of the Buddha's teachings was the result of others' past actions, then participation in the continued flourishing of the teachings provided a powerful identity and common purpose, one Berkwitz argues was stronger than regional, family, and caste identities in premodern Sri Lanka.

> Starting with accounts of the bodhisattva, whose selfless actions are said to have been done for the benefit of all beings, through episodes in which the Buddha shows his gratitude to those who assisted him, and up to accounts where later Buddhists enshrine and venerate relics of the Buddha out of joy and gratitude, audiences of Buddhist *vaṃsa*s are repeatedly conditioned to feel grateful for having had their welfare facilitated by others. Thus, having been implicated in the narratives of Buddhist history, contemporary readers and listeners are grouped together into a moral community that shares the distinction of having been acted on by virtuous Buddhist agents in the past.[11]

Just as gratitude for this past action and an ethical obligation to continue the benefits for the future generations bound medieval Sinhala Buddhists together, the concern for the state of the *sāsana* and the obligation to ensure its future bound colonial-era Burmese Buddhists together.

While the connections of moral community tied Buddhists to those who came before, the means of imagining themselves shifted in colonial Burma. The Burmese cultivated a sense of moral community through conversations carried out in the pages of newspapers and in Buddhist journals, tracts, and reports of popular preaching. Buddhist identity came to be shaped by membership organizations and moral reform campaigns. These technologies for organizing and preserving the *sāsana* came with new forms of self-reflection. They produced new ethics and new modes of subjectivity. The discourse of moral community that emerged was flexible enough to offer diverse internal interpretations and bring together broad swaths of the Burmese population, from the educated elite to villagers. The real product of these collective endeavors was not so much resistance to colonialism as a sense of belonging derived from Buddhist discourse. The moral community offered not just an alternative mode of identity and mobilization; it oriented Burmese in a larger history of Buddhist reform and offered a means to negotiate broader shifts in orienting categories.

Religion

In colonial Burma, as elsewhere, "religion" was not a distinct mode of human practice and thought but a powerful taxonomy whose contents and value could be leveraged for a variety of goals. What would count as religion became a site of contention where the relative status of the moral community and its autonomy could be worked out. Like *sāsana* and identity, the colonial category of religion was fluid in this period, coming to be shaped by conflicts and interactions across the colonial divide. Drawing on the work of Talal Asad and Tomoko Masuzawa, who analyze the category of religion as a technique of colonial power—one mode of defining and thus containing and limiting aspects of thought and practice—I am interested in understanding how debates over which aspects of Burmese lives would be considered "religion" invoked politics of colonial authority and autonomy.[12] Religion was not a singular or universal category of human practice, but something particular, historical, changeable, and malleable in its application vis-à-vis a variety of interests.[13]

Despite the common gloss of *sāsana* as religion, the two were distinct, if overlapping, categories operating at the time. Placing the focus on *sāsana* allows us to question religion as a universal comparative frame. Viewed this way, we see that religion as a category was not static but a moving container for a variety of discourses and projects that was itself undergoing continuing redefinition. Setting aside religion as a framework of analysis illuminates how those oriented in the dynamics of *sāsana* engaged the category of religion as a means to contest power and interests.

Religion was central in the colonial encounter as part of the cultural modes of power and hegemony. What stands out in the Burmese case, however, is how the process of defining religion was itself a technique of power. State secularism (noninterference in religious affairs, as it was phrased in British colonial territories) was well-defined official policy and rhetoric that had to be respected in reports to Calcutta or London. On the ground, however, agents of the state were deeply implicated in Buddhist affairs, and it was never exactly clear what fell into the protected category of religion. The colonial state engaged Buddhist discourses and institutions in various ways because Buddhism held a serious appeal for agents tasked with the transformative projects of governmentality: creating educated and disciplined subjects. The ambiguity of the category meant that Burmese Buddhists and colonial actors alike in this period could actively contest "religion" as a means of promoting, resisting, and/or renegotiating the power of the state and the cultural projects of colonialism.

The loss of the Buddhist king in 1885 required rethinking the paradigm for supporting the *sāsana*. The years immediately after the fall of the monarchy show the first attempts to construct a new model for the promotion of the *sāsana*. They also offer a glimpse of Burmese Buddhists' creative responses and the ways in which the concepts of *sāsana,* identity, and religion were set in motion.

THE THATHANABAING ON A STEAMER: A PRELUDE

In February of 1887, a little over a year after the fall of the Burmese monarchy, the Taungdaw Sayadaw, who had been appointed as the Thudhamma Thathanabaing—head of the Thudhamma monastic lineage—by King Thibaw, traveled from Mandalay to Rangoon. He traveled with a retinue of forty-five monks and twenty-seven attendants down the Irrawaddy by riverboat steamer from Mandalay to Prome, and from there to Rangoon by rail. The trip was momentous; the arrival of the Buddhist dignitary in Rangoon was the biggest public event since the British had escorted King Thibaw into exile, and the first time such a large contingent of high-ranking Thudhamma

monks had traveled to the colonial capital. The province had been in turmoil for much of the past year, torn apart by insurgencies fighting against
colonial, non-Buddhist rule and the bloody "pacification" by the colonial
military. In Rangoon the colonial government built a temporary monastery
on the grounds of the Shwedagon Pagoda especially for the visit, a symbolic
balance to the military barracks stationed on the pagoda's hillside. The Thathanabaing was welcomed at a grand reception organized by the Shwedagon
Pagoda trustees, allowing the Buddhists of Lower Burma to pay their re-
spects. Far from a spontaneous outpouring of the local Buddhist community, the financial sponsorship for this merit making came in a grant of five
hundred rupees from the colonial government.[14]

During the visit, the chief commissioner and the Taungdaw Thathanabaing issued two related statements. The first indicated that the "British government recognizes the Thathanabaing as the head of the Buddhist
religion in Lower and Upper Burma and desires to see his authority respected
and supported in all matters concerning the Buddhist religion."[15] As the
chief commissioner explained, the government agreed to this recognition because "much benefit will result from the help which he hopes the Thathanabaing will give in pacifying the country, bringing the people to accept
British rule and convincing them that the British Government in no way
desires to subvert the Buddhist religion."[16] The second, announced by the
Thathanabaing, offered amnesty to all dacoit insurgents who surrendered
by February 16, with a call for peace and equality under the new colonial
state. The visit put a public face on the direct ties between the creation of a
government-recognized religious authority and the end of a bloody insurgency that threatened colonial stability. The colonial government had sought
the Taungdaw Thathanabaing's help in quelling the often monastic-led insurgencies, and he had actively negotiated with the insurgents over the past
year. In exchange, he asked for continued government patronage for Buddhism and a grant of legal authority over the whole of the sangha.

Although the colonial government's recognition was phrased as simply an acknowledgment of an existing status, Alexey Kirichenko has demonstrated it was instead the creation of a new position and new kind of
authority.[17] In the past, the role of Thathanabaing had been much more
limited, with discretion only over the affairs of the Thudhamma lineage
and few actual powers of sanction. There had been a separate royally recognized head of the Shwegyin lineage, and most of the new monastic sects
in Lower Burma had not recognized the Thudhamma Thathanabaing's
authority at all. Yet the growing English-language interpretation of the

Taungdaw Thathanabaing as the singular Buddhist "Archbishop" constructed the power of the position as broad reaching and absolute. In this, the colonial government's recognition was an innovation in Burmese religious authority, carried out as one of the first acts of the new government that claimed a policy of noninterference in religious affairs.

When the Thathanabaing traveled south from Mandalay to Rangoon, he covered the same route as another portentous religious mission three decades earlier. After the defeat in which he lost political control of Lower Burma to the British in 1852, King Mindon sought to assert his legitimacy as a Buddhist monarch. As part of his status as the chief patron of Buddhism for all of Burma, he commissioned a new *htee*, or golden umbrella, to be erected on the top of the Shwedagon Pagoda in Rangoon.[18] The British would not allow him to be physically present for the ceremony, but the symbolic message was clear: the British may have had the military and technological superiority, but King Mindon retained the karmic authority to preserve and promote the Buddha's *sāsana*. Like Mindon's *htee,* the Taungdaw Thathanabaing traveled from the royal, cultural, and monastic center to the new center of cosmopolitan colonial authority—the source of new foreign goods and desires, and the material and political authority of the empire. And, like the golden *htee,* he came on a mission that exploited the ambiguities of political and religious authority.

However, the Thathanabaing arrived to a very different world. Exposure to new ideas and new orientations over the past three decades, as well as the distance from royal authority, had produced movements in Lower Burma that were disconcerting to the Thudhamma monastic authorities of Mandalay. Despite King Mindon's best efforts, it seemed from their perspective that the *sāsana* and respect for the teachings had begun to wane. A number of new monastic sects had formed in Lower Burma outside royal and Thudhamma control. These understood themselves as efforts to return to monastic orthodoxy and to preserve Buddhism under colonial conditions, but they created factions among the laity with fierce public disputes. The Taungdaw Thathanabaing had sent the Thingaza Sayadaw on a mission to British Burma to return the monks and laity to the correct practices, but the problem proved too great. From the Thingaza Sayadaw's perspective, the *sāsana* was already in irreparable decline. In 1885 the Thingaza Sayadaw offered this parable about the future of Buddhism under British rule to Theosophist Col. H. S. Olcott:

> Great Layman, at the beginning of the rainy season, the farmer plows his
> large field and, at the same time, in one small corner he makes a nursery of

small paddy plants. As the rain continues to fall, he anxiously digs drains around his nursery to keep away the water. In ordinary times he can manage to keep his nursery above water, but, in a year of a catastrophic deluge, floods will occur, the young plants in the nursery will die, and after the floods have abated the fields will remain barren because no transplanting can take place. Great Layman, I am the farmer, the monasteries are my nurseries, and Lower Burma is my field. I could have dealt with an ordinary deluge of new ideas but not with a catastrophic flood. Alas, as you have noted, my nurseries are now underwater and I cannot hope to drain it out.[19]

Now with the loss of the king as royal patron, the threat seemed even greater. The arrival of new ideas and practices was an onslaught the *sāsana* would not be able to withstand.

When the British took Lower Burma in 1852, they were content with economic and political control as modes of power. Their main concern was with the spread of European commerce and taxation. However, over the coming decades, colonialism would see an important shift in orientation. John S. Furnivall has argued that around 1870, the British administration in Burma shifted from a laissez-faire approach to one that sought to intervene to improve the welfare of the population.[20] The British colonial administration began to develop an infrastructure to shape the lives of individual Burmese, including social welfare projects in agriculture, sanitation, education, and public health.[21] In Foucaultian terms, the colonial state became engaged in the projects of "governmentality," shaping orderly and self-regulating subjects, ones who would internalize and embody the values of liberal modernity in its colonial modes.[22] It was a massive project, one in which the colonies frequently became a laboratory for projects that would later be tried at home.[23] It required a new machinery for empire. Whereas the military, taxation, and police infrastructure had been sufficient for colonial government in its extractive and repressive roles, now the colonial project needed schools, universities, community organizations, awards and honors, pageants, and libraries to train new Burmese colonial subjects in the correct introspection and self-governance.

At the same time, after the 1857 mutiny, it became Indian government policy that the state could no longer manage religious temples or appoint religious authorities. This cut the state off from one of the most effective means of shaping sensibilities and subjectivity: religion. The ostensive policy of "noninterference in religious affairs" on its surface meant that religion could not be used in the service of the projects of the colonial state. But on the ground, things were never so clear. Burma, now all of Lower and Upper

Burma, was part of British India, and the policies of the Indian government had to appear to be respected. However, colonial officials appointed to Burma often contended that a different set of rules should apply, arguing that an overwhelming Buddhist majority meant that policies created to mediate between Hindus and Muslims could be adjusted in this context.

This ambiguity opened up the question of what would count as religion and what would be excluded from state intervention. A look at the discussions that preceded the Taungdaw Thathanabaing's trip to Rangoon and his recognition provides a glimpse of the multiple definitions of religion operating at the time and the ways in which the defense of *sāsana* and Burmese identity were becoming intermeshed. The origin of the Thathanabaing's visit was a proposal in January of 1886 by the viceroy in India. The viceroy worried that the overthrow of the Burmese monarch by the British would upset the Chinese emperor, because the Burmese throne had made minor gifts to the Imperial throne in the past. The viceroy wrote to the chief commissioner of Burma asking if it would be possible to find "an ecclesiastical dignitary as the ostensible representative of the Burmese nation who would send the ten yearly presents to China without compromising the Queen's dignity?"[24] He explained that the idea "seems to have taken the fancy of both the Chinese Ambassador and of the English Cabinet."[25] The chief commissioner, with his eyes on local issues, suggested that the Chinese emperor, as "the greatest of all Buddhist monarchs," could appoint the Burmese Thathanabaing, who could make the gifts, help quell the insurgency, and pacify monastic factionalism. Where the viceroy and the Cabinet had sought to use religion and religious authority as a proxy for the Burmese culture and people, one that was devoid of political ties to shield the dignity of their empire, the chief commissioner sought a religious authority who could have influence in sticky local political affairs and become central to the broader civilizing efforts of the colonial state.[26] The viceroy agreed to this plan, but warned that he was "very desirous that the action of the Government should not be interpreted as establishing a new church or setting up an altar to Baal."[27] Thus, while professing strict religious neutrality, the idea of Buddhism as a handmaiden of the state was active at the earliest moment of a unified colonial Burma. Implicit in the discussion was the concept that under British rule, religion's powers of persuasion and authority could be engaged for projects of governmentality.

With the permission of the viceroy, the chief commissioner sought consultation with Buddhist representatives in Rangoon. The reactions he received show that the question of religion was equally ambiguous for the many Burmese factions. The chief commissioner gathered a group of local monastic leaders, the Shwedagon Pagoda trustees, and lay patrons in Rangoon. The group had gathered before the meeting to come to a consensus. Sayadaw U Meda presented their position, that the appointment of a Thathanabaing for all of Burma was vital for Buddhism, but because the Chinese emperor belonged to a sect that "the Burmese do not regard as orthodox," he "should not be allowed to interfere in the religious concerns of Burma."[28] Sidestepping the chief commissioner's concern that a Thathanabaing could only be appointed by a monarch, U Meda argued, "The English Government, in their not molesting the Buddhist religion, are, so to speak, supporters of that religion. Their recognition of a Thathanabaing nominated by the people, therefore need not be a difficult matter," adding that the choice of the Thathanabaing had been the result of an election by a council in the past. Sayadaw U Kawthan La further noted that political authority had significant impact on religious authority in the past; just as the Thathanabaing appointed by King Thibaw had not had jurisdiction in Lower Burma because he was not recognized by British political authority, a Thathanabaing appointed by a Chinese emperor would not have recognizable jurisdiction in British Burma.[29] In this way, these monks reworked the religious neutrality that the British policy treasured as a pillar of liberal colonial rule to construct a new type of patronage of the *sāsana*—one where political authority and noninterference made possible the flourishing of Buddhism. Although this was quite different from the Asokan ideal of a Buddhist monarch, it was a workable solution to preserve the *sāsana* under these conditions. Far from being set on reviving "traditional" conditions, these Rangoon Buddhist representatives were deeply engaged in the processes of defining religion and the boundaries of religious authority in innovative ways.

They were not the only innovators at work. The limits of the new patronage were tested in the coming weeks. Monks requested free passage on government railroads, claiming a right to state patronage. Similarly, a local group of lay Buddhists in Thaton asked the government to appoint a local Thathanabaing for the ethnic Mons of their region. Both incidents contested the universal nature of the Thathanabaing's authority and sought to push the new understanding of *sāsana* patronage in the mode of religious neutrality.[30]

Although the focus was on monastic authority in these early days, the central presence of laymen in these discussions is telling. Over the next three decades, laypeople would offer the most fervent opinions and sway the debate. The Burmese-language *Burmah Herald* editorial the day after the meeting offers a window into the types of hybrid interpretations that were coming to shape the face of Buddhism. The article argued that a Thathanabaing "should be vested with executive authority" to enforce the rules for the sangha.

> The Mahadan's (ecclesiastical censor) subordinates are like policemen, the Mahadan is like the jailor, the Gaingoks and Gaingdauks, who decide cases are like Sessions Judges, and the archbishop [Thathanabaing] himself exercises his power of revision and supervision. The person by whose authority that Thathanabaing is appointed should not only possess power to give secular aid but also be able to provide for the wants of priests, deacons, novices, and school boys who may be receiving their education.[31]

Rather than appealing to Pali texts or past royal administration to argue for greater authority for the Thathanabaing, the author chose a comparison to the judicial model of the colonial state. The judicial machinery was a more familiar mode of governance for this Lower Burman author and his presumed audience, and it offered a suitable model for how religious authority should operate. Religious authority in this sense was an innovation, and one that could easily be understood and molded in the terms of colonial administration.

Another article under the heading "*Sāsana* Affairs" argued "the splendor of the religion can be promoted only by the lay supporters in authority" and boldly challenged the colonial state to furnish the Thathanabaing with a "grand imposing gilt monastery of fine architecture" and provide rice and financial support for eighty or ninety *sayadaw*s, the monastic members of the Thudhamma council, the Thathanabaing, and all the junior monks and novices dependent on them "so that they may be enabled to study and learn the Pitaka books."[32] Here the call for the state to serve as the patron of the *sāsana* more explicitly reflected the royal model, as the donor that could ensure the financial security of monastic *pariyatti* scriptural study. This was a model of support for religion that the colonial state was loathe to embrace; the chief commissioner approved instead a modest twenty-five bags of rice per year to the Thathanabaing and twenty bags each for two senior *sayadaw*s. He refused to fund any further resplendent monasteries.

The state found a position of nominal patronage in its recognition of the Thathanabaing, one that was less than what many Burmese would have desired. The influence of the Thathanabaing would quickly wane in coming years, as the model of monastic leadership began to recede in favor of lay Buddhist initiatives. However, these early negotiations demonstrate the ways in which concern for patronage of the *sāsana* and fluid definitions of

religion had already come to define colonial interactions. Out of these negotiations it became clear that neither the colonial state nor the newly empow-
ered Thathanabaing would be able to assume the duties of royal patron and
protector of the *sāsana*.

The fear of a vacuum in patronage and the new colonial conditions led
laypeople to step in. As much as they argued in these early days for the state
as patron, worry about a lack of sponsorship created new possibilities for
laypeople to understand themselves and their role in the life of the *sāsana*.
The issue of the Thathanabaing and his jurisdiction would remain a concern
for certain groups of laypeople, who would ask for greater British colonial
acknowledgment of Buddhism and greater centralization, but the type of
Buddhist leadership he represented would recede in importance. Just as the
Thathanabaing and the state were inventing modes of defining religion and
religious authority, laypeople would soon step in to offer their own innovations. In these new projects, concern for the *sāsana* remained central, but it
was not yet exactly clear what the promotion of *sāsana* would mean or how
it would be carried out. It was a time of adaptation on both sides of the colonial divide, one in which new groups of leaders and new ways of understanding oneself as Buddhist emerged. Burmese laypeople became deeply involved
in the game of redefining how the religion would operate in the new circumstances and how the protection and promotion of the *sāsana* could be carried out, with innovative and hybrid interpretations.

BUDDHIST ASSOCIATIONS AND THEIR MULTIPLE
SUBJECTS, VOICES, AND SOURCES

The Buddhist lay associations at the center of these changes emerged
out of interactions with a wide range of cultures. The ethnic and cultural
diversity that had long been a feature of the port cities of Southeast Asia was
only intensified by British colonialism. The major Burmese cities of the period, Rangoon, Mandalay, Akyab, and Moulmein, were all meeting grounds
for a variety of Asian and European cultures. One missionary described
Mandalay as a mixture of Shans, English, French, Italians, Greeks, Jews, Ar-
menians, Parsees, Manipuri Brahmins, Gujaratis, Persians, Chettiars, Ben-
galis, Goorkhas, Sikhs, and Chinese.[33] This rich diversity offered a wide variety of influences on Burmese Buddhists in the last decade of the nineteenth
century.[34] The technologies of travel and communication worked to create
cosmopolitan and hybrid identities in ways that scholars are only recently

beginning to explore. Recent work by Su Lin Lewis on colonial cities in Southeast Asia and work by Penny Edwards on hybrid cultures and networks of Sino-Burmese intellectuals like Taw Sein Ko and the movements in support of the Mingun Prince provide a window into the diverse interactions that form a background to these associations.[35] Similarly, colonial Burma was awash in a variety of foreign religious expressions, from orthodox forms of missionary Christianity to reform and heterodox movements like the Arya Samaj, Theosophy, Freemasons, spiritualists, Swedenborgians, and atheist freethinkers.[36] The urban Burmese interacted with this wide variety of interpretations and absorbed something of their approaches.

Technologies of communication made the cultural world inside of Burma smaller and more interconnected as well. The rise of Burmese-language newspapers and Buddhist journals as well as a sharp increase in the number of Buddhist books and tracts allowed for the rapid spread of ideas between villages and towns. Such media helped to create a sense of collective endeavor among Burmese Buddhists. Publications also put Burmese Buddhists in touch with the new transnational Buddhist networks like Col. H. S. Olcott and Anagarika Dharmapala's Maha Bodhi Society. Burmese, particularly those in Rangoon and Arakan, were initially quite taken with Olcott's rhetoric and Dharmapala's efforts, creating the first branches of the Maha Bodhi Society and providing much of the early funding for the fledging association. However, by the late 1890s, such international projects no longer held the Burmese imagination. They were overshadowed by more pressing local problems and local efforts. The internationally focused Buddhist efforts that gained longer support came from two of the earliest Europeans to ordain monks: U Dhammaloka, an Irish sailor who became a popular preacher and reformer, railing against the threats of Christian missionaries and the dangers of drink, and Ananda Metteyya, a Scottish chemist and occult practitioner who sought to create a Buddhist mission to Europe based out of Rangoon.[37] Although Burmese laypeople were at times enthusiastic supporters of these two figures, their popularity came mainly from their presence in local Burmese Buddhist affairs and the symbolic role they played in the preservation of the *sāsana*. Burmese were aware of these larger translocal networks and participated when they seemed advantageous, but the nexus of the problem lay in the preservation of Buddhism locally.

Locally organized and locally oriented Buddhist associations became the dominant and motivating force in Burmese society at the turn of the twentieth century. Buddhist associations became not just wildly popular (surviving records document nearly two hundred of the likely hundreds of associations created), but offered mechanisms for innovation and intervention in Burmese society. Although united by a discourse of preserving the *sāsana*, Buddhist lay associations represented a wide variety of approaches and members. They ranged from small local associations that gathered to take precepts, recite chants, and listen to sermons to large organizations with branches across Burma and ambitious agendas. Some sought to preserve older models of Buddhist practice, like the Malunze Rice Donating Society, which organized rice donations to monks previously supported by the monarchy. Others envisioned new models of Buddhist leadership, insisting that finding a productive balance of European education with Buddhist ideas was vital for the future of Burmese Buddhism. Many organizations came together simply to combine their efforts, whether it was to supply running water to monasteries, to clean and restore the pagoda grounds, or to create libraries of printed Buddhist texts.

Education and scholarship were particular concerns: the creation of Buddhist primary and secondary schools was a central project, as was promoting Pali study among both the laity and the sangha. Some groups were led by Western-educated members and discussed Buddhism in English, like the Rangoon College Buddhist Association and the Young Men's Buddhist Association (YMBA).[38] However, there was a complementary trend to bring Buddhist ideas in the vernacular to those in small towns and villages. Monastic preachers on tours would draw thousands from the countryside to hear their moral exhortations.

Older incarnations of Buddhist organizing focused on special types of donation and merit making, such as pagoda festival committees and the Satuditha organizations that would collect donations to offer food to anyone, especially the poor, who came "from the four directions."[39] In this period, however, associations took on a new character. They transformed from groups who would gather to recite precepts to organizations designed for study and debate, from those responsible for organizing local festivals to those who organized Pali examinations and schools for the entire province. The Rangoon Satuditha is a good example of this: while there were still organizations that offered food to the poor in Rangoon, by 1905 this organization had become a prominent gathering of Burmese who worked to preserve Buddhist monuments and intervene in colonial policy on Buddhist wills. A few of the Buddhist associations established during this period have survived to the present day and served as dominant Buddhist institutions during the twentieth century. Most, however, have long since been forgotten, their purposes lost with the arrival of new priorities and motivations.

Records of the Buddhist associations and their conflicts with colonial authority survive primarily in newspaper accounts and colonial reports.[40] The journals and other publications of the associations or, in rare cases, their surviving records are the best sources for understanding their goals, membership, and activities. The archival record offers a view of official colonial policy and some internal government debates on these issues.[41] Newspapers in English and Burmese proved valuable resources not just for understanding the events that unfolded, but for seeing the multiplicity of perspectives in cosmopolitan colonial society. Different newspapers appealed to varied constituencies and included authors and correspondents from different ethnic, geographic, and social positions. Letters to the Editor, mainly anonymous, allowed the authors to present opinions that conflicted with those of the official representatives of their community, offering insight into differences inside the European and Burmese communities.

Nonetheless, this study is limited by the sources available. It is disproportionately focused on the activities of ethnic Burmans in the larger towns and cities of the Irrawaddy valley.[42] The sources for the towns outside this area are limited: although there were flourishing newspapers and presses in these towns, few if any of their publications have been preserved.[43] This does not mean that all record of their activities has been lost, however. The Rangoon newspapers all included sections of "mofussil" news from outside the capital in which they would reprint articles from newspapers in the smaller cities together with reports from amateur correspondents stationed in small towns across the province. These reports often provide more detailed accounts of the Buddhist associations than those in Rangoon, given that in the smallest towns there was often little else deemed newsworthy.

I hope to present the diversity of approaches represented by the Buddhists active in this time period: from villagers gathering by the hundreds to hear popular preachers and those who recited Pali chants to repel cholera to the Rangoon College students debating Buddhist ideas in English. However, the voices presented come almost exclusively from printed sources, which always have the problem of representation. More often than not, the sources presented here offer statements made in the aggregate, representations made on behalf of a group with a specific audience and purpose in mind. In this, they tend to be expressions of the leadership and elite of these groups rather than popular voices. The sources we have filter the multitude of Burmese voices, but diverse concerns come through vibrantly nonetheless.

In the stories of Buddhist efforts that I tell in this book, I have tried to highlight certain characters to provide a sense of the diversity of agency and interpretation that animated this period. A few of these are well-known monastic figures that are typical of studies of colonial Buddhism, such as the Taungdaw Thathanabaing discussed above and the meditation master and scholar Ledi Sayadaw, the subject of Erik Braun's excellent recent biography.[44] The majority of the figures I highlight were laypeople who found themselves positioned at the crossroads and connections between changes and cultures. A few are wealthy patrons like Daw Mya May, who founded Buddhist schools, and privileged self-taught scholars like Maung Hpo Hmyin, who was involved with international Buddhist efforts. More common, however, are school inspectors and teachers like U Kyaw Yan, and businessmen like U Tun, who founded the Pariyatti Thathanahita. There are a number of Europeans who figure in the story—colonial administrators and education officials, as well as a Russian Pali scholar. However, the most common agents in these stories often are not named, and their biographies have not been recorded by history—they were schoolboys writing to the newspapers and active in strikes, young women who gathered in the hundreds to memorize Buddhist texts, and, above all, Buddhists who subscribed and joined the new Buddhist associations. I have tried to highlight biographical details to provide more background wherever possible, but have chosen not to focus on specific individuals and lives, in an attempt to forefront the cacophony of voices and agents that engendered the key changes of this period.

This book explores the stories of these many voices through four thematically organized chapters. Chapter 2 discusses the discourse of the decline of the *sāsana* and the longer history of *sāsana* reform in Burma, locating the developing sense of moral community as a rearticulation of existing elements in the tradition of reform. Burmese and Pali textual sources on the decline of the *sāsana* and their changing interpretations over the previous century illuminate how the narrative of decline offered a language and structure to make sense of the changes of the colonial encounter. In this context, groups of lay Buddhists adapted techniques from earlier periods of reform to respond to the colonial condition. Changing approaches to Pali examinations developed in conversation and unlikely collaboration with the colonial state, revealing new emphases within the discourse of *sāsana* and the community responsible for its promotion.

Education became a key issue for many of the new Buddhist associations as a site of the production and reproduction of moral community, and Chapter 3 traces education as a place of miscommunication and mistaken identity across the colonial divide. British officials from the education department, like Buddhist reformers, were entranced with the power of Buddhism to shape subjectivity. The colonial state viewed teaching literacy in monasteries as the same as secular education and sought to bring Buddhist practice into the service of colonial ends by turning monasteries into government-sponsored schools. Within the conflicts over education that ensued, the boundaries and capacities of religion were negotiated beyond the official rhetoric of state nonintervention. In the wake of the failures of efforts to bring the monasteries into the state program, the Buddhist associations took up the mantle of creating a modern Buddhist education system, ultimately reshaping the role of religion in public life.

Chapter 4 explores Buddhist lay associations and their campaigns to reform morals and manners among Buddhists, shaping a growing sense of moral community. Working from previously unexamined primary sources, the chapter investigates how joining Buddhist associations elevated members to the state of patrons of the *sāsana,* making the moral community visible in donation and subscription lists. It explores how a perceived crisis of morals among Burmese Buddhists focused the reform efforts inward: Buddhists came to see *sāsana* decline not just as the product of external colonial impetus, but as stemming from their own personal moral failings. Participation in the moral community thus required policing one's own behavior in new ways. Following Buddhist efforts to curb meat eating and alcohol use, the chapter explores how moral reform campaigns constructed new modes of Buddhist subjectivity, teaching Buddhists to view themselves as individually capable of preserving the Buddha's teachings when embedded within the larger community.

Chapter 5 wades into a series of conflicts between Burmese and Europeans over demonstrations of respect that encoded broader issues of subordination and the politics of colonial difference. It demonstrates how Buddhists used the changing terms of official religious neutrality to stake claims to autonomy. The chapter explores how the issue of what counted as religion and religious practice changed over twenty years through clashes across the colonial divide. Religion was carefully negotiated through these conflicts to serve a number of different interests, with Burmese and European actors alike learning to exploit the limits of colonial secularist discourse. These conflicts became a means to realign the status of the moral community and create space for contingent autonomy in relation to colonial power. The Conclusion returns to the three themes outlined in this Introduction: the ongoing and labile tradition of *sāsana* reform, multiple modes of collective identity, and religion as locus of conflict.

2

Sāsana Decline and Traditions of Reform

"There is an end of teaching," the yellow robes whisper privately.

—Ivan Pavlovich Minayeff, *Travels in and Diaries of India and Burma*

In January of 1886, a Russian scholar traveled to Burma in search of Pali manuscripts, arriving just after the British annexation of Upper Burma and the fall of Burmese King Thibaw. Ivan Minayeff's diary records the political turmoil and fears of dacoit insurgents that continued to obsess Europeans. The worries expressed by the majority of Burmese monks and laypeople he met, however, were not fears of political change or violence, but fear for the future of Buddhism: an overarching concern that contemporary events had larger cosmological significance. One English-educated intellectual in Rangoon explained to him, "Panic reigns over Mandalay. The country is completely ravaged. The Burmese do not at all want annexation. They are afraid of the British; they are afraid of the violence and annihilation of their faith. The monks dread particularly the fate of Buddhism."[1] In Mandalay, laypeople reported that, with the loss of royal patronage, scholar-monks had retreated from the city. They told him of "Buddhism in agony" and worries about the death of the *dhamma* in Burma.[2] Minayeff's own assessment was that Buddhism "is struggling desperately but is losing ground under its feet. It could still have got on peacefully with Christianity, but western culture and unbelief are striking its death-blows."[3] He reflected that "people, who are religious minded, do not want the annexation because they think that this would bring about the end of Buddhism. And of course they are right."[4]

Of course, Buddhism did not end. Buddhist thought and practice persisted in the colonial fray. Within a decade, observers would herald a moment of Buddhist resurgence and revival. The certainty of loss and the challenge of change at the moment of colonial takeover had spurred a movement that would come to define much of Burmese society at the turn of the twentieth century. How do we account for the turnaround? Or, perhaps more importantly, how do we understand the perception of loss and the Buddhist response? Was it caused by the persistence of the Buddhist tradition, or was it the product of colonial assimilation? Is it possible to understand this movement in a way that renders it neither simply an adaptation of colonial models nor wholly independent, the product of unchanging Buddhist ideals? Emphasizing external colonial forces as the impetus for change risks presenting colonialism as a radical break in Burmese history or granting colonial power a hegemonic impact it sought but never fully achieved. Alternatively, the inclination to turn to Burmese culture as the catalyst risks reifying an image of "traditional Buddhism" as a single unchanging institution.

Buddhist movements did not simply react to universal forces of colonial modernity but nor were they static, seeking to return only to an invented past. They responded with the tools for intervention that had served them in the past. Understanding these movements requires a perspective that leaves us not, with Minayeff, nostalgic for an imagined ideal Buddhist tradition lost in colonial decadence, but attentive to the means of transformation and production of tradition. It lies, as Anne Blackburn has proposed, in taking Buddhist perceptions and discourse about decline seriously, not as a description of history, but as an active and motivating force in Buddhist history.[5]

This was a time of rapid change in Burma. The fall of the Burmese monarchy in 1885 was just one aspect; colonial rule brought with it wide and pervasive challenges in Burmese daily life. New economic structures produced new sets of desires, there were new configurations of authority, and educational systems shifted emphasis away from the monastery toward a bewildering bureaucratic machinery. In need of a frame of reference in which to interpret these changes, Burmese turned to Buddhist discourse and the practices of Buddhist reform in past times of crisis.

The myth of a singular traditional Buddhism quickly falls away in light of the history of nineteenth-century Burmese Buddhism that this movement inherited. Unlike the material, economic, and political changes brought by the impositions of the colonial encounter, the idea of a Buddhist revival and the need for reform would have been deeply familiar for many Burmese. The nineteenth century had been dominated by a long series of *sāsana* reforms, sets of transformations that continuously examined and redefined Buddhist orthodoxy and practice. Starting from debates over monastic dress and practice, through the creation of royally sanctioned and reformist monastic sects and the mid-century Fifth Buddhist Council convened to recite the Pali *tipiṭaka,* the century had seen multiple rearticulations of correct Buddhist performance. The impetus toward reform and the types of innovations offered echoed those across Buddhist Southeast Asia and Sri Lanka in the eighteenth and nineteenth centuries. If anything, the Buddhists organizing at the turn of the twentieth century had inherited not a single orthodox Buddhist heritage in need of preservation, but a tradition of reform, a process of continuously reexamined and redefined orthodoxy driven by a concern to prevent the decline of the *sāsana.*

PRESERVING *SĀSANA* AS AN ENGINE OF CHANGE

Framed in terms of protecting the Buddha's dispensation and teachings, the discourse about the Buddha's *sāsana* was dynamic and multivalent, serving as much as a means of innovation as an orienting frame. Throughout generations of Buddhist reforms, it had historically offered Burmese Buddhists a means of making sense of their changing world. Any instance of uncertainty could be made intelligible in the longer history of the life of the *sāsana* and its gradual passing away. Interpreted as signs of decline, what would otherwise seem foreign or challenging, be it a rival monastic practice in the eighteenth century or changing aspirations of young men at the turn of the twentieth century, became a comprehensible and predictable part of the decadence of the *sāsana*—a sign of a problem but not a threat to the larger worldview. Rallying calls for change were phrased in terms of the need to ward against its degeneration. In this, the call to preserve the *sāsana* and resist anything that might hasten its decline had served as a central means of innovation in Burmese history.

Based on the model of Asoka, kings undertook campaigns to reform the sangha and promote perceived orthodoxy with the explicit purpose of ensuring conditions in which the *sāsana* could thrive. In the Kalyani Inscriptions from 1476, Mon King Dhammaceti announced that he "purified the *sāsana* so that it would endure five thousand years," a trope found in dedicatory inscriptions from the Pagan period through the nineteenth century.[6] Throughout Burmese history, new capitals, major donations, and construction and renovation projects had been mobilized by calls to ensure the *sāsana* would endure. Reconfigurations of monastic authority, the continual redefinition of lax practices, and repeated calls for correct adherence to the ascetic rules of the Vinaya all came about from claims that poor monastic performance precipitated the loss of the Buddha's teachings. The mid-nineteenth century also saw the rise of a number of monastic reform sects that argued that the practices of the monks had become lax and needed reform to preserve Buddhism in these changing times. The Thudhamma majority sect was a product of an early nineteenth-century effort by a royally sponsored monastic council to reform deteriorating monastic practice and revive the *sāsana*. The Shwegyin, Ngettwin, and Dwaya monastic sects in turn broke off from the Thudhamma in the middle of the century, finding the Thudhamma practices too lax and looking instead to create strict adherence to preserve the Buddha's teachings.[7] Each instance of reform formulated new interpretations of orthodoxy. The need to resist decline provided a reason to intervene—a powerful means for innovation in Burmese history. Thus, reform to preserve the *sāsana* became an engine of change, a technique of living and continually redefined orthodoxies.

Sāsana offered a framework for understanding the present in broader historical perspective. Buddhist temporal cosmology adopts Indian ideas of a cyclical progression of eons of decline, destruction, and renewal, termed "*kalpas*" (Pali: *kappa*). *Kalpas* are further broken down by the appearance of Buddhas and their dispensations. Each *kalpa* may see the appearance of a number of different Buddhas, or no Buddhas at all. The most relevant and orienting division of time becomes the era of each Buddha's enlightenment and the duration of his teachings: his *sāsana*. While *sāsana* translates literally as "teachings" or "instructions," the concept of the Buddhist *sāsana* has come to include not just his teachings as a body of knowledge but the living practice of following the teachings and the conditions of their flourishing. The current era is the *sāsana* of the Buddha Sakyamuni, and time is made meaningful and intelligible in relation to his enlightenment and the continuation of his teachings.

In line with the fundamental doctrine of impermanence, a Buddha's teachings themselves are not eternal, but in a slow process of decay leading to their eventual loss. Enlightenment and realization of the stages of the path are most easily achieved when the Buddha is present on earth, and they become progressively more difficult as time passes. From the moment of the Buddha's enlightenment, the *sāsana* begins a process of inevitable decline in which the teachings are forgotten and the practices abandoned.

Despite this overarching narrative of decline, the *sāsana* takes on a life of its own in descriptions of Buddhist history, flourishing more or less in different regions and time periods given the support of people. Local chronicles herald the establishment of the *sāsana* in different kingdoms through contact with monks and texts. The local health of the *sāsana* offers an immediate referendum on the moral legitimacy of the king and political power, as responsibility for preserving and promoting the *sāsana* is central to Buddhist kingship.

Buddhist sources offer multiple chronologies for the eventual loss of the *sāsana,* ranging from one hundred to five thousand years.[8] Pali texts that narrate this disappearance offer various formulas for stages and length of this decline, but all agree that the *sāsana* will eventually disappear completely when all knowledge of the texts and practices is lost, setting the stage for the arrival of the next Buddha, Metteyya. The *Milinda pañha,* for example, describes three stages of decline lasting five hundred years.[9] The most detailed account of decline appears in the *Manoratha pūraṇī* commentary on the Aṅguttara Nikāya, attributed to the medieval Indian commentator Buddhaghosa. It describes a five-tiered sequence through which the *sāsana* will be lost, including the loss of the attainment of insight (*adhigama*), monastic practices (*paṭipatti*), textual knowledge (*pariyatti*), characteristics of the ascetic life (*liṅga*), and finally the Buddha's relics (*dhātu*).[10]

The discourses of the decline of the *sāsana* and its preservation are multiple and varied in Buddhist history, evolving in consort with the goals of each instance of reform. Discussions of *sāsana* decline were shaped in response to specific historical challenges with slightly different emphases and concerns. Anne Blackburn has shown how in eighteenth-century Sri Lanka a shift in emphasis from the issue of monastic performance to concern for monastic scholarship "altered the terms in which desirable and authoritative Buddhist monasticism was understood," promoting the scholasticism of the Siyam Nikaya monastic sect.[11] Similarly, the dual emphasis on monastic performance and the preservation of textual knowledge as the core of the *sāsana,* Jason Carbine explains, produced the Shwegyin monastic self-understandings as sons of the Buddha in twentieth-century Burma.[12] Each moment of reform drew on ideas of decline present in canonical and commentarial sources to offer new interpretations and inflections of the visible signs of decline and new definitions of the most essential aspects of *sāsana.* These changing interpretations produced *sāsana* as a living and adaptive discourse, one able to interpret change and drive reform, whose development offers insights into how Buddhists understood and reshaped their world.

In Burma, the trope of *sāsana* decline had driven reform and patronage for centuries, but the late eighteenth and early nineteenth centuries saw an increase in writings about the stages of the *sāsana*'s future demise. Earlier Burmese chronicles and inscriptions made reference to the *sāsana* lasting five thousand years, with a vague reference to a future decline. This began to change in the eighteenth century, with a growing focus on determining whether the true sangha, as a cardinal sign of the *sāsana*'s status, had died out. The decades surrounding the turn of the nineteenth century saw a discussion of the specific evidence of decline in greater detail. This focus stemmed from controversies over monastic performance and debates as to whether monks were sufficiently orthodox to carry out their duties. King Bodawpaya, in a falling out with his own monastic authorities, briefly flirted with an interpretation that the true sangha had died out and the higher attainments on the path to enlightenment were no longer possible.[13] Such an interpretation would have facilitated the creation of a new monastic order under his rule and a radical reconfiguration of authority. Refuting this interpretation required more detailed research into the signs and stages of decline, and subsequent chronicles and debates about monastic reform demonstrate greater focus on these issues. Whereas prior chronicles had offered only broad discussions, there was a shift from abstract concern about *sāsana* decline to a more concrete discussion.[14] Patrick Pranke has observed that prior to *Thathanalankara sadan,* written in 1831 partially in response to Bodawpaya's problematic interpretation, Konbaung era monastic chronicles did not specifically discuss the stages of the decline of the *sāsana* as laid out in the commentaries.[15] However, the discussion of the specific signs of the *sāsana*'s decline became a recurrent theme in the coming decades.

THE DECLINE OF THE *SĀSANA* AND THE LOSS OF LEARNING

Burmese and Pali sources on *sāsana* decline became well known by the end of the nineteenth century, offering detailed narratives that could be used both to explain the problems of colonialism and to offer modes of response. The *Thathanalankara sadan* was the first of a series of nineteenth-century texts to discuss the stages in detail. This monastic chronicle offered two separate discussions of decline. The first addressed commentarial sources that state the *sāsana* will last one thousand years for each of five different levels of soteriological achievement.[16] The second account offered a Burmese translation of the five stages of decline listed in the Pali *Sārasaṅgaha,* a thirteenth- to fourteenth-century Sri Lankan compendium, which itself draws from the

Manoratha pūranī.[17] The *Sāsanavaṃsa*, composed in 1861, repeated the first discussion of decline, but not the second.[18] By the end of the nineteenth century, there was a growing emphasis on a different family of texts that addressed the end of the *sāsana*, known under the name *Anāgata vaṃsa*.

An Indologist with a particular interest in Buddhism, Ivan Minayeff traveled from Russia to Burma in 1886 to collect Pali manuscripts and study the Burmese monastic education system. However, the Burmese concerns he encountered and his own reading of the situation shaped the texts he collected. Later that year he published two pieces in the *Journal of the Pali Text Society:* an edition of the *Gandha vaṃsa* (Book History) and versions of *Anāgata vaṃsa* (History of the Future) collected from four different manuscript recensions. Although Minayeff did not record any explicit connection between the situation in Burma and the texts he collected, the *Anāgata vaṃsa* texts must have held an interest and urgency for him or his Burmese informants.

The manuscripts Minayeff collected during that trip represent the range of texts that fall under the title *Anāgata vaṃsa*.[19] The first and longest came from the library of a former Burmese court official in Mandalay and discusses the coming of the future Buddha Metteyya in great detail. Most of the texts known under the title *Anāgata vaṃsa* from Sri Lanka and elsewhere reflect the content of this manuscript and emphasize the hopeful predictions of Metteyya's arrival, and such discussion forms an important subcategory of *Anāgata* literature in Burma.[20] The second and third manuscripts, on the other hand, incorporated Metteyya's arrival into a detailed discussion of the decline of the *sāsana*. The second manuscript offered an extended set of predictions given by the Buddha to Sariputta describing how his *sāsana* will be lost in the world. The third, found in a monastic library in Prome, offered a Burmese commentary on the second manuscript.[21]

These different versions of the *Anāgata vaṃsa* were copied in numerous manuscript collections in nineteenth-century Burma and would have been recognizable to scholars and authors.[22] Moreover, Minayeff's source for the second manuscript demonstrates that the discussion of decline was known and valued well beyond the circles of monastic scholasticism. He obtained the copy from Maung Hpo Hmyin, a Rangoon colonial magistrate who represented what Minayeff referred to as an English-educated "intelligentsia," that is, those who sought to promote ideas of Buddhism as known through English books and translations. Like many of the earliest generation of colonial Burmese Buddhist organizers, Maung Hpo Hmyin came from wealth and was deeply allied with the British colonial administration in Lower Burma. He was awarded the KSM "gold chain of honour" from the viceroy of India and was said to be deeply loyal to Sir Charles Bernard and Sir Charles Crosswaite, the chief commissioners of Burma in the 1880s.[23] He was appointed as the only Burmese representative on the Rangoon Ports Commission and later to the Rangoon Municipal Council, as well as serving on the Educational Syndicate, the Text Book Committee, and as a Shwedagon Pagoda Trustee. Well educated and widely read, he was one of the few of his generation to receive a Western education. He collected Pali manuscripts and became an expert in "Buddhist psychology" with a strong interest in comparative religion, making a massive donation of manuscripts to the Bernard Free Library in the 1890s.[24] His affiliation with Europeans interested in Buddhism expanded in the years after his meeting with Minayeff. He hosted Col. H. S. Olcott, cofounder of Theosophy and acclaimed hero of Buddhists in Ceylon, at his Rangoon mansion during Olcott's visit in 1885. Olcott described him as "one of the best men I have met in the East—generous, courteous, pious and honourable."[25] Active in Theosophy and the largest Burmese donor to the Pali Text Society, he met Anagarika Dharmapala in 1891. According to Dharmapala, Maung Hpo Hmyin was one of his strongest supporters and closest allies, the first donor to support the fledgling Maha Bodhi Society, the first to encourage him to secure Bodh Gaya, and the impetus for Dharmapala's presence at the momentous Parliament of World Religions in Chicago in 1893.[26] In these pursuits, Maung Hpo Hmyin was ahead of his time in Burma: active in international Buddhist causes and Buddhist associations before the majority of his compatriots discovered their importance. Although by the late 1890s the influence of international organizations like Theosophy and the Maha Bodhi Society would fade in Burma in favor of locally organized Buddhist associations, Maung Hpo Hmyin's networks set the stage for the later Buddhist associations that would shape the Burmese colonial experience.[27]

The presence of this version of the *Anāgata vaṃsa* in Maung Hpo Hmyin's collection tells us something about his interests and inclinations. Maung Hpo Hmyin was one of the old guard, who had achieved both wealth and prominence through his loyalty to the colonial administration and his openness to new ideas like Theosophy and comparative religion. And yet, he could see the rapid changes happening around him and looked to the Pali texts for a framework of interpretation. That the *Anāgata vaṃsa* factored so prominently in the exchange between Minayeff and Maung Hpo Hmyin indicates that this discussion of decline had currency at this moment of turmoil, and that he felt that the text had something to offer those interested in understanding a Buddhist interpretation of the world. Far from being a popular superstition or concern limited to monastic scholars, the text and its narrative of decline were deeply entangled in the origins of Buddhist revival and associations in Burma from their earliest days among the most elite and well-educated worldly Buddhists.

In the next decades, the *Anāgata vaṃsa* and its Burmese commentaries would be published in multiple editions, popularizing this rendition of the narrative of the decline.[28] It became widely available through inexpensive print technology. The 1907 edition was published in ten thousand copies, each costing only six *pya*, a publishing run rivaled only by the largest missionary tracts.[29] The narrative had resonance for many, offering an explanation for their tumultuous world and a means for intervention. The *Anāgata* texts provide an insight into Burmese thinking about the decline of the *sāsana* at the end of the nineteenth century and a glimpse of the lenses through which they interpreted their changing condition.

The *Anāgata vaṃsa,* in the version preserved by Maung Hpo Hmyin, repeats the five stages of loss, known as *antaradhānas*, as presented in the *Manoratha pūraṇī.*[30] The Burmese commentary, *Anagatawin kyan,* reproduces these stages of decline as well, changing the order and offering one substitution to shift greater emphasis onto the sangha.[31] The first disappearance, or *antaradhāna,* described in the *Anāgata vaṃsa* is the loss of attainments (*adhigama*): the end of the ability of monks to achieve the four final stages on the path to *nibbāna,* which means the end of the presence of enlightened arhats. This signals the conclusion of the period that began following the Buddha's enlightenment, when it was possible to become enlightened. The next stage is the loss of *paṭipatti,* conduct or practice, in which monks progressively become unable to practice meditation and keep the rules of conduct until the last monk ultimately violates all of the rules.[32] The loss of learning, *pariyatti,* the third stage, narrates the eventual loss of all the books of the Pali *tipiṭaka.* The fourth stage, the loss of the outward appearances (*liṅga*), describes the decline in performative terms, addressing the manners of monks, their dress, their livelihood, and their decline in morals. It paints a shocking picture of married, working monks who have forgotten even the basics of monastic propriety: essentially monks who have ceased to behave as monks. The final stage, the disappearance of the relics (*dhātu*), offers a supernatural crescendo in which all of the Buddha's relics, heralded by the gods, magically reunite at the site of the Buddha's enlightenment and are consumed in flames.

Each of these stages of decline paralleled a number of Burmese Buddhist concerns in the nineteenth century, offering a cosmological orientation for colonial changes. The concern for the attainments of monks coincided with late eighteenth- and nineteenth-century monastic reform movements. The discussions of the declining morals foreshadowed growing concerns about lay behavior and morality. The idea of the relics ultimately reuniting at Bodh Gaya would have inspired those trying to wrest control of the site from non-Buddhists and provided an incentive to renovate other monuments.[33] However, the loss of *pariyatti* corresponded most directly with the concern that the loss of royal patronage meant a decline of monastic scholarship and a broader knowledge of the *dhamma*. As Minayeff reported, there was a perception that *pariyatti* was particularly threatened with the arrival of colonial power. In a haunting passage, his diary reported monastic fears that characterized the moment. " 'There is an end of teaching,' the yellow robes whisper privately."[34] The loss of learning had perhaps the most bearing on the Burmese Buddhist anxieties of the last decades of the nineteenth century. This aspect of decline offered both a means for understanding contemporary events and a template for projects to preserve *sāsana* under colonial rule.

The section on the loss of *pariyatti* in the *Anāgata vaṃsa* stands out with its vivid description of society and the signs of decline that had direct implications for laypeople.[35] The section provides a chain of causation with links to specific social concerns.

> As time goes on there will be base-born kings, not Dhamma-men; their ministers and so on will not be Dhamma-men, and consequently the inhabitants of the kingdom and so on will not be Dhamma-men. Because they are not Dhamma-men it will not rain properly. Therefore the crops will not flourish well, and in consequence the donors of the requisites to the community of monks will not be able to give them the requisites. Not receiving the requisites the monks will not receive pupils. As time goes on and on learning will decay.[36]

The text paints a picture in which a crisis of the state (the loss of a *dhammic* king) precipitates a social crisis (ministers and inhabitants not being *dhammic*), and in turn an economic crisis (famine). The collapse of the society provides a material explanation for the loss of learning: an impoverished laity cannot sustain their donations to the sangha, who in turn will not be able to afford to take on students.

The text is explicit about how the loss of learning will progress: starting with the loss of the *Paṭṭhāna,* the books of the Abhidhamma Piṭaka will be lost in the reverse order of their appearance. Next, the works of the Sutta Piṭaka, followed by the Jātakas and the Vinaya Piṭaka, will be lost, until only four verses of the teachings can be recalled.[37] The final stage describes preserving the teachings as a social and political concern.

> When a king who has faith has had a purse containing a thousand (coins) placed in a golden casket on an elephant's back, and has the drum (of proclamation) sounded in the city up to the second or third time, to the effect that: "Whoever knows a stanza uttered by the Buddhas, let him take these thousand coins together with the royal elephant"—but yet finding no one knowing a four-line stanza, the purse containing the thousand (coins) must be taken back into the palace again—then will be the disappearance of learning.[38]

This passage offers a test to determine the survival of the teachings as well as a means to provide incentives for their preservation. The offer of large donations as a reward for reciting texts was a central method for preserving learning before and after the fall of the monarchy.

Buddhist texts, both Pali texts and those preserved in Mahayana traditions, are ambivalent about whether human intervention has an impact on the decline of the *sāsana.* Many texts, like this version of the *Anāgata vaṃsa,* narrate social and political causes of decline. And yet, as Jan Nattier explains, even these explanations operate within a system in which decline is unavoidable. "In a number of narrative texts where the effects of human actions are the center of attention, we find specific timetables for the duration of the Dharma. Yet the very existence of these timetables suggests that the lifespan of the Dharma is fixed, and thus not subject to human intervention."[39] The ambivalence in these contradictory explanations opens the narratives to multiple readings, depending on the contemporary conditions. Some of the texts Nattier discusses focus on foreign invasion as an impetus for decline, an interpretation that was certainly on the minds of the Burmese in 1885. Often, however, as is the case in this version of the *Anāgata vaṃsa,* these political causes are linked with the moral decline of Buddhists themselves. In laying the fault at the feet of Buddhists, narratives can operate both as cautionary tales for Buddhists as well as directions for intervention.

The structure of the narrative offers the opportunity to read the text backwards as a prescription, suggesting interventions to slow the decline and resist the conditions of the *sāsana*'s demise. There are numerous points to interrupt the process, particularly in the detailed chain of causation leading to the loss of *pariyatti*. The first cause, the rule of an *adhammic* king, would have been on the minds of the Burmese with the arrival of British rule. Much of the discourse of *sāsana* decline evoked by lay Buddhist associations makes direct reference to the loss of a Buddhist king as the first threat to the *sāsana*.[40] The causal chain of an *adhammic* king, ministers, and population could potentially be interrupted at any stage. With the fall of the monarchy, the focus turned to the lay population. If preserving the *dhammic* nature of the people could prevent famine, the impoverishment of the sangha could be preempted by the continued generosity of the laity, ensuring that the sangha could continue to teach students and thus prevent the loss of the texts. This reading offers three points of intervention: the preservation of lay morality, the continued generosity of the laity, and the promotion of *pariyatti* education. These provided fallback positions to preserve the *sāsana* after the loss of a Buddhist king—a fail-safe mechanism for the *sāsana*.

EXAMINING AUTHORITY TO PRESERVE THE *SĀSANA*

The *Anāgata vaṃsa* version of the stages of decline offered a framework for understanding the conditions of colonialism, but also provided a specific course of action. With the loss of the monarchy and the disorganized state of the sangha, prominent laymen decided the responsibility to preserve the *sāsana* had fallen to them. Over the course of the next two decades, they appealed to their fellow Buddhists to come together to create organizations for the preservation of the *sāsana*. The morality of lay Buddhists and their performances would become important for many of the new Buddhist associations. Others would focus on promoting the longevity of the sangha, or the Buddha's reliquaries. In their first decade, however, the loss of *pariyatti* was the most pressing issue for many in these new Buddhist organizations. They placed increasing emphasis on the study of Abhidhamma philosophical texts, and especially the knowledge contained in the *Paṭṭhāna*, the first book prophesized to disappear, and increased interest in Pali scholarship by the laity in general. These new efforts looked to the past for their inspiration, drawing on the techniques of previous instances of *sāsana* reform. Royal patronage of *pariyatti*, especially the practice of sponsoring Pali examinations, served as models. Yet even where their discourses and procedures sought to be closest to those of the former monarchy, their efforts brought reconfigurations of the means of preserving the *sāsana* and its meaning in the colonial context.

Promoting scholarship as a means of preserving the *sāsana* was not itself an innovation. Pali examinations, like the offer of gold coins described in the *Anāgata vaṃsa,* had been a central technique of *sāsana* reform and preservation under the Burmese kings. Khammai Dhammasami argues that Pali examinations began in the seventeenth century under King Thalun as a means for the king to limit the number of men ordained as monks to maintain a large pool for military conscription.[41] The relationship between royal control of the sangha and Pali examinations became stronger in the late eighteenth century when King Bodawpaya and the Thudhamma monastic council began to hold systematized examinations for royally sponsored monks. They instituted two sets of examinations: Vinaya examinations on knowledge of monastic rules and Patamabyan examinations that were divided into different levels and encouraged participation with rewards of royal patronage.[42]

These examinations persisted through the nineteenth century. Among his many Buddhist projects in the middle of the nineteenth century, King Mindon turned to examinations to foster a sense of collective engagement in preserving the teachings, emphasizing examinations as a means of promoting virtuoso scholarship. Mindon built special halls and promoted attendance as a means of public merit making.

> The examination halls were highly decorated and the recitations by the candidates were held solemnly in front of a Buddha image. The ceremony also had the flavor of royalty, because the candidates patronized by high-ranking court officials were well dressed and entered the examination hall under golden umbrellas. The first grade of candidate was allowed to use a palanquin sheltered with four golden umbrellas and the junior grade on horseback under two umbrellas. The whole scene of ceremony was therefore glittering with golden umbrellas and the area was filled up with palanquins, giving the impression of grandeur and affluence in the kingdom.[43]

Successful candidates were awarded prestigious titles as well as royal donations of alms, including "one thousand silver coins and clothing" for the lower and middle grades and "one thousand five hundred silver coins and a ring with a precious stone, red in color" for the higher grades."[44] In addition, the families of successful candidates would be exempt from taxation. Like the image of the king offering a bag of a thousand coins in the *Anāgata vaṃsa,* Mindon's examinations held out incentives for monastic scholarship in order to preserve the teachings, bringing the public directly into the effort to preserve the *sāsana.*

Royal sponsorship for examinations ended when the British deposed King Thibaw in 1885. The end of the monarchy meant the end of not just examinations, but the entire system of royally sponsored monasteries and scholar-monks. Such a loss of patronage not only created an exodus of monks from Mandalay in the years after annexation, but had a ripple effect through the rest of the economy and society. Merchants and artisans who had relied on a steady stream of religious donations for trade prior to 1885 felt the shift of power. Over the next decade, Burmese laypeople became increasingly concerned about the implications of fewer monks dedicated to the study of Buddhist knowledge. Just as the *Anāgata vaṃsa* described, the loss of Buddhist authority at the top had corroded the influence of Buddhism at lower levels and dried up the stream of donations to the monks, who could no longer take students.

By the late 1890s, men in Mandalay, and to a lesser extent Rangoon, felt they must step in to address the situation. Although they persisted in appeals to the colonial government to revive the state financial support for scholar-monks, these men realized that the responsibility would now fall to them.[45] U Tun, a prosperous merchant, brought together twelve businessmen and professionals from Mandalay in 1898 to form the Pariyatti Thathanahita Society with the intent of reviving Pali scholarship among monks.[46] The twelve men were mostly merchants and brokers in trades such as rice, silk, and monk's requisites who had seen annexation's economic impact on Buddhist monks firsthand. U Tun, while prosperous in his business connections, held no particular social prominence. In a city that had been dominated by sartorial hierarchies of ministers, princes, and royalty a few years prior, U Tun and his colleagues were only lowly businessmen, with no claim of being former officials. They are listed in founding journals and commemorative volumes by their occupation, not by title, representative of the identity of a rising Burmese middle class. The only two who held any official status were chief clerks in government offices—humble compared to the ministerial and royal donors prior to 1885. Nonetheless, U Tun was convinced that they could come together to stem the tide and promote Pali study. To bolster their authority, he sought out the patronage of the unofficial Thathanabaing, the Pakhan Sayadaw, and eight prominent *sayadaws* (chief abbots), including the Minekhine Sayadaw.[47]

U Tun described the situation as he saw it in a memorial to Lord Curzon in 1902, decrying that:

> The number of members of the Buddhist Clergy in the city during Mindon's time is roughly computed at 70,000, and of these no less than 2,000 were learned Bhikkhus, scholarly teachers who were beacons of wisdom and holiness to the younger generation of monks and the laity. The thirst for the knowledge of the Sacred Scriptures was then so keen, and reputation of some of the Pongyis so widely extended that eager disciples flocked to Mandalay from all parts of further India and Ceylon to drink in the teachings of the Omniscient Thathagata at their purest fount. Many of the venerable masters had each between five to six hundred pupils hanging eagerly on their lips at their lectures. . . .
>
> [N]ow the city barely counts 100 Bikkhus of the old stamp famed for any extraordinary eminence in wisdom and sanctity, with barely a tenth of the number of novices students that crowded the kyaungs in Mindon's reign. Some of the venerable prelates who sat at the Fifth Great Synod and identified themselves with the Golden Age of Buddhist literature are still alive imparting their stores of knowledge to their future successors between four to five hundred at each lecture. But these holy men are in the eve of life and with their death the shining lights of the Revival Era of Buddhism will be extinguished forever.
>
> That the painful and sad inference to be drawn from this is that the zeal for the study of the Dharma and Buddhist literature is on the decline, which is attributable to—
>
>   1. The discontinuance of State aid and the absence of active interest in these matters of monarchs like Bodawpaya and Mindon.
>   2. The poverty of the people who are barely able to keep the pongyis in the necessaries of life.
>   3. The growing want of zeal on the part of the pongyis themselves.[48]

These last three causes could have been inspired by the discussion of decline in the *Anāgata vaṃsa*—a tragic chain reaction that could only lead to the decline of the *sāsana*. And yet, U Tun and his colleagues developed a plan to address the catastrophe they foresaw. The twelve men set as their goals:

(a) To furnish Bhikkhu lecturers and novices of the Buddhist scriptures with a monthly supply of provisions and medicines.
(b) To support a picked number of Bhikkhus to keep up the main of well-educated and scholarly Teachers of Buddhist scriptures.

(c) To bring under repairs any monastic school building wanting in repairs or in case of insufficient class rooms to erect new ones if necessary.

(d) To establish a library of such copies of the Pitaktas written at the insistence of the Society as are useful to such students and also to receive and keep in said library any kind of books or palm leaf manuscripts of Buddhist scriptures, donated or entrusted for safe custody by the people.[49]

U Tun became a consummate organizer and fund-raiser, making public appeals for funds to his coreligionists not just across the city, but around the colonial province.[50] The organization flourished, creating a systematic program for promoting monastic teachers and students.

U Tun and his colleagues were not alone. In 1896, merchants from the Malun market in Mandalay had gathered to coordinate rice donations to the forest monks in the Sagaing and Mingun hills who had previously been supported by the king.[51] They sought to directly replace the royal rice donations to scholar-monks that the colonial government had ended. In a similar vein, in 1894 a number of prominent men in Rangoon, including Shwedagon Pagoda trustees, established the Zediyingana (Cetiyangaṇa) Pariyatti Nuggaha Association.[52] Its stated purpose was "to donate such that the *sāsana* could endure into the future without the Burmese king as its chief patron."[53] In its early years, members gathered for study and discussion at the Shwedagon Pagoda. Eventually they began to collect books and funds for *pariyatti* study and erected a building on the pagoda platform. In 1909, they opened the Dhammanuggha Kuthodaw Pitaka Taik, a free Buddhist library that became a center for those seeking books and manuscripts.[54] By 1915, their library had come to replace the European-run Bernard Free Library (which held the manuscripts of the former royal collection) as the source for monks preparing for examinations and consulting manuscripts for editing printed editions.[55]

Through all of this organizing, Pali examinations remained a key interest. After many years of requests by Burmese leaders, and one failed attempt at cooperation between the Department of Public Instruction and the Thathanabaing, the colonial government revived the state-sponsored Patamabyan Pali examinations in 1895.[56] The examinations proved extremely popular with monks throughout the province.[57] One hundred and six candidates sat for the first Patamabyan examinations, and by 1905 that number had quadrupled.[58] After only the first year, Mon monks were asking to have the examinations offered in Mon as well as Burmese, and soon the examinations had to be extended to multiple sites around the province to respond to the monastic demand.[59] The government offered all those who passed the examinations monetary awards, ranging from 50 to 150 rupees, and gifts in kind to monks who would not receive cash. The examinations again became an issue of public prestige; the candidate who scored the best at the highest level was awarded the title *Patamakyaw* and presented with a certificate from the lieutenant governor at a special awards ceremony. The names of successful candidates were published in the official *Burma Gazette* and lauded in the Burmese-language newspapers.[60]

Because examinations had been prominent public events under the monarchy and were lost with the arrival of colonial rule, Burmese were drawn to the prospect of reviving them as a means of preserving the *sāsana*. While the examinations attracted strong participation from monks in the early years, they produced even more enthusiastic attention from the community of lay Buddhists. From the beginning, the government had enlisted the help of local Buddhists to support the monastic candidates. The original proposal for the examinations invited the public to "extend hospitality to the candidates who come up from outlying districts," and it was hoped that the community would "be able to raise funds for defraying the traveling expenses of students too poor to go to Mandalay at their own expense."[61] The Buddhist laity more than exceeded this request. The Patamabyan examinations, and especially the conferral of the *Patamakyaw*, offered an opportunity for the colonial government to display its generosity and values. However, the laity expanded and transformed these events into celebrations of Burmese dedication to Buddhism and *pariyatti* study.[62] Held at the major pagodas, they became opportunities for public merit making; what began as simply offering meals expanded eventually into large-scale donation ceremonies.[63]

Leading Buddhist laypeople offered their time and expertise to organize the events. Preparations required coordination and organization; Buddhists in the towns offering examinations created *Patamabyan dayaka* (sponsors) associations. These coordinated the efforts of individual Buddhists and solicited donations and volunteers in the Burmese-language newspapers.[64] The newspapers in turn were assiduous in reporting donations to the cause; the Burmese-language *Maha-Bodhi News* dedicated a special section of each issue to record these donations. In addition to monastic scholars, the colonial Patamabyan examinations were now open to nuns, laymen, and laywomen, all of whom came in increasing numbers to participate in the preservation of the *dhamma*.[65] While the monks were the object of the broader public support and celebrated with top honors, this opened the opportunity for other groups within the Buddhist community to participate more directly.

The laity's enthusiasm for preserving *pariyatti* scholarship was not sated by the opportunities provided by the government's Patamabyan examinations. They continued their efforts in new lay associations, whose massive popularity was driven by a growing sense of lay responsibility for the *sāsana* in the absence of a Buddhist king. The Buddhist associations soon came to sponsor their own Pali examinations, which operated not as alternatives to the government's examinations, but supplements, since there seemed to be no shortage of interest in examinations among the monks or the laity. The examinations were organized and administered by volunteer laypeople and drew their support not by soliciting large donations from prestigious patrons but by requiring small donations and subscriptions for membership in the organization.

By 1903, the Pariyatti Thathanahita Society began offering regular Pali examinations for monks to qualify as teachers of the *dhamma*. The written question-answer examinations, at two grades, qualified the successful candidate for recognition as a *pariyatti* teacher and earned him a monthly stipend to promote his teaching.[66] In 1913, the Zediyingana expanded their scope to offer their own Pali examinations for monks. These consisted of both Vinaya recitation examinations and written examinations at graded levels covering questions on the Sutta, Vinaya, and Abhidhamma Pitakas. Successful candidates were awarded the title of Dhammacariya, teacher of the *dhamma*, and were accepted as the most respected of monastic instructors.

The Zediyingana and the Pariyatti Thathanahita continue to be the preeminent Pali examinations today, but they were only two of many at the time. Independent Pali examinations flowered in small towns across Burma, sponsored by Buddhist associations. Through the first decades of the twentieth century these exams multiplied; some of the larger towns sponsored two or three examinations per year.[67] Buddhists in Yenangyaung were bold enough to create their own exams and generously invite the government to participate.[68]

PARIYATTI PRESERVED IN THE PEOPLE: EXAMINING THE LAITY ITSELF

The narrative of decline incited a concern for *pariyatti* that was not quelled by the encouragement of monastic scholarship, but spilled over into efforts to instruct the laity in Buddhist concepts and texts. Many of the

Buddhist associations, like the Zediyingaṇa, began as small groups that gathered to recite precepts and study simple texts. These *dhamma wut* associations expanded at the turn of the twentieth century as laypeople became increasingly interested in gaining the knowledge of the Pali texts themselves. The Dhammathawana Association (Buddhist Propaganda Society) responded to this interest by sponsoring monastic preachers who could explain Buddhist philosophical concepts to the laity in simplified Burmese. Whereas preaching had previously been dominated by recitation, this association promoted preachers who started "bringing home the truths of the law to their minds in plain, earnest language."[69] The Dhammathawana's preaching monks and the articles explicating philosophical points that began to appear in newspapers and Buddhist associations' journals all responded to a desire to preserve the teachings.

The weight of the responsibility for the *sāsana* shifted down the social hierarchy to the broad base of the Buddhist laity. As lay Buddhists claimed greater responsibility for the preservation of the *sāsana,* their ideas about what constituted the life of the teachings and how they should be preserved changed as well. Laypeople felt they could take on new duties and modes of preserving the teachings. It was no longer enough to promote the *pariyatti* learning of monks; the laity began to preserve that knowledge themselves.

In the first decades of the twentieth century there was an almost insatiable desire to examine and be examined on Buddhist knowledge. Smaller organizations arose that proposed public examinations for groups of laypeople. Some of these offered tests for women on Burmese translations of Pali texts or treatises explicating Buddhist thought; others offered recitation examinations on simple Burmese Buddhist texts for children. The most widespread of these by far were the Paramattha Thankheip societies formed by Ledi Sayadaw.[70] Ledi Sayadaw, himself a virtuoso scholar-monk heralded in Mindon's Pali examinations, promoted simple Burmese translations and explanations of Pali texts and lay meditation. He condensed the basis of Abhidhamma knowledge contained in the *Abhidhammatthasaṅgaha* into a simple Burmese poem that could be memorized by the masses. The resulting text, the *Paramattha thankheip,* offered easily memorized verses that, it was alleged, even young women could learn.[71]

In terms of publishing, the *Paramattha thankheip* was Ledi Sayadaw's most popular work of the time. Between 1904 and 1907, 51,000 copies of the text were published by four different publishers, the cheapest costing only three *annas.*[72] With Ledi Sayadaw's encouragement, societies focused on studying and memorizing the text formed in almost every town. These associations attracted teenage girls and young women in particular, who could now recite and comprehend the most important of Buddhist insights.[73] The associations' emphasis on memorization in turn sparked an interest in examination. As Ledi Sayadaw or his deputies traveled from town to town to preach, they would adjudicate memorization and comprehension examinations for the local association.[74] During his visit, the members of the association had the opportunity to show off their accomplishments to the great monk himself. The successful girls had the privilege of following in his procession, reciting the verses as he departed the town.[75]

The impact of these changes on the perspective of a young woman from a small town would have been substantial. The dominant monastery school system was open exclusively to her brothers, although the system of lay-run "house schools" would have offered her a training in literacy and some of the most basic texts of the monastery curriculum. However, other than opting to become a *thila shin* nun, the serious work (and merit) of memorizing Pali texts would have remained outside the grasp of most women, reserved for male monks with extended years in the robes. The technological changes of the colonial era would have had significant impact on the lives of these young women. In the past, the Pali palm leaf manuscripts were guarded in a manuscript cabinet in the monasteries, available to monks, but unavailable to women. Now print technology churned out hundreds and thousands of copies of Buddhist texts. While the published editions of the *tipitaka* texts were still so expensive as to be well beyond their means, newly written Burmese-language texts on Buddhist topics were printed by the thousands, sponsored by Buddhist associations and their presses. And here, Ledi Sayadaw had condensed the knowledge of the most complicated Abhidhamma text into a short poem available for only three *annas*—a sum that could be easily earned by women in the markets or trading, arenas long dominated by Burmese women, young women included. Moreover, given the easily memorized structure, a group of women could easily share one text, spreading the knowledge much further.

The advancements in transportation and communication that the British lauded for their economic and political implications had significant impact on the Buddhist lives of these women as well. Better roads, not to mention ferries, trams, and railways, meant that it was easier to travel to the next town to hear the esteemed scholar preach and to participate in the memorization examinations. And no longer were they reliant on word-of-mouth news from travelers to hear of upcoming preaching events or examinations. Now the news arrived daily in the newspapers and Buddhist journals efficiently delivered to their town by the postal service. Such opportunities would have radically expanded the scope of participation by young Burmese Buddhist women.

Young women came in droves to participate in the *Paramattha thankheip* recitations. At one event in Moulmein, for example, seventy-five horse carts full of women arrived at the site of the examinations two nights in a row.[76] The desire to learn the knowledge of the Abhidhamma and to preserve it in one's own memory, thus safeguarding *pariyatti* teaching and the *sāsana*, drove the massive turnout. It offered both the opportunity to create personal merit through knowledge of the Abhidhamma and to gain social recognition by becoming a central participant in the preservation of the *sāsana*. The efforts of associations that focused on lay study transformed the preservation of the teachings from an effort the laity could support to a good they could embody. The body of lay Buddhists could now become self-sufficient in its efforts to preserve the *sāsana*—the knowledge being redundantly inscribed in every member, ensuring it could never be lost.

The image of the young women reciting the *Paramattha thankheip* for Ledi Sayadaw and processing with him brings the issue of Buddhist examinations full circle. These examinations proposed an inversion of the fundamental monastic, gendered, and age hierarchies of Burmese society. Whereas in royal times the laity listened to monastic exam recitations to gain merit, here young female laypersons recited the text for an audience of esteemed male monks. The weight of responsibility for preserving the *pariyatti* teachings had shifted from the highest social elite to the lowest base of society. These new examinations offered a celebration of students not for their individual virtuoso achievements, but for their ability to collectively reproduce the text and their contribution to the massive reproduction and preservation of *pariyatti* knowledge.

CONCLUSION

Pali examinations offer one example of the projects undertaken by the Buddhist lay associations in colonial Burma. Over the next few decades, lay Buddhists would mobilize around a number of issues, each understood as a sign of decline, and offer means of preserving the *sāsana* for the Burmese community. Techniques of *sāsana* preservation offered continuity in the midst of colonial changes. Pali examinations provided lay Buddhists a strong connection to earlier instances of *sāsana* reform, allowing them to locate their efforts in a tradition of reform driven by larger cosmological conditions. More than this, understanding the shifts in economic, political, and cultural systems, such as the loss of support for monastic scholarship, in terms of predictable developments in a larger cosmological-historical frame, provided a means to make sense of colonialism and its increasing impositions on Burmese lives.

These signs of decline, in turn, required intervention on behalf of the *sāsana* and opened the door to a wide range of cultural and religious innovations. Even as they appealed directly to the *sāsana* reform of the past, the new Buddhist organizers inflected the meaning of *sāsana* and how it would be preserved to their colonial context. Buddhist associations claimed techniques of past reforms, but transformed these in their application, creating new modes of lay authority and bringing new technologies of voluntary associations and print media to the center of Buddhist practice. The claim to purify the *sāsana* and return to traditional Buddhist practice or orthodoxy became itself an engine of change. In this, the discourse of *sāsana* proved to be dynamic and responsive—open to be inflected to respond to contemporary conditions and flexible enough to be read in a variety of unprecedented conditions. In this sense, *sāsana* was both the means and the product of a continuing process of reform and reimagining. *Sāsana* was an active and adaptive discourse, shaped by the efforts of lay Buddhists to transform their world. Locating these Buddhist movements as part of a longer history of *sāsana* reform and driven by a larger cosmological framework of decline offers a vantage point on the dynamic responses to colonialism. Concern for the *sāsana* proved to be a robust worldview that offered continuity with the past and yet could be molded to fit colonial conditions.

3

Buddhist Education

> The ear is deafened by a chorus of children's voices repeating
> with the full power of their lungs the traditional Burmese
> spelling book. As we enter, the voices, now raised higher than
> ever, are found to issue from forty or fifty boys recumbent on
> the bare floor in regular ranks, each having before him a
> small oblong black board which serves the purpose of a slate.
> —Peter Hordern, "Buddhist Schools in Burmah"

The nineteenth-century world of Burmese Buddhism, in
many ways, centered around these boys, lying on the floor, learning to possess and embody the teachings of the Buddha. For centuries prior to the arrival of British colonialism, Burmese boys had learned to read in the monasteries as preparation for their ordination as novices. This training was key to
Burmese acculturation and foundational for preserving the Buddha's words
and his *sāsana* in the world—it created civilized Burmese and ensured the
future of Buddhism.

This monastery scene was deceptively familiar to many in the colonial
administration. It resembled what these utilitarian-trained officials imagined as an ideal, simplistic system of education—one that instilled discipline
together with literacy and was capable of producing compliant colonial subjects. At the same time, education in the village monastery could be unset-
tling to colonial administrators. A later colonial report would deride the
"babel of voices" coming from the monastery: "It is not generally known . . .
that this discordant noise represents the preparation of lessons and however
unsuitable it may seem for this object to the average European, there is no
doubt that the Burman does not see it in this light."[1] The methods seemed
unorthodox, but the potential of an existing education system housed in

religious institutions was particularly enticing to colonial administrators charged with creating a school system. Yet, the gulf between training boys in the monasteries and a colonial education system proved much wider than they judged. The four-decade encounter between the two was fueled by mis-communication and misidentification of common purpose. Colonial educa-tion presumed conceptual categories and divisions that could not be readily translated into the life of the monastery. The similarities between Buddhist monasteries and colonial schools were deceptive; their projects were oriented toward very different, and in the monks' analysis, ultimately opposing ends. Combining the two required reconceiving and reordering the practices of the monastery to fit with a specific definition of religion, one that the monks judged to be a threat to their larger purposes.

And yet, education and the formation of boys remained central to the cause of preserving the *sāsana*. The monastery schools could not meet the demands of the colonial era and were quickly undercut by government and missionary schools. As the colonial system eclipsed monastery education, Buddhist associations' projects for preserving Buddhist knowledge expanded to include the creation of schools that could ensure the future of Buddhism in the hands of the next generation. Adopting the methods of the colonial education system required adapting to its underlying conceptual categories. If the new Buddhist leaders chose to participate in the system, they would have to grapple with definitions of religion without detracting from their larger project of protecting the *sāsana*.

"THE MOST LITERATE OF ALL THE LANDS OF THE EAST": FASCINATION WITH BURMESE EDUCATION

The British perceived the Burmese to be highly educated, an advantage in a Victorian value system that fashioned education, and literacy in particu-lar, as a marker of civilization and modernity. Late eighteenth- and nineteenth-century European observers were impressed with the ubiquity of the ability to read and write in Burma. Explorers, diplomats, and missionaries alike were astounded at how common literacy was among men, and often women, of all classes. Michael Symes remarked in 1795 that "a knowledge of letters is so widely diffused, that there are no mechanics, few of the peasantry, or even the common watermen (usually the most illiterate class) who cannot read and write in the vulgar tongue."[2] Wide-eyed reports such as this cultivated the European image of the Burmese as a highly literate culture.[3]

The origin of this universal literacy, European observers explained, was the institution of the village monastery and the practice of sending all young boys to the monastery to receive elementary training prior to their ordination as novices. Father Sangermano, writing of Burma at the turn of the nineteenth century, explained:

> It must be acknowledged that the Burmese owe much to the Talapoins [monks], for the whole of the youth of the Empire is educated by them. Scarcely are the children arrived at the age of reason when they are consigned to their care; and after a few years most of them put on the dress of a Talapoin, that they may be taught to read and write, and may also acquire merit for themselves and their relations.[4]

Although few boys stayed past their novice ordination, the system was effective in educating the majority of the male population.

Building on these early descriptions, discussions of Burmese literacy and monastery schools became standard fare for travelers' accounts and colonial reminiscences published back home.[5] Almost every account of Burma published in the second half of the nineteenth century included a few pages on education, with the most famous dedicating whole chapters to the subject, projecting an image of the Burmese as particularly progressive in the area of education.[6] Popular magazines ran articles on Burmese schools and published reviews of even the driest text on the subject: the government's *Report on Public Instruction in Burma*.[7] The interest was not limited to England; the Russian Indologist Ivan Minayeff visited Burma to observe primary education in the monasteries.[8]

The idea of near universal literacy was so strongly embedded in the consciousness of Europeans in Burma that it outweighed that quintessential mode of colonial knowledge—the census.[9] When the first census of British Burma was taken in 1872, the results showed that only 24.37 percent of men and 1.37 percent of women could read and write.[10] Although these figures were higher than those for the rest of British India, the census takers themselves disputed their accuracy, citing personal experience over their scientific enumeration methods.[11] They claimed it was rare to meet a Burmese man who could not read and write, and refused to believe the numbers that were, in other areas, an article of faith for colonial bureaucrats. The census report of 1872 dedicated two full pages to reconciling how they could have arrived at what were, to the authors, such clearly false numbers. They speculated on the modesty of the Burmese population in reporting their educational accomplishments and the laxity of the district administrators in asking the questions, but never questioned the accuracy of the received knowledge that the Burmese as a culture were well educated and valued education.

The British were quick to place the Burmese system of monastery education as superior to any other system in the colonies. Burma was "one of the most literate of all the lands of the East," a comparison that could be used both to praise Burmese civilization and to justify further civilizing efforts elsewhere in India.[12] This fascination with widespread literacy did not limit itself to comparison with other colonial possessions. Observers compared the Burmese system favorably to those of Europe.[13] Henry Gouger remarked of his time in Mandalay in the 1820s that "my impression was that a larger proportion of the common people could read and write in Burmah than could be found among similar classes in our own country."[14] John S. Furnivall, writing in the 1930s to correct earlier claims, argued that "a hundred years ago the first English Commissioner reported that almost every one could read and write and, even if this report may have been touched with exaggeration, it is certain that the proportion of people who could read and write was then far higher in Burma than in England."[15] The evidence supports a claim that late nineteenth-century Burmese literacy rates were much higher than those of the rest of British India and higher than some countries in Europe.[16] However, for our purposes, the empirical literacy rates are less interesting than the British perceptions, because conflicting conceptions of literacy and religion lay at the heart of the conflict over education policy.

Education was quickly becoming a key value for Victorian society, one that was central to its duties to civilize both its colonial possessions and its underclasses at home. The developing system of mass primary education in England had its origin in the Sunday and charity schools created in the early nineteenth century to teach poor children to read the Bible and limit the threat of immorality and criminality among the new masses of poor urban youth.[17] As the nineteenth century progressed, a consensus developed that education, and literacy in particular, was central to both the moral betterment of the individual and the proper regulation of society. The creation of a system of primary education in England and the development of education as a key value is part of the familiar story of the rise of modern governmentality and the new responsibility of the modern state for the self-improvement of the people.[18] Within these changes there were debates over whether education should be the purview of the state or of religious institutions, a conflict that shaped expectations of religion and the limits of its influence in public life in England. These tensions at home colored perceptions of Burmese education.

Despite the value placed on education in contemporary discourse, the educational system in England in the nineteenth century developed unevenly, with a patchwork of different schools and systems for different classes and state funding for schools run by Christian associations. It was not until the end of the nineteenth century that the state attempted a universal system of primary education. In this context, George E. R. Grant Brown's claim "It is a remarkable fact that the Burmese had universal education of a sort long before anything of the kind existed in any European country" is not entirely an exaggeration.[19] In the projects at home, those advocating a universal free system of primary education were considered the most progressive. And here, much to their surprise, the British had discovered a culture that had exceeded even England itself in this key index of civilization.

Literacy was one of three areas in which British observers labeled the Burmese as modern as the West. In the spread of education, the social position of women, and the rational, scientific nature perceived in Buddhism, many Europeans saw the Burmese not only as embracing the values of Victorian civilization, but as occasionally exceeding the British themselves.[20] Yet these were never unalloyed perceptions. In daily interactions, a very different set of perceptions dominated for many Europeans. The complement to Burmese women's freedom was the perceived laziness and sloth of Burmese men. And many British felt the great ethical tradition of Buddhism was lost in the hands of indolent monks who spent their time sleeping and reciting "meaningless chants." In equal fashion, the promise of the Burmese education system eventually proved hollow for the British colonial administration.

EVERY LETTER EQUALS A PAGODA: MONASTERY EDUCATION AND LITERACY

Monastery school education, as a product of Buddhist practice and reform, created the scholarly culture much admired by the British, but its purpose was to preserve the *sāsana* and create good merit for both the boys and their parents. Prior to British colonialism, the village monastery was the primary source of education in Burma.[21] The association between monasteries and primary education is so strong that the contemporary word for school is the same as that for monastery. Monks taught all of the boys of the village to read, write, and recite Burmese and Pali as preparation for ordination and to create merit.[22] Young boys were sent to the monasteries around age six or seven. Most studied there during the day and returned home at night to eat their evening meal, although some lived at the monastery full time.[23] When the parents felt a child was ready to begin his education, they would ask permission from the head of the monastery, who would then select the proper day.[24] Parents would make a special donation of food to mark the occasion and bring the boy to the monastery to begin his education.[25]

The curriculum for boys started with tracing the letters on a slate. "When a boy enters the monastery as student, the teacher places in his hand a piece of blackened board, whereupon are written the first letters of the alphabet. The poor lad has to repeat over and over the name of the letters, crying aloud with all the powers of his lungs."[26] To learn all of the letters, their names, and vowel combinations, students would work their way through a *thinbongyi*, or spelling book, that often also included simple verses.[27] After learning to recognize and write the letters, students would proceed in the same manner through other texts, copying from palm leaves and reciting aloud, until they had memorized them completely. Each evening the monks would correct their recitations.

The first text memorized in this fashion was the *Maṅgala Sutta* (Burmese: *Mingala*), a verse text of moral admonishments, followed by the *Sigālovāda Sutta,* a text on the ethics of social relationships for laypeople, the *Mahāparinibbāna Sutta,* and the *Dhammapada.*[28] When students had mastered these, which would be a matter of years, they were allowed to study the Jātakas, and in particular the last ten Jātakas.[29] These early texts were primarily ethical prescriptions, some specifically focused on the ethics of lay life. The curriculum was supplemented by treatises intended for the edification of young men, including the *Lokanīti* and the *Puttovada son ma sa.*[30]

Much of the learning the boys gained in the monasteries was not from texts but from participation in the monks' daily rituals. Jeffrey Samuels has argued that teaching boys in monasteries "is largely based on an action-oriented pedagogy, a system of learning that is centered around doing, performing and speaking."[31] While the young boys held the status of laity, they joined in the daily rituals of the monastery—they learned ritual formulae, including the precepts and *paritta* texts, by taking part in these rituals.[32] Participating in the life of the monastery, they learned the practices and postures of the monastic life they were expected to join as well as the correct language and behavior for laypeople in their interactions with monks. This practical education was as influential as the assimilation of the content of texts. As Samuels argues, this does not mean that "these texts have no place in the lives of newcomers to the sangha," but that "the pedagogical function of these texts has more to do with their performance than it does with studying their content."[33] Texts were important to monastery pedagogy, but the goals of monastery education were not limited to assimilating content.

Boys learned to read by memorizing first the Pali of each text and then a *nissaya* version that interspersed a Burmese translation with each word of the Pali text, teaching the meaning of the Pali through the *nissaya* text.[34] Comprehension came through memorization and only at the end of a long process of learning texts, listening to sermons, and interacting with learned monks. Memorizing the words and sounds of a text allowed the student to interiorize the text for future reference. Beyond the *nissaya,* the meaning of the Pali was not directly addressed. For the young scholars, questions about meaning would be posed not to the monks but to less intimidating parents.[35] Memorization of texts became the central object of education because memorization preserved the textual aspects of the *sāsana* within the student himself and was the foundation for the much longer, gradual process of comprehension.

The scholarly culture the Europeans admired was represented literally in the treatment of texts. Texts themselves, palm leaf manuscripts and, later, printed books, were objects of reverence. They were kept in a special manuscript cabinet, and students had to pay homage to the book before removing it. Students were reminded of the *Dhammanīti* proverb "akkharaṃ ekamekañ ca buddharūpaṃ samaṃ siya," translated by one former monastery school student as "every letter is worth a pagoda," or "one letter means one Buddha."[36] Reverence for the texts, reading, and copying them were means of paying respect to the Buddha and his teachings and of producing merit. In monastery education, texts and reading were not simply means to acquire knowledge, but were themselves integrated into the economy of merit and the preservation of the teachings.

In many villages, the monastery schools were supplemented by lay-run house schools that offered similar training to girls and young boys.[37] These schools were run as acts of merit by respected laymen or laywomen and taught the same curriculum as the monastery schools, but operated outside of the monastery restrictions that limited girls' access. The lay house schools expanded the system of monastery education and were likely responsible for the relatively high rates of female literacy.

The history and development of this system of education is unclear, but it seems to have been shaped by the new textual emphases of the preceding 150 years.[38] This form of education is common to other polities in South and

Southeast Asia, and the methods of education employed in Burma are very similar to those described in Sri Lanka, although as Heinz Bechert notes, the Burmese system never had the same emphasis on Sanskrit education.[39] In Burma, this system of education was likely shaped by changes in the seventeenth century and the series of monastic reforms beginning in the 1780s.

Victor Lieberman and Patrick Pranke argue that a shift in the demographics of Buddhist monasticism in the late seventeenth century led to new educational patterns. Political and economic shifts in the sixteenth century created a proliferation of monasteries in villages, shifting emphasis away from monasteries in royal centers.[40] Combined with evidence of increased popular literacy, this allows them to argue that a greater number of boys were educated in village monasteries and interacted with flows of knowledge among monastic centers starting from this time. Likewise, the use of *nissaya* operated for cultural integration in much the same way that, as Anne Blackburn has explained, the *sutra sannaya* texts operated in Lanka, facilitating the spread of ideas and standardizing curriculum among villages, representing the new sorts of textual emphases evident in Buddhist reforms of this period across Southeast Asia and Sri Lanka.[41] If the evidence bears these hypotheses out, it would mean that the mass literacy the British so admired, far from being the innate trait dating back to the birth of Burmese culture in Pagan, was the product of a fairly recent set of Buddhist historical innovations.

The monastic reforms beginning in the 1780s likely also shaped the education of young boys. The Thudhamma reformers of King Bodawpaya's time argued that the decline in the *sāsana* was due to the fact that novices were poorly trained in the Pali texts and insisted that new novices must learn the words and the letters of the texts.[42] This concern created the curriculum of the Patamabyan Pali examinations discussed in Chapter 2 and elevated reciting Pali texts to the pinnacle of monastic practice.[43] Reform ideals established curriculum and education as central issues for the *sāsana* and mandated memorization as a pedagogical method.

In addition, part of these reforms was a process of purging monastic curriculum of lay-oriented and practical forms of knowledge. Reformist monks accused their opponents of teaching skills that were directed toward earning a living as a layperson and specialized sciences not directly related to Buddhist textual reflection or monastic practice. Such knowledge was rejected as corrupting, and monks accused of teaching it were defrocked, practices that would have consequences for the colonial engagement of monastery education.[44]

Monastery education in Burma placed a premium on literacy, as the British perceived. Through the history of reform and the tradition of respect for texts, literacy pedagogy was elevated to the heart of Buddhist practice and the preservation of the *sāsana,* and refined into a core institution of the village. However, literacy in this system was not understood primarily as a means to the content of texts but as a practice of creating merit and preserving Buddhism. In fact, those aspects of previous pedagogy that had focused on lay and practical knowledge detached from the system of merit making had been denounced. Literacy was for the preservation of the *sāsana,* which claimed universal and highest import in both political discourse and the daily life of the village. This was the world to which the British arrived, understanding little of its history or internal logic.

Turning Monasteries into Schools?

The village monastery system of education was so impressive to the colonial administrators that when they were forced to implement a system of primary education, it seemed obvious to promote the monastery schools. The prospect of colonial education through monastery schools, however, was destined to fail because officials misunderstood the purposes of Buddhist education. In 1864, Arthur Phayre, the chief commissioner of British Burma, in response to pressure from the government in India to create a system of education in Burma, proposed to offer the monks free textbooks in Burmese.[45] He wanted to use the monastery schools as the basis for a near-universal system of primary education that would expand the current monastery curriculum in areas where European knowledge would be helpful to the people: specifically arithmetic, geography, and land-measuring. He wrote in 1865, "It is believed that if books on the subjects above mentioned were furnished to the Chief Phongyee [monk] of each Monastery, and a qualified Burmese teacher were engaged to superintend the studies occasionally, that the books would be willingly used."[46] Adding European content to Buddhist practices of teaching, he believed, would both make monastic schools more productive and bring their project under the regulation of the colonial state.

Phayre's plan rested on the idea of encouraging the existing native system and convincing the population that the government shared their educational goals.[47] The gift of books seemed the perfect means of engaging monks with a new curriculum. Making donations to monks was one of the most basic acts of Buddhist piety and one that was expected from a sympathetic state. Intellectual materials, in particular the most highly prized new technology of the time, printed books, were especially appropriate donations.

The Department of Public Instruction officials quickly discovered, however, that while for the most part the monks were happy to receive the books, since in a Buddhist economy of merit no such gift could be refused, they were slow to employ them in their teaching. The Director of Public Instruction complained that monks, "who have taken our books, have let them lie unused in the manuscript chest owing to their indolence."[48] Choosing to store the government's donated books together with Pali texts in the manuscript chest demonstrated the respect due to precious intellectual artifacts for the monks. It was not likely meant as resistance to the scheme. The officials' response demonstrated how little they understood the role of texts in Burmese Buddhism. To their dismay, the monks never responded with the desired enthusiasm to the gift of books or the offer to participate in the government's system; they did not necessarily share the government's ideas of education nor were they interested in its teaching methods.

While the monastery schools were reticent to engage the colonial system, the lay-run house schools took well to government encouragement. Early colonial discussions put the emphasis on the monastery schools, mentioning house-schools as minor classes set up to provide education for girls excluded from monasteries. However, Burmese sources indicate that the lay schools had a long history, likely given encouragement under the late eighteenth-century reforms.[49] Peter Hordern, disappointed with the prospects of the monastery schools, discovered the lay schools early in his tenure as Director of Public Instruction and set about to encourage them as an alternative.[50]

In 1872, he initiated a new system for education in Lower Burma. In addition to the free textbooks, the Department of Public Instruction created a series of grants to schools based on the performance of students on new standardized examinations. The lay schools flourished under this system. Their previous volunteer work had become lucrative, further fueled by government requirements that they charge the parents fees. Grants to monastery schools were more difficult, given that monks could not accept money in exchange for their efforts. The government attempted to circumvent this by offering the equivalent in gifts of rice or books or by making donations to the monastery stewards who dealt with money. They found, however, that "the offer of grants is no inducement to Buddhist monks whose vows forbid them to receive money and the curriculum of the Department is not always approved by those who believe that the sole object of education is to enable their pupils to understand the truths of religion."[51]

Colonial officials were stymied in their efforts to motivate the monks, for whom neither gifts nor government recognition were incentive to engage the new pedagogy. The thriving lay schools began to attract boys away from the monastery schools, highlighting the shift from an educational economy of merit to a capitalist system. Monastery pedagogy, driven by the ability to facilitate merit making for parents and donors and the need to preserve the Buddha's teachings, resisted transition to a paid system, because its educational goals were inconceivable in those terms. While colonial officials were well aware that the Burmese population needed training in capitalist values, they were unprepared for monks whose status rested on the resistance of sensual motivations. All of the colonial technologies for the production of desires seem to have little effect on a body of men who understood their ultimate goal to be overcoming desire. While a less diligent colonizer might have dismissed these monks as irredeemable, the colonial education system in Burma was convinced that the monks shared fundamental modern values of education and literacy.

Over the next fifty years, the Department of Public Instruction tried dozens of programs to bring the monastery schools into the system, each with a determination in the logic of Phayre's original plan—that if only the monastery schools could be modernized they would create a massive universal primary education system and gain the sympathy of the people.[52] As one report put it, "If anything can be done to encourage the monks to take a greater interest in secular education, which they might easily do without interference with their religious duties, Burma will possess a system of vernacular education such as exists no where else in the East."[53] Yet, according to the statistics they reported each year, all of their attempts were a failure. The number of participating monastery schools never significantly grew, and increasing attendance at the lay and missionary schools meant that monastery schools had an ever-declining influence on the youth of the province.[54]

Education officials were inconsistent in their support for the program. The plan to engage the monastery schools was met with skepticism from some colonial officials from the very beginning, and this doubt was a powerful presence throughout the next half century.[55] While the frequent initiatives would bring some monastery schools onto the Department's register, within a couple of years a frustration with the quality of education in monastery schools would create a tightening of the rules and purge hundreds of monastery schools from the rolls.[56] This pattern was repeated over and over. The annual *Report on Public Instruction in Burma* contained frequent outbursts of optimism followed immediately with despair that the system would never work. Whereas the monasteries were discussed as seats of native learning on the verge of becoming great schools, there were equally expressions of disillusionment and frustration—that the monks were lazy, ignorant, and completely unreformable.[57] This contradictory approach was expressed not just from one director to the next, or one year to the next, but from one page to the next in the annual reports.[58] Reading the reports, it becomes clear that the colonial education officials simultaneously held two contradictory views of the monks: that they were both potential educationalists of the greatest stature and useless idlers who slept and recited meaningless chants.

Despite the persistent prejudice against the monks, doubts about the viability of the system, and the very real failings of its projects, attempts to bring the monastery schools into the colonial education system persisted unabated for more than a half century. The issue remained at the forefront of educational concerns into the late 1930s, when the lay schools offering English education had all but destroyed attendance at monastery schools.[59] This ambivalence and persistent hope in the monks as educators stemmed from a fundamental misunderstanding of the monastic practices of literacy education.

A Case of Mistaken Identity of Purpose

They looked on education as the main instrument of freedom.
　—John S. Furnivall, *Colonial Policy and Practice* [60]

Many discussions of the plan to build a colonial education system from the monastery schools emphasize efficiency and economy as motivating factors for the colonial officials. Monastery schools had the great advantage that they required no investment in infrastructure and very little state aid for instructors. Colonial administrators in a utilitarian-fashioned system could not go wrong arguing for the efficient and inexpensive nature of a program; thus economic factors were a frequent rationale in requests sent to Calcutta and London. However, Phayre's original plan presented a second reason that was a deeper motivating factor for many in the Burmese colonial administration. In his early letters on the issue to the Home Department in India, Phayre expressed concern that the only contact the majority of the Burmese had with colonial power was through its coercive aspects. "The people of British Burma as yet know very little of the British Government except as a Police, a Revenue, and a Judicial power. . . . The masses of the agricultural population know nothing of the desire of the British Government to educate and to raise them in the scale of civilization."[61] He was worried that the face of the colonial state in British Burma was, to put it in Foucault's terms, purely juridical, whereas the intent of the colonial state was the improvement of the people. The reason for implementing a system of education was to show the population the true nature and purpose of the modern state.[62]

For Phayre this meant not only creating European model schools in the larger towns to demonstrate the best in British education, but actively engaging the monasteries to convince the people that the government's projects were not in competition with the monasteries but engaged in the same project with the same ends. His early memos refer to the monasteries as "national schools" and emphasize that the government's educational projects would succeed only if they were understood as augmenting and complementing the monasteries.[63] Colonial officials and British observers had commented for decades that the monasteries were already engaged in one of the most important civilizing projects of modernity. For Phayre, all that was left to do was to demonstrate to the monks that they shared a common project and a common goal.

When Phayre saw boys tracing letters on black *parabaik* and reciting sentences at the top of their lungs, he saw education. He, as did generations of officials that followed him, saw monks engaged in the improvement of the people through teaching them to read, a project identical to that of the modern state. Thus to him it seemed only logical to convince the monks that they could become partners in what was now the legitimate concern of the state.

For the British government, the goal of colonial education was explicitly framed in terms of the "moral and intellectual improvement of the people."[64] As L. E. Bagshawe has pointed out, these two were taken to be fundamentally identical: intellectual improvement was understood in terms of productivity and usefulness in society, and the Protestant ethic had elevated industry to be the central moral value of society.[65] Both projects to educate poor children at home and missionary education abroad centered on forming useful and productive subjects. The National Society for Promoting Education of the Poor, which founded schools in England, gave its purpose explicitly as, "to confer on the Children of the Poor the Inestimable Benefits of Religious Instruction, combined with such other Acquirements as may be suitable to their stations in Life and calculated to render them useful and productive Members of Society."[66] These values are reflected in the subjects Phayre chose for the book-donation program—geography, land-measuring, and arithmetic—topics that were suited to making an agricultural population more productive in its labor. Officials viewed the monks and monastery education through this interpretation of productivity. Throughout the annual *Report on Public Instruction in Burma,* the directors and inspectors lament the decline of the monastery school because they saw it as the monks' only productive contribution. They worried that the rise of secular schools served "to deprive the vast army of pongyis of what is perhaps their greatest sphere of usefulness to the community."[67] Usefulness in the officials' minds was located solely in social, and not religious, contributions.

Material productivity and engagement, however, were not the goals of the monastery. The monks whom these education officials decried as detached and indolent were cultivating this detachment. The status monks held, and the merit that respect for them produced, relied upon their disengagement from the world. Yet colonial officials failed to grasp how intentional disengagement could be a value. They commonly accused the monks of not participating in the education system out of apathy—even in those moments when the monks were most actively engaged in resisting the plan.[68] Accusations of apathy, laziness, and indolence, high crimes from a Victorian sensibility, demonstrate how little the education officials understood the purpose and nature of the sangha.

The misunderstanding ran deeper. For the officials of the education department, there was no conflict between teaching the government's curriculum and the religious goals of the monks, because they understood education and literacy to be universal projects that work toward a universal good of progress and modernity. Furthermore, they understood the Buddhist aspects of the monks' teaching to be limited to the *content* of what the students read, while having no effect on the universal *practice* of learning to read. Religion here was one compartmentalized aspect of social life, not a set of practices and ideals that permeated and shaped all aspects of life, as the monks would understand it. Pedagogy and literacy were secular universal practices to which religious particularities could be added or neglected without changing the basic goal. Religion, in this way, was limited to the particular content. The purpose of education was to form modern productive subjects; its religious content could inflect these as productive Buddhist subjects or productive Christian subjects, but the learning itself was not a religious practice. It was unthinkable that religion, understood as a general good but one with a specifically limited scope, could conflict with the greater good of education.

Officials from the education department insisted that monks could teach "without interfering with their religious duties," but this meant a recognition of religious duties that were somehow separate from their teaching. It required adopting European conceptual divisions between activities that were religious and those that were secular. A successful project engaging the monks in a colonial education system would require that they recognize the betterment of society as the legitimate responsibility of the colonial government. This in turn required a redefinition of the capacities of Buddhism and its location in a sphere known as "religion," whose responsibilities were for individual moral betterment and soteriology. Buddhism as a religion, in this definition, could operate as an adjunct to the state's projects, as Christian missionaries did, but education was not a religious project or a religious good. Phayre's plan required teaching the monks the proper categorization of their pedagogy. If they could learn the correct boundaries between the religious and the secular, two goals would be achieved at once: the state could further the improvement of the people through the institution of monastery education, and the people would learn about the true nature of the modern colonial state. This was simply a matter of asking the monks to recognize the correct and universal categories that should shape their actions and, from the state's perspective, need not threaten their practices.

The education department's intervention in monastery education can be read as a colonial attempt to propose a particular definition of religion—one that divided religious discourse from secular social universal goods with a stark boundary. Projects such as providing textbooks or registering monasteries as government schools were the mechanics of producing a conceptual scheme in which Buddhism could operate as a "religion," properly bounded off from the secular concerns of society. It was one of many interpretations of what religion should mean operative in Burma and the broader British colonial world. Their plan sought to produce a conceptual scheme in which the Buddhism in the monasteries operated as a religion, with its capacities and contributions located in doctrine, ethics, and textual content, and identified projects for the material and moral betterment of the people in a secular category that was inside the purview and mandate of the colonial state. Religion, defined this way, limited the impact of the teaching in monasteries and denied the universality of categories like *sāsana*. The education officials' frustrations came from the monks' inability, or unwillingness, to recognize and participate in these "universal" categories.

Monastic Resistance and the Limitations of "Religion"

The monastic response to the government's education scheme was mixed. There were a few monks who welcomed the books and the new curriculum, but they were the minority. Monastic resistance to the plan was much more common, and fell into two broad types: those who expressed no open resistance to the plan but did not comply with the rules set out by the Department of Public Instruction, and those who rejected the plan and organized their opposition along a discourse that labeled the government's efforts harmful to Buddhism.[69]

The former consisted of monks who accepted the government's gifts or acquiesced to participate but never allowed their teaching to be shaped by the new rules. These monks were often simply not willing to take attendance and keep the records required for registration.[70] Unlike the training in the daily practices of the monastery, the disciplinary acts of pedagogy required by the government served no educational end that the monks could see. Monastery education had its own disciplinary formation, and its ethics and discipline were something the colonial officials much admired, but its logic was quite different from that of the colonial state. The organizing and surveillance technologies of examinations, records, and attendance did not in any way help to preserve the teachings or make their students better Buddhists. This resistance was about opposing the ethical and disciplinary system the government's education system was predicated on and not allowing it to supplant the ethical project of the monastery. The transformation of ethical and disciplinary techniques that the government sought failed because the new techniques could not correspond to the ethical project of the monastery.

The second category of opposition was much more organized and explicitly contested the categories the government's plan sought to instill. While the largest monastic sect at first offered no direct opposition to the plan, in 1887 a group of monks publicized a statement that teaching math and other subjects on the government's curriculum, or accepting a government lay teacher into the monastery, was a violation of the Vinaya.[71] This forced the more government-inclined monks to refuse the assistance they had requested and resulted in one monk being defrocked.[72]

The Pakhan Sayadaw, an influential abbot in Mandalay, led the charge.[73] He was the center of the old guard of the Thudhamma hierarchy and a man many considered should rightly hold the title of Thathanabaing.[74] Unlike the Taungdaw Sayadaw, who King Thibaw had appointed (and the later

British recognized) as Thathanabaing largely because he had been the royal preceptor, the Pakhan Sayadaw was a scholar and savvy leader and was the chosen successor of the second Maungdaung Sayadaw, the Thudhamma Thathanabaing under King Mindon.[75] From 1885 to 1895, the Pakhan Sayadaw remained more influential than the Thathanabaing, and many Burmese recognized him as de facto Thathanabaing after the Taungdaw Sayadaw's death in 1895. However, the Pakhan Sayadaw's opposition to the government's education efforts meant that the British refused their recognition and ignored the result of monastic elections that would have given him the title.[76] Moreover, the government refused to take up the issue of appointing a new Thathanabaing until after the Pakhan Sayadaw's death in 1900.[77] The Pakhan Sayadaw's long experience on the Thudhamma Council, the appointed keepers of monastic orthodoxy, meant that he was deeply resistant to colonial intervention inside the monasteries and able to quickly organize other senior monks to support his position. By 1891, even the Thathanabaing had acceded to the Pakhan Sayadaw's will. He issued a circular discouraging monks from participating in the colonial government's plan to make the monasteries into primary schools, with a reference to the authority of the Thudhamma Council—a nod to the Pakhan Sayadaw's influence.[78]

The Pakhan Sayadaw commissioned the Minekhine Sayadaw to write a treatise on the types of knowledge contained in the government's curriculum and whether monks could teach these subjects according to Vinaya law.[79] Unfortunately, the Minekhine Sayadaw died before he finished the treatise, but his draft of the text was published in the *Maha-Bodhi News* in 1913.[80] The text labeled the government's curriculum as *lokāyata* knowledge, knowledge that, because it did not assist in teaching people to strive for either *nibbāna* or a better rebirth, instead worked to prevent progress toward these goals by distracting from the teachings. The monastic leaders argued that monks should not participate in the government's education scheme because its teaching did not further the goals of the *sāsana* and the karmic betterment of their students.

Juliane Schober has argued that the monks' resistance was a shortsighted evaluation of the impact of colonial forms of knowledge, which defined opposition to colonial rule in premodern terms and precipitated the decline of monastic authority.[81] Like Donald Smith, she sees in the monks' decision a lack of understanding of the consequences of colonial ideas.[82] I would argue instead that the monks proved acutely aware of the fundamental shifts the government's plan required, and their formulation of the problem in terms of *lokāyata* knowledge was an innovative response that sought to preserve the centrality of *sāsana* as a worldview and conceptual framework.

This group of monks rejected the idea that they could participate in secular acts of teaching without violating their religious goals. I see in their resistance not just a rejection of the plan, but a rejection of the classificatory scheme the government's proposal presumed. The plan required that the monks be formed not only by the disciplinary procedures of taking attendance and keeping records, but also by the conceptual scheme that recognized secular and religious spheres and produced Buddhism as a religion bounded off from other aspects of life. Monks like the Pakhan Sayadaw resisted the conceptual subordination of the purpose for their pedagogy to a competing claim of universality. For them, their teaching had meaning relative to the category of the *sāsana,* not subordinated and located in a universal category of religion. The monks were not interested in participating in the creation of Buddhism as a religion because this did not serve their ends. They were not willing to engage a system in which the preservation of the *sāsana* was a peripheral consequence of a larger project of creating productive, modern colonial subjects. The monks experienced the category shift that the colonial system required as a shift in the nature of Buddhist practice. While the government claimed it simply wanted to embrace the system that was already in place, the monks understood the threatening potential of this conceptual change. As the organized monastic opposition argued, teaching and learning in this system was not just indifferent to the cause of creating merit and preserving the *sāsana;* it detracted from those projects by classifying their pedagogy as directed toward other ends. Despite the colonial officials' hopes, it turned out that the engine of Burmese society's perceived progressive civilization was at its core opposed to the civilizing mission.

MODERN BUDDHIST EDUCATION AND THE FUTURE OF THE *SĀSANA*

The disconnect between the colonial state and the monks as to what constituted education and Buddhist practice led to a dramatic decline in the monastery school as a social institution. Although the preservation of the *sāsana* remained the pressing issue for the Buddhist majority, parents abandoned the monastery schools and sent their children to the secular lay schools that taught the government curriculum to prepare them for the economic changes sweeping through the colonial province. They especially sought out the Anglo-vernacular schools that taught both Burmese and English so that students could prepare for lucrative careers. However, the move to new schools created new anxieties. Many worried that boys trained in English would not support Buddhism and would lose all knowledge of the Buddha's teachings.

The popularity of the lay schools and their government and missionary school counterparts quickly created a new class of student in the local imaginary—the Burmese Anglo-vernacular schoolboy. Trained in the best learning of the new colonial state, these boys were seen as the cadre of future leaders and became the image of progress in the discourse of both Burmese and Europeans in Burma.[83] However, this position carried great responsibility for the future of Burma and Buddhism and created concern about how these boys were being shaped.

As we will see in Chapters 4 and 5, schoolboys became pivotal characters in the stories Burmese Buddhists told themselves about the decline of the *sāsana* and its future prospects. These boys held a unique position as both mediators between changing worlds and agents of change in their own right. Their fathers, both the prominent and the lowly, would have been educated in the monastery system, but had chosen something different for their sons. New economic configurations and the changing social and political conditions meant that parents and many of the boys themselves aspired to the possibilities opened up by government education. Formal education, and especially Anglo-vernacular schools, offered the tantalizing prospect of a position as a clerk, in business or government, a place with both economic opportunity and the status and respect of being an intermediary between communities and cultures.

Some Burmese Buddhist leaders faulted parents for seeking to promote the economic and not the spiritual welfare of their children by sending them to the new schools.[84] They argued that with the new emphasis on gaining English, the purpose of education had become the mere pursuit of jobs.[85] More to the point, they argued that this situation had taught boys to replace the Buddhist religion of their ancestors with the pursuit of wealth.

> Every day the number of our children learning in these English-teaching schools is increasing, every day the necessity of an English education is becoming more and more felt: and the children who to-day are thus growing up without any Religion will be the leaders of the people, members of the professions and the moulders of the national opinions and beliefs. . . . We

are this day supporting the Priests of our Lord,—our children to-morrow will be leaving them to starve; to-day we are building Cetiyas and Temples, and to-morrow the Temples will be untenanted ruins, and our grandchildren will not worship at our Shrines; worse still, we are letting our children grow up without any knowledge of Religion in its deeper sense and meaning, we are letting them enshrine in their hearts the gaining of wealth and power in place of the Most Excellent Law and the Memory of our Master; and in so doing, we are preparing for them lives of sorrow instead of lives of happiness and peace.[86]

Many Buddhist parents felt that English education was necessary for the future of Buddhism—that the changing conditions of colonialism had placed the *sāsana* in a double bind. Whereas under the monarchy there had been general prosperity among the laity and sufficient patronage from the king to support the monasteries and pagodas, the colonial system posed a new risk. If the next generation only learned English and the skills of the colonizer, they might become rich but abandon the teachings, leaving the monks to starve. On the other hand, if the next generation could not compete in the new economic system, the laity would become impoverished and not have enough to support the sangha.[87] Unlike the objections of the monks to the government curriculum, these Buddhists directly tied the ability to earn a good livelihood as a layperson to the status of the *sāsana* and argued for a need to adapt to current conditions.[88]

Writing to the *Times of Burma* in 1900, one young man boldly asserted that the new education system "does not tend in any way to better the intellectual and moral condition of the people but that it is pointing out the way to speedy demoralization."[89] This man would go on to become the famous U May Oung, a key nationalist, founding member of the Young Men's Buddhist Association and the Burma Research Society, respected attorney and judge, Buddhist legal scholar, and Home Member. But at this point, he was simply Maung May Oung, born in Arakan, educated in Calcutta and at Rangoon Government High School where he won honors, who had dropped out of Rangoon College before completing the BA.[90] At the turn of the century, he was working as a schoolmaster in Mergui. He was undoubtedly elite, with his English education, the product of the very secular government education system that he critiqued as degrading Burmese morals and religion. Yet he was an outspoken and ardent activist during his foray into education before beginning his legal career in 1902. In a series of letters to the newspapers, he pushed for the creation of an educational reform society and for a radical transformation of the education system, using his own name in a day when most signed such critiques with a pseudonym.[91]

For these concerned Buddhists like Maung May Oung, the new economic and educational situation constituted a crisis for Buddhism in Burma. They argued that the *sāsana* was in danger because this cadre of boys who were being trained to be the future leaders of Burmese society knew only a smattering of Buddhist concepts and literature. As early as 1883, leaders in the Burmese community expressed a great concern that the new educational realities could spell the death of the *sāsana*. By the 1890s, education, and the lack of Buddhist education, in a rising generation of boys was a central issue in newspapers in English and Burmese, and the subject of public meetings, lectures, and new Buddhist associations.

It was a lack of understanding of Buddhist ideas that drove the concerns over the place of Buddhism in education. Maung May Oung complained, "he had met some who had no knowledge even of the Life of the Buddha, others who recited their prayers were ignorant of their meaning, still more, those who, when asked to explain their religion for the benefit of an enquirer, hopelessly failed in the attempt."[92] The impulse toward knowledge was the same as that toward Pali examinations for laypeople, but in this context it was not enough for the children to know the text; they needed to understand and internalize it.[93] This lack of understanding was in part a product of the circumstances. Boys enrolled in government and missionary schools only remained in the monasteries for a few weeks during school breaks for their temporary ordinations. This was long enough to learn the prayers and precepts, but little else. The pedagogical practices of monastery education placed comprehension and reflection at the end of a long process of memorization, a process that was not possible on the calendar of the Anglo-vernacular schools. The type of knowledge necessary to preserve the *sāsana* shifted. Parents and Buddhist leaders wanted the boys to be able to explicate doctrine and apply it to their daily lives. Whereas in monastery education, Buddhist concepts were embodied in the boys through memorization and the practices of the monastery, now the Buddhist leaders sought boys who could embody the *sāsana* in ethical practice as the result of intellectual reflection. Knowledge of the words of the text or the ability to recite them was no longer sufficient to prevent the decline of the Buddha's teachings.

The colonial condition had created an untenable position for the future of the *sāsana*. Sino-Burmese author and government translator Taw Sein Ko asked:

Is it not a patent fact that the Burman youths of the present day receive no religious or moral training at home, that being brought up in no religion at all, they look upon pagoda-going as orthodox Buddhism?...Go to any English school and ask the Burman boys what they know of Buddhism, what the Buddhistic rules of conduct are, and we are quite sure that nine out of every ten boys examined will answer with gaping mouths and wondering eyes, that they do not even know exactly what the ten Buddhist commandments are; and yet on every Sabbath day they go to *kyaungs* and solemnly promise to abide by promises they do not know![94]

Buddhists recognized a need for laypeople to receive the education offered at the new schools so that they could financially support the *sāsana,* and yet these schools superseded Buddhist training and left the children ignorant of the most basic Buddhist ideas. This lack of Buddhist knowledge, formulated in the new terms of comprehension and ethical reflection, became the acute concern of Buddhist associations worried about the status of the *sāsana* in the generations to come.

TEACHING BUDDHISM IN A HALF HOUR A DAY

The problems of education and *sāsana* under colonial conditions required a creative engagement of colonial forms for Buddhist ends, a process that in turn shaped the nature of what was taught as Buddhism. Starting in 1897, a number of prominent Buddhists decided to address the increasing anxiety over the education of Buddhist children with concrete action. The solution was not a return to monastery education, but new Buddhist schools and the introduction of Buddhist education into secular schools. For many, the creation of Buddhist Anglo-vernacular schools took precedence.

The first two Buddhist Anglo-vernacular schools were created by wealthy individuals. Daw Mya May, who often signed as Mrs. M. M. Hla Oung in a hybrid colonial fashion of naming, was the daughter of a key Mon general who had supported the British and the wife of U Hla Oung, the Comptroller of Indian Treasuries and the highest ranking Burmese in the colonial government. Although these two connections give an indication of both her wealth and prominence and her loyalty to empire, she was anything but defined by the men in her life. She became a hub of Rangoon social and cultural life and a patron of many of the most important projects of the first decade of the twentieth century.[95] She was known as a benefactor of the nascent Burmese modernist painting tradition, and her portrait still hangs in the National Museum in tribute to this work. She traveled widely, was presented to royalty twice in England, and hosted the Prince of Wales at a party in Rangoon. She supported a variety of Buddhist causes, including the European monk Ananda Metteyya and his Buddhist mission to England, which established the Buddhist Society of Great Britain and Ireland. She would later be sought out as the representative of Burmese women at the Burma Round Table talks on Burma's independence from India.[96]

However, her first project, and the one that would come to define her life and work, was the creation of two Buddhist schools. She shared with her nephew, Maung May Oung, the sentiment that government education was undermining Buddhism in Burma. Daw Mya May and her husband U Hla Oung founded the Empress Victoria Buddhist Boys' School in 1897.[97] The name itself suggested what they understood to be its innovation—a strong positive identification with both empire and Buddhism. Moreover, she had the vision to create a Buddhist school specifically for girls: later the same year she opened the Empress Victoria Buddhist Girls' School.[98] The boys' school taught to the seventh standard in Burmese and English, and the girls' school taught to the fifth standard, both under the supervision of European headmasters. Both schools taught the government's curriculum but employed a Burmese layman to give Buddhist religious instruction for an hour and a half each morning.[99]

The desire to provide an education that offered both the social advancement of English training without sacrificing a foundation in Buddhism was shared by Buddhist organizers around the country. Buddhist Anglo-vernacular schools in Moulmein and Mandalay, important cultural and economic centers of the time, quickly followed this experiment in Rangoon. In 1899, a group of laymen gathered in Moulmein to form the Sasanadara Society, which took as its first project the creation of the Shin Buddhaghosa School.[100] This school also followed the government curriculum and offered English instruction to the fifth standard for boys and girls, and provided religious instruction for a half hour daily, with lay Pali teachers providing lessons once a week and the abbot of the nearby Pagandaung monastery preaching twice a month.[101] One of its first headmasters was Maung May Oung himself.

Whereas Daw Mya May and Maung May Oung, like Maung Hpo Hmyin (discussed in Chapter 2), represented an elite defined by its wealth, position, and loyalty to the British administration, they were not the majority of those active in founding new Buddhist schools. Far more typical was

U Kyaw Yan, who came from a more modest background. He was educated not in Calcutta or a Rangoon high school but by a local village abbot in a monastery school before entering a government normal school in 1882. From there, he went on to become a teacher and then a school inspector in the government system as it grew in the 1880s and 1890s.[102] In this, he was perhaps exactly the model of what many parents hoped for with Anglo-vernacular education in this period—a boy who gained mobility out of the village and into a secure, if low-level, position in government service. And yet, he was attuned to the sentiment that education was undermining Buddhism.

U Kyaw Yan would go on to a storied career as Buddhist revivalist and later nationalist, but this pivotal moment of his influence came mainly from his cautious position between cultures. He was fluent in both the culture of colonial bureaucracy and the values and practices of the previous Buddhist monastery education. More than this, however, like many of this era, he fashioned himself as a self-taught intellectual, developing expertise in multiple registers, from science, astrology, and traditional medicine to business and Buddhist ethics.

Although he was deeply embedded in the system, as the Department of Public Instruction grew, so did U Kyaw Yan's dissatisfaction with the impact of education separated from religion. By 1897 he was serving as deputy inspector of schools in the thriving transit town of Myingyan. There he rallied local Buddhists to found the Kalyanathingaha Society, and in turn opened the Buddha Thathana Noggaha Anglo-vernacular School.[103] The school had not been running long when its founder was transferred to Mandalay, much to the dismay of the Buddhists in Myingyan, who protested the transfer.[104] Nevertheless, the school in Myingyan prospered, and U Kyaw Yan continued his work.[105] In February of 1901, a group of merchants and civil servants in Mandalay established the Buddha Thathana Noggaha Association, with the first goal of creating a Buddhist Anglo-vernacular school.[106] They founded the Buddha Thathana Noggaha School in Mandalay, which became one of the most important of the Buddhist schools and the only one for which a complete curriculum survives.[107] U Kyaw Yan became involved with this school and published a number of books on Buddhism and ethics for Burmese youth.[108]

The next few years saw the creation of schools throughout the province. The schools and the associations that founded them quickly became centers of Buddhist organizing and activity, engaging the students in the other projects of the Buddhist associations. Records survive from fifteen of these Buddhist Anglo-vernacular schools, although there are indications they were a widespread phenomenon.[109] Some of the schools, such as those associated with U Kyaw Yan's organization, the Society for Promoting Buddhism, became franchise operations, with branches in multiple towns.[110] By 1910 there were at least three different Anglo-vernacular Buddhist schools in Moulmein and four in Rangoon. In certain areas Burmese leaders fought with the colonial administration for funding to open and run Buddhist schools as alternatives to Christian missionary schools.[111] And at schools where the parents were pleased with the education but not the religious content, special associations were created for the Buddhist students.[112] In other places where they could not find competent English teachers, associations created Burmese-language vernacular Buddhist schools.[113] From the records available it seems clear that by 1915 there was at least one Buddhist Anglo-vernacular school in all of the major towns of the province.[114]

The Christian missionary schools provided an example for religious education, but were one of many influences. There were schools for Indian Muslim communities in Rangoon by the 1860s, and by 1900 there were schools sponsored by various groups of Hindus, Chinese, and Theosophists for their children. Sri Lankan monks as well as Col. H. S. Olcott and Anagarika Dharmapala had discussed Buddhist schools in their travels in Burma. The monk Ananda Metteyya published a pamphlet entitled *On Religious Education in Burma* in English in 1903, proposing weekly instruction for children at pagodas, Buddhist education in government schools, Buddhist Anglo-vernacular schools, and a Buddhist University.[115] In addition, Buddhist schools in Sri Lanka were cited as an inspiration for those in Burma.[116]

The momentum that drove the creation of the Buddhist Anglo-vernacular schools also prompted a program of Buddhist education in the government schools. The public concern that secular schools were turning out unruly students encouraged a search for ways to return moral education to the system.[117] While some Burmese had called for an inclusion of Buddhist religious instruction in the government schools as early as 1883, the first program was started in 1902.[118] At the instigation of two Burmese men, the Pegu municipal government allowed a monk to offer religious instruction at the municipal Anglo-vernacular school for a half hour a day. These first lessons involved collective recitation of the Three Gems and the Five Precepts, followed by sermons on the precepts, the *Sigālovāda Sutta,* and the ethical duties of boys, each lesson ending with a statement of gratitude and respect for the government, and "a prayer for the welfare of the King-Emperor."[119]

It was not until 1907 that the Department of Public Instruction seriously considered the measure and surveyed the district commissioners as to its feasibility.[120] Religious neutrality had been a bedrock principle of British policy in India, and religious instruction had been specifically banned in government schools in 1854.[121] However, officials in Burma questioned whether this policy was appropriate for a country with a 90 percent Buddhist population and petitioned authorities for an exception. In 1909, the government allowed religious instruction on school grounds, so long as it was not supported by public funds, was initiated by parents, was provided outside of school hours, and, unlike the first lessons in Pegu, included "no public religious ceremony or act of worship or ritual."[122]

Those active in the Buddhist associations strongly welcomed the new policy; the YMBA printed ten thousand copies of the announcement in Burmese and quickly set up the courses and examinations in the schools.[123] While the option of religious instruction was open to all religions, in practice only Buddhists took advantage of it; Muslims, Hindus, and Christians preferred to make their own arrangements elsewhere.[124] In addition, the program, ostensibly only to be initiated at the request of parents, was strongly supported by the colonial officials to the extent that "it was made clear that whether arrangements were made for instruction in Buddhism at a given school was definitely not a matter of indifference to the department."[125]

To teach Buddhism in a half hour a day, without the practices and postures of the monastery, required a new method. The Buddha Thathana Noggaha Association commissioned U Tilawka to draft a curriculum for its schools in 1901. Instead of adapting the monastery curriculum to be taught in a new context, U Tilawka created a series of lessons divided by grade level. The content he used shared little with that of the monastery schools. The *Mangala Sutta* was required for the third grade, but the *paritta,* the *Sigālovāda Sutta,* the *Lokanīti,* and the *Dhammapada* were eliminated. In their place, U Tilawka composed his own reader, with lessons on the qualities of the Three Gems and the precepts, along with excerpts from other *suttas.* The methods of teaching were changed as well; students learned the Pali text one year and its Burmese translation the next, but no Burmese *nissaya.* The largest change was an assimilation of the government's pedagogical methods; instead of emphasis on textual memorization, once a year students were examined orally on their comprehension of the meaning of the texts, and monetary prizes were awarded to those students who passed.[126]

U Tilawka's curriculum was fairly representative of the new Buddhist Anglo-vernacular schools. The Empress Victoria Buddhist Schools used a catechism-like text in which the students learned responses to a set of questions.[127] The other texts that have survived and the curriculum for Buddhism in government schools are similar to U Tilawka's curriculum, with lessons divided by grade levels and annual exams.[128] All of these, like the 1909 policy on Buddhist education in government schools, shared a concern for dividing instruction in the content of Buddhist doctrine from any practice that might appear to be ritual.

The change in the curriculum engaged larger changes in the methods of teaching Buddhism.[129] In adopting the government's pedagogical methods, Buddhist reformers seem to have agreed with the assessments of the Europeans trying to reform monastery education that located religion in the content and not the practices of learning. Learning to read was no longer a Buddhist practice; it was a secular skill that could be applied to texts with Buddhist content. The new idea of teaching Buddhism in a half hour a day, as a set of doctrines and content divorced from the practices and postures of the monastery, worked to define Buddhism as a discrete object—one that was engaged primarily, if not exclusively, intellectually. Like the 1909 order, the new Buddhist pedagogy actively rejected the inclusion of anything that it understood to fall in an ill-defined category of ritual. Reciting precepts and listening to sermons were sufficiently content focused, but ordinations, pagoda attendance, and anything that could be called worship were not productive for teaching Buddhism.

Many of these changes were the result, not of conscious reflection either on the part of the colonial state or the Buddhist reformers, but the product of adapting to the circumstances of the day, the changes necessitated by the government rules for funding and the structure of the school day. For the Buddhist Anglo-vernacular schools, and the projects for religious instruction in other schools, simply the need to constrain Buddhist teaching to a short period during the day and separate it from the secular curriculum changed Buddhist instruction from an integrated part of life to a discrete subject that could be learned from books. Other aspects represented a broader shift in thinking and engagements with the categories of the colonial encounter. The focus on comprehension was the product of the involvement of Buddhist leaders with both the colonial administration, especially the education department, and the new international dialogue of Buddhists and Buddhist sympathizers in Asia and Europe. Although the Buddhist associations had succeeded in making Buddhism integral to their children's education, their efforts had shaped the terms through which Buddhism was perceived.

CONCLUSION

Europeans, deeply impressed with Burmese literacy, had taken the values of monastery pedagogy to be identical to the colonial state's civilizing goals. They sought to employ monastery schools to carry out these goals, but failed to comprehend the concepts of literacy and *sāsana* foundational to monastery education. Even where projects looked similar to the disciplinary and civilizing efforts back home, as was particularly the case with British perceptions of Burmese Buddhist literacy education, local categories and conceptual frameworks were resistant to colonial projects. The perception of similarity proved deceptive; the projects were oriented toward very different and, ultimately, in the monks' analysis, opposing ends. Embracing the colonial system required accepting concepts that were not only foreign, but, the monks argued, antithetical to the purposes of monastery education.

The monks refused the scheme for primary education and with it the categories of religion and the secular. The production of religion as a category required a shift and reformulation of the efforts that counted as religious. Locating Buddhist practices and thought within this sphere required reformulating those goals in relation to that category. Religious discourses and projects could not be contained in the category of "religion" and come out unchanged. The Buddhist goals became provincialized in relation to the universal modern goals of education. Their meaning had to take on a new location in the formation of the subject and collective identity. The education officials only wanted the monks to recognize Buddhism as a religion; the monks, however, understood that the plan required that they reformulate much more. They rejected the new categories because these required a new system of universalities that were in conflict with the monks' concerns for the *sāsana* and efforts for its preservation.

These conflicting purposes and frameworks remained an issue for Buddhist parents and community leaders. Their concerns about the future of the *sāsana* were inextricable from concerns for economic prosperity. Old modes of education and *sāsana* promotion were no longer viable, but neither could the government's education program meet their larger goals. The Buddhist schools and programs for Buddhist education offered a means of accommodating the colonial pedagogical forms and content that offered access to the economic opportunities and yet produced alternative means of forming children as Buddhists who could preserve the *sāsana*. This assimilation of colonial forms, however, forced the new Buddhist pedagogy to operate in the conceptual frameworks the monks had rejected. Learning Buddhism as content from books in a period set aside each day created a conceptual separation of religion from other aspects of life and a perception of literacy as an instrumental practice detached from merit making. The goals the monks saw as central remained alive but changed by the encounter with the new framework. This meant that the Buddhist schools and Buddhist leaders had to adopt the colonial definition of religion that emphasized content, but adapt it to their own purposes. The modes of learning for the new Buddhist schools changed the ways in which Burmese conceptualized the *sāsana* and its place in daily life, but they did not alter the centrality of *sāsana* preservation.

Although the Buddhist associations used the European methods and their evaluative principles, ultimately these were undertaken strategically with another goal in sight—the preservation of the *sāsana*. They were willing to engage in the projects of the modern colonial state, but they did not necessarily agree with its assessment of universal values. The Buddhist Anglo-vernacular schools assisted in the creation of productive modern colonial subjects, but only because they understood this to be the best means to promote both a standard of livelihood and a level of literacy that would produce good Buddhists and keep the Buddha's teachings alive. Like the monks, they would not acquiesce to a categorization that put the status of the *sāsana* subordinate to universalized secular values.

Like the crisis of morals I will discuss in Chapter 4, the concern over the decline of Buddhism under colonial rule was recognized not just by Burmese Buddhists, but also by a range of other observers. Sympathizers and detractors alike theorized as to whether Buddhism could survive the changing conditions of colonialism. H. Fielding Hall, thought to be a favorable observer of the Burmese, asked of Buddhism:

> What are the tendencies in future? Will it die? I do not think so. Why should it die? It is not untrue. It is as true as any faith can be—truer to them than any other. It is certainly more akin to them than any other faith. It is a very beautiful faith. No greater disaster could be imagined to them than that they should forget it or disown it, that they should become without religion or adopt an alien one. This one has in many ways grown into their hearts, it should never be removed. But it should take its place below the greater truths. If it is to live, it must adapt itself and incorporate itself into the national needs. It must put a national truth above a scriptural reading. It must remember there are higher truths than religion. It must do as ours does.[130]

This, however, was precisely the position that the Buddhist associations were organizing against. While the associations may have been happy to take up the teaching methods and practices of the colonial administration, happy to extol its virtues and pray for the welfare of its emperor-king, they would not substitute its values for their own. The history of primary education had required a major shift in methods to preserve the *sāsana,* but, for now at least, the teachings of the Buddha remained their "greater truths."

4

Morals, Conduct, and Community

At the end of the nineteenth century, associations were quite the fashion in Rangoon. Forming or joining an organization became wildly popular. As the *Burma Star* reported, tongue in cheek, by the early 1880s, founding a new association was a popular cure for all manner of social ills:

> Moulmein is celebrated for its public meetings. It believes in them as a panacea for all the evils that affect a community. Should rulers tyrannize, institutions go wrong or dangers threaten, the *tocsin* is rung, and the residents hasten from Mopoon and Dine-woon-Quin to the hall of meeting. Resolutions are framed, speeches made, the evil denounced, and its remedy agreed upon. After which, each speaker retires to his home and his slumber. . . . Further measures are seldom deemed necessary; the resolutions and the speeches are supposed to effect the cure.
>
> Here we have our public meetings but they are not looked upon as the guards of the province. Our greatest strength lies in Institutions.[1]

Our Monthly, a Rangoon magazine that reprinted this witty barb from the *Burma Star*, listed a number of literary, social, and service institutions that represented the cosmopolitan communities of Rangoon. From this start, the inclination to form associations became contagious, spreading, in the coming decades, through all of Rangoon's ethnic and religious communities. Not only did European associations grow and multiply—adding Theosophical lodges, Freemasons, racing clubs, and temperance lodges—but Hindus and Muslims founded their own associations. By the turn of the century, the grand new Young Men's Christian Association (YMCA) building and the Maduray Pillay (Tamil) high school competed to host the most important associational gatherings in Rangoon.

The fashion for organizing spread well beyond Rangoon. In 1899 the western city of Akyab could boast of the presence of the Arakan Jubilee Club, the Hypocris Club, a literary society, and a half dozen others, not to mention the presence of the Young Arakanese Student's Club of Rangoon. A report from the far northern outpost of Meiktila in 1900 sums up how infectious the eagerness for creating associations had become:

> Societies and clubs are now all the go and the people employed in the government service have founded a few:
> (a) Thathana anokgaha Dimitea Society,
> (b) The Union Reading club,
> (c) The Y. M. Foot-ball club,
> The clerks in the office of the deputy commissioner take a keen interest in them all.[2]

Although the literary and sporting incarnations may have drawn the attention of these young men, by the late 1890s Buddhist organizations would eclipse all others in the number of associations, membership, and activity.

Buddhist associations sprung up across colonial Burma in the hundreds at the turn of the twentieth century. As E. J. Colston, discussing the broad impact of this Buddhist revival, reported, "there was scarcely any pagoda without one."[3] While some of these were large-scale organizations with branches in multiple towns, like the educational, Pali-examination, and rice-donating associations discussed in Chapters 2 and 3, these were well outnumbered by the local and spontaneously formed associations of lay Buddhists that peppered the small towns and villages. Associations became not just the focus of much popular attention, but the driving force behind social movement and innovation.

The center of all of this activity was not the Buddhist monks or any proxy for the king, but laypeople, who emerged to become a dominant Buddhist force in the twentieth century. Their rise is part of the now familiar story of the birth of Buddhist modernism and Buddhist modernities across Asia. Lay involvement has become the sine qua non of Buddhism enmeshed with modernity. Much of the rhetoric surrounding the rise of the laity emphasizes the ways that Buddhist laypeople took over the role of the king or adopted Protestant modes of religiosity, but little has investigated the means through which the laity came to prominence. If in 1885 the king and the sangha were the two key driving forces behind Burmese Buddhism, how, less than a decade later, could they be replaced by mere laypeople—and ones as lowly as schoolteachers, shopkeepers, and low-level bureaucrats? What were the motivations, sentiments, and mechanisms that allowed for such a sea change? How did Buddhists come to think of themselves in new terms that would allow for such a revolution in leadership?

This period in Burmese history transformed not just how Buddhists interpreted the *sāsana* and developing concepts of religion, but the ways that Burmese Buddhists thought about themselves and their connections to each other. Through the Buddhist associations, Burmese laypeople developed new modes of identity. Like Benedict Anderson's concept of nation as an imagined community, Burmese Buddhists came to sense a series of horizontal bonds between them, forming a community that was larger than the sum of its parts.[4] And yet, this imagining operated not through the metaphysics of nation, but through a distinct set of cosmological parameters. The growing sense of connection between Burmese Buddhists was imagined and carried out through a common ethical project—the preservation of the *sāsana*.

Through this ethical project, and the sense of moral community it engendered, Burmese Buddhists transformed not just the traditional Buddhist roles—those of king as patron of the *sāsana* and the sangha as objects and agents of reform—but also transformed how lay Buddhists situated themselves and their actions. This new sense of identity relied on the technologies of the age for its forms of imagining, including not just print media but the techniques of the voluntary association and the practices of Victorian moral reform. However, these were brought in conversation with older local Buddhist practices of *sāsana* reform to produce new modes of ethical subjectivity. The sense of belonging to a moral community responsible for the preservation of the *sāsana* situated a new self-perception at the center of Burmese practice.

A SMALL ARMY OF VICE-PRESIDENTS AND HONORARY SECRETARIES

Coming together as a loose body to carry out a specific task, particularly one focused around donations or the renovation of a pagoda, was not an innovation in Burmese society. Village leaders had long organized groups to plan pagoda festivals and major donation ceremonies. Moreover, there were traditional bands that came together for specific acts of merit, including the Satuditha societies that collected donations to distribute food to the needy. Buddhists frequently gathered in groups to recite precepts on half-

and full-moon days—informal groups that later evolved into more organized bodies. However, the types of and enthusiasm for organizations
changed substantially at the end of the nineteenth century.

Clerks like those in Meiktila were a common constituency for new Buddhist associations, and their group was fairly typical of the early structures
and goals. The newspaper article quoted above reported that the Buddhist
association in Meiktila "propose[s] building a *kyoung* (rest house) in Kanna
Taik at a cost of over Rs. 3000" and had set to collect one-eighth of the salary
of all members for the project.[5] The newspaper further described how
"Members of this society every Sunday meet in a *zayat;* observing the *At-
thanga Sila* of Eight-fold precepts; and they spend the day discussing the
doctrine of the Buddha."[6] Many of the Buddhist associations began as similar simple *dhamma wut* societies, whose members gathered to recite precepts in
this way, but, like the Meiktila group, evolved into something more. The Sedi-
yingana association formed in the small central town of Minbu in September of 1900 is typical of the associations in their early stages. The *Times of
Burma* reported:

> Every Saturday evening the members in white dresses go round the town
> begging for alms; and on the following Sunday they assemble at "Thud-
> hamma Zayat" on the platform of the Chanthagyi Pagoda, to hear the
> preaching of very learned Phongyis and make various offerings to them. . . .
> The Society ever since its start has been flourishing in this manner, and the
> members consisting of resident clerks, leading advocates and elders of the
> town, take a keen interest in the welfare of the society.[7]

However, by 1901, the good folks of Minbu and Meiktila were a bit behind the times. Associations in Rangoon, Akyab, and Bassein and even in
the smaller towns of Myingyan and Sagaing had taken on much more ambitious agendas—founding Buddhist schools, organizing elaborate systems
for collecting and donating rice to monks, organizing Pali examinations,
and considering Buddhist missionary activity abroad. The Minbu and
Meiktila focus on study and precept taking was a more modest incarnation
of an impulse in larger organizations to host public lectures and debates on
Buddhist ideas and morals, and to create their own publishing arms, starting first with the associations' journal and then moving on to tracts and
books. In the smaller towns, the orientation to organize festivals merged
in associations that sponsored massive events to host traveling preaching
monks. As one European observed, "Religious societies are being formed

with astonishing rapidity with the one object of strengthening the religion of the people."[8]

In 1896, merchants from the Malun market in Mandalay organized to coordinate rice donations to the forest monks in the Sagaing and Mingun hills who had previously been supported by the king, forming the Malunze Rice Donating Society.[9] The Buddhabatha Thathana Pyu Association (Society for Promoting Buddhism), formed in 1900 in Mandalay, set out at first to support the monks with donations, but soon sought to promote scholarship among the laity with a Buddhist printing press, schools for children, and a monthly journal.[10] The Dhammathawana Association (later known in English as the Buddhist Propaganda Society) focused on sponsoring monastic preachers.[11] It also published a monthly journal that reprinted the sermons for wider distribution and sponsored a preaching hall and monastery for preaching monks.[12]

Buddhist organizations were flowering all across the colonial province, and representing every possible constituency. As one Buddhist organizer writing to the *Times of Burma* explained,

> Now-a-days, the light of Buddhism is beginning to shine in almost every hole and corner of the world; and Societies spreading this ancient Religion, far and wide throughout the Earth, are now so numerous, that it would be almost impossible for anyone to describe them all even in their barest details. But alas! There are but very few societies of young boys of about 14 or 15 years old that have been formed to co-operate in this noble undertaking.[13]

Lest the reader worry, the author had founded the Selarakkheta Society for fourteen- to fifteen-year-old boys in Bassein. Apparently, the thirteen-year-olds and sixteen-year-olds there were already well served.

Given that many of the early founders were government servants, clerks, and schoolteachers, groups particularly well trained in the new bureaucratic technologies, it is not surprising that the associations quickly became formalized and rule driven with written constitutions, membership rules, and elected officers. These bureaucratic techniques were novel and highly attractive to organizers, because they signaled the seriousness of their mission and their "modern" approach. The descriptions of associations mentioned their "well-kept subscription books and accounts" alongside "the usual beautiful images of Buddha."[14] Between 1887 and 1906, the official *Catalogue of Books and Pamphlets Published in Burma* is riddled with entries like *Sediya noggatha upathaka thamuha athin upade* (Rules for the Society for Protecting Pagodas) and *Rules and Regulations of the Dhamma Suka Society.*[15] At the turn of the century it appeared that the fate of Buddhism lay not in the benevolence of esteemed patrons and preachers but in the organizational efficiency of a small army of presidents, vice-presidents, honorary and recording secretaries, and subcommittee chairmen.

As the organizations grew in popularity, their leaders gained social status and respect. While the early supporters of the government's Patamabyan examinations were drawn from those who already enjoyed a dominant role in society—pagoda trustees and community leaders—these organizations offered leadership roles to less-well-known government clerks, teachers, attorneys, and merchants. Such groups already enjoyed respect for their ability to interact with Europeans, but the Buddhist associations became a path to greater prominence in the Burmese community. The portraits of the past chairmen printed in the journals of later decades, and those still hanging in the buildings of surviving associations, testify to the ways that the organizations facilitated new social and business networks and became a means to social visibility.[16]

Women played an important, although not prominent, role in the Buddhist associations. The leadership of the major organizations was almost exclusively male, but Buddhist women were major contributors and carried out many of the details of the projects. Women like Daw Mya May, the founder of the Empress Victoria Buddhist Schools, served as patrons for a number of new associations. Women were an important audience for these programs, and often sought out preachers, journals, and tracts with a greater enthusiasm than men. Some organizations excluded female membership, but those that did not had long lists of women eager to participate in the work of preserving Buddhism.[17]

THE MEMBERSHIP-SUBSCRIPTION ORGANIZATION: MORAL COMMUNITY MADE VISIBLE

By the turn of the twentieth century, the newspapers had christened this fervor for publishing and founding associations a "Buddhist Revival." Europeans looking to explain the phenomenon to those back home, as well as Buddhist propagandists seeking to build international connections, opted for the language of revival to explain the rapid rise of Buddhist enthusiasm. As E. J. Colston, writing about "recent social movements in Burma," explained, "the world movement which was caused by the success of Japan transmuted as it broke on our shores into a general desire for social betterment, and into what, with Buddhists, is almost the same thing—what is known as religious revival."[18] Yet, the language of revival presumes a previous decline. What drove the Buddhist enthusiasm of this period, however, was not so much an actual historical or material decline in terms of lay practice or emphasis on Buddhism in daily life, but a rhetoric of decline, an intuition that the state of Buddhism was deteriorating, born out of the larger worldview of the life of the *sāsana* discussed in Chapter 2.[19] The need to slow the decline linked Buddhists together in a common project with a common goal. However, as much as there was not a specific set of material changes that constituted decline, there was not a single pristine past state that could or would be revived. Thus the revival did not just reanimate old forms, but gave life to new modes of being and interaction in the Burmese world.

In colonial Burma, the obligation Buddhists felt for ethical intervention on behalf of the *sāsana* created a sense of moral connection and community. The Burmese who joined associations and promoted Buddhist revival at the turn of the century felt that their privileged enjoyment of the fruits of the Buddha's teachings was the result of past patronage by kings and others, now lost. The only way to preserve this essential moral condition was for individuals to come together and take responsibility as a collective. The Buddhist associations thus forged a community out of moral necessity and collective action.

Buddhists in colonial Burma physically came together in association meetings, massive preaching events, Pali examinations, and study and chanting groups. The Buddhist "revival" of 1890 to 1920 involved collective gatherings through which Buddhists came to see each other in a new light. More than these physical gatherings, associations produced emotive and imagined collectives. Buddhists came to understand themselves as linked by their membership and common efforts in specific projects and by a larger link sensed in the collective project of preserving the *sāsana*. Buddhist associations operated not just to preserve the teachings, but also to produce a body of Buddhists who understood themselves to be directly connected through their responsibility for the *sāsana*. The pageantry of celebrating the Patamabyan examinations and the organizing efforts of the Pariyatti Thathanahita, Zediyingana, and other associations all inculcated not only a desire for greater Buddhist practice among the Burmese but a self-understanding as members of a community brought together for a cosmological purpose. Buddhist associations allowed individual lay Buddhists to see themselves as part of the life of the *sāsana* in a way not possible under the monarchy. The shared responsibility of preserving the *sāsana* produced a moral community that became a powerful source of identity, motivation, and shared sentiment for Buddhists in colonial Burma.

Some of the sense of connection and belonging came out of the organizational technologies they adopted. Although they had evolved from the older village committees, the form of the Buddhist associations changed radically at the end of the nineteenth century, adopting the form of the membership-subscription organization—a key innovative technology for Buddhists in the early twentieth century. Burmese imported this organizational framework and translated it from its European context, where it had dominated civic life in the nineteenth century, into a Buddhist idiom. The organizational rules provided a structure that not only allowed the association to make claims on its members, but gave individuals a stature that came with membership. Through such an organization, the simple act of becoming a member (and paying one's dues, of course) transformed a mere individual Buddhist into an official patron of the *sāsana*.

In addition, the bureaucratic and democratic structure that appealed so much to clerks and schoolteachers required a formal membership that could vote and be solicited for funds. By its bureaucratic rules, an association consisted of nothing but its members. Creating a bounded and identifiable membership fashioned a discrete image of community and a concrete means of visualizing the bonds between disparate Buddhists.[20]

The list of subscribers and donors was the heart of the Buddhist associations. It stood not only as the record of the collective body but as a means of shaping subjectivity and desire. Paying a subscription to the association offered individual Buddhist laypeople membership and an acknowledgment of their participation. Donation had long been the center of *sāsana* reform and Buddhist practice, but it took on a new twist. For centuries, Buddhist kings, ministers, and wealthy laypeople had publicly recorded their donations as a part of making merit, so that their efforts would be known well into the future. *Dāna,* or donation, was central to Buddhist merit making, and records of donations littered the walls of temples and monasteries. Frequently these inscriptions record that the donations were made explicitly "for the long establishment of the *sāsana*."[21] This familiar undertaking was reproduced in the new donation and subscription lists that publicized the contributions not of exceptional donors but of the masses of individual lay Buddhists.

The monthly journals sent to all subscribing members listed every member or donor, his or her status, and the donation made, ranging from five hundred rupees to just a few *annas*. Even those who could afford only a tiny donation had their name included in the lists that came to dominate the journals. The December 1908 journal of the Pariyatti Thathanahita dedicated eight of its twenty-one pages to donation lists, dwarfing the three pages each allocated for explicating the scriptures and listing the monks whom they supported.[22] The lists organized donors by geographic region and town, with the names of large donors appearing next to those who gave only a little. Those with titles of respect for age or learning (Saya, U, Bho, or Daw) were listed next to younger people with lower (Maung, Ko, Ma) or no titles.[23] The Dhammathawana association's journal, *Dhammadethana,* dispensed with listing the amount of the donation and listed all male members by occupation. Women were not granted membership, but their names were listed with their donations, ranging from seventy-five rupees to just a few *annas.*[24] A tiny few of those included were of such low social standing that they did not warrant a name but only a collective title: the "actresses of the Banyan tree troupe" or the "children at the Buddhist Girls' School."[25] In this, the journals presented Buddhists connected in horizontal relationships as a collective body, in such a way that placed emphasis not on individual karmic acts or social status but on the contribution to the collective project.

The subscription list brought Buddhist traditions together with a hybrid of colonial technologies. Lists reprised the long history of recording acts of Buddhist merit in inscriptions and memorials, but fused this with the homogenizing statistical epistemology of the census, which Bernard Cohn and Nicholas Dirks have identified as a key technique of colonial power in India and the subject-forming viewpoint of the panopticon identified by Foucault as a central disciplinary mechanism of modernity.[26] The lists did not simply record various acts of merit; they equated them as statistical parts of the whole. More than this, as public lists, they made individual members aware of the eyes of a host of others observing their conduct. Seeing one's name on the list not only internalized identification with the group and its projects, but also opened the individual to public scrutiny and/or praise. Becoming a member meant shaping one's self to be a collaborator in the collective project for preserving the *sāsana.*

Like Bible societies in Britain that collected penny-a-week subscriptions from poor Christians to mark their participation in the missionary endeavor, the membership subscriptions and the small donations sought by the Buddhist associations offered participation in a larger moral project of preserving the *sāsana.*[27] Building on both the ritualized practice of Buddhist donations and the history of recording acts of merit, they offered the possibility for a low-level clerk or shopkeeper to serve a crucial role in a project that had been until recently the purview of the king, ministers, and senior monks. Their voluntary participation and the individual discipline of saving and donating funds marked them as members of a collective body that was striving to keep the teachings alive. The individual's merit and karmic intention mattered because they gave life to the collective ability to preserve the *sāsana*. Choosing to form oneself as a subject of the collective concern for the *sāsana* in this way forged a new way of being for the laity.

This sense of Buddhist moral community, that is, the collective body constituted from these individual subscriptions, became the driving force of the Buddhist projects of the next two decades. The concern for the *sāsana* and identity reprised some of the techniques of earlier *sāsana* reforms. However, it came to change how the laity constituted Buddhism, less as patrons and more as constitutive participants, whose impact existed in aggregate, not personal, form. This was a collective identity, a way of belonging that in some ways anticipates national identity. It was a means for Buddhists to understand themselves as patrons now responsible for the *sāsana* in a collective body, driven by the metaphysics not of colonial modernity or nation, but of concern for the *sāsana*.

BEHAVIOR AS BAROMETER: DECLINE OF MORALS AND STATUS OF THE *SĀSANA*

Some of the new Buddhist associations focused on the work of Buddhist patronage, collecting donations in an attempt to fill the gap left by the fall of the Buddhist monarchy. Organizations like the Malunze Rice Donating Society, the Zediyingana Pariyatti Association, and the Pariyatti Thathanahita offered financial support and sponsorship for monastic scholars, taking over the patronage role of the king. But for the vast majority of associations, the most pressing concern was not the loss of the king but the behavior of Buddhists themselves.

At the turn of the twentieth century, Burmese were deeply troubled by a seeming decline in Buddhist morality. Journals and newspapers overflowed with letters decrying the lax behavior of Buddhists: complaining that Buddhist youth were becoming less and less respectful of their parents and elders, that Buddhists were drinking alcohol, frequenting billiard parlors and opium shops, and gambling in numbers shocking to the older generation. The challenges and changes of the colonial condition, these Buddhist critics argued, were undermining the moral fiber of Buddhists in Burma, and there was an urgent need to reform behavior and manners.

The moral community turned its critical gaze inward and determined that the behaviors of Buddhist laypeople themselves posed a threat to the *sāsana*. The problems of the age, vague and amorphous as they were, seemed to reside not in Burma's political situation or changing economic or social conditions, but inside the collective body of Buddhists themselves. Unlike the program for Buddhist education, the campaigns to address this perceived crisis of morals among Burmese Buddhists focused the reform efforts on internal reflection, defining the problem of *sāsana* decline as residing within the body of the moral community.

To Burmese association organizers at the turn of the twentieth century, evidence of moral decline was everywhere: from their perspective Buddhists were behaving badly in almost every arena of life. Concerned Buddhists writing to the newspapers and Buddhist journals decried what they saw as Burmese abandoning the Buddhist values of precolonial times, their behavior heralding an era of moral decay. In Lower Burma the worries began in the late 1870s. Charles Forbes reported that "Elders tell with sorrow the common tale, the English spirits and opium are gradually destroying their native good qualities in the rising generation. A feebler constitution, greater ignorance, disrespect of parents and elders, and disregard of religion are fast becoming the characteristics of young Burma in the British province."[28] By the 1880s and 1890s, Burmese journals published letters arguing that changes in education had ruined the character of Burmese youth.[29] Newspapers ran articles expressing worry that Burmese sons and daughters had become rude, arrogant, and immoral.[30] By the turn of the century, the Burmese press was full of complaints of drinking, rude speech, extravagance in spending, and impropriety in manners.[31]

These anxious Buddhists focused on actions that demonstrated a violation of Buddhist precepts or a more general lack of restraint and decorum they felt was required of good Buddhists. Alcohol, opium, and gambling were targets of great concern, but consuming meat, and, in particular, beef, were no less so. Moralists complained that young people had abandoned the manners and postures that communicated respect to elders and taken up coarse and rude language. Likewise, boisterous and unruly conduct at pagoda festivals and *pwe* theatrical performances was taken as clear evidence of collective moral decline. The concern for restraint extended to other aspects of public performance as well: Buddhist associations issued calls to curtail lavish spending on Buddhist rituals and sumptuous jewelry and promoted thrift as a private virtue. Evidence of moral decline did not come from a single register or tradition but from a range of actions, new and old, that juxtaposed the reality of changing cosmopolitan colonial life with a newly imagined Buddhist moral purity.

Changes in behavior are difficult for a historian to measure, but actual changes mattered less than the growing perception of moral decline that became a recurrent theme in public discourse. Burmese and Europeans alike came to believe that crime and delinquency had increased radically in the preceding decades. Historical evidence does not seem to bear this out, but the belief did much to shape Burmese perception of the colonial condition.[32] The anxiety over moral performance and the efforts at reform, rather than the behavior itself, shaped Burmese identity and the moral community.

Buddhist reformers writing to the newspapers were agitated by all of these activities. Whereas in the past Buddhists might have seen personal failings, now they perceived a collective and communal moral problem. Together these behaviors seemed to point to a much larger problem for the Buddhist community.

DISOBEDIENT AND DISRESPECTFUL LADS

Social critics singled out groups who were most affected by the colonial changes for concerns about moral laxity. Students, especially those attending Anglo-vernacular schools, were particularly troubling. Schoolboys came under greater scrutiny because they were undergoing the greatest transition in manners and behavior. In the move from the monastery to schools on the government's model, boys no longer benefited from a Buddhist setting where they could embody the postures of respect and language expected to mark them as cultured and polite. Instead they interacted with European teachers for whom respect was equally important but embodied in radically different ways. The difference between how one sat politely on the floor of the monastery and how one sat politely at a desk was a gulf young Burmese were quickly learning to cross, but one that produced much moral anxiety.

As we saw in Chapter 3, the Buddhist schoolboy became a key character in the anxieties and the interventions of this period. Schoolboys were the first scouts sent out by the Buddhist community into the new and unpredictable prospects of colonial modernity. They necessarily became quite adept cultural translators, but also bricoleurs and inventors in their own right. At the same time, however, they were also the most highly scrutinized by Buddhist leaders and association members to see what their actions and intentions could portend about the path that lay ahead.

Over the last two decades of the nineteenth century, concerns grew. Buddhists worried about the effect colonial education was having on their children. In 1883, Taw Sein Ko reported,

> Now-a-days in Burma, old men and women complain that youths in general, who have a smattering knowledge of the English language, and who are not acquainted with Buddhistic doctrines, are apt to despise their national religion and their paternal calling, that they are not docile and obedient as before, but rash, independent and conceited. The little secular knowledge they have received must have inflated their youthful minds and changed their entire character.[33]

Complaints of the bad behavior mounted; concerns in the 1880s that boys were no longer polite and obedient shifted in the 1890s to frustration at boys wielding peashooters and stones, parading around using coarse language and harassing girls.[34] By the turn of the century, newspapers reported gambling, stabbings, drunkenness, and arrests of schoolboys.[35]

For their part, Buddhist parents argued that where the Buddhist texts of the monastery system had instilled good manners and morals, the government's texts offered nothing in its place. They protested,

> What do they teach the boys? Nothing of course in the shape of Burmese morals! Yet the Education and other Government Departments expect their subordinates and pupils to show them the greatest respect. But the old style courtesy is being obliterated, without substituting anything to serve the same purpose in its stead. I would ask whether it is not ridiculous to expect old forms from those who are not taught them.[36]

In these indictments the Department of Public Instruction was responsible for boys who "turn out to be drunkards, disobedient and disrespectful lads ... bringing miseries, troubles and sorrows on their families, and on themselves and their fellows subjects."[37]

Buddhist training in the older monastery education system offered a moral framework for civilized behavior; without this framework the Buddhist reformers saw only moral decay. Government schools were threatening because they took the students away from the Buddhist community and worked to reshape their dispositions and orientations toward a different set of norms and assumptions. This was exactly the disciplinary project the colonial state understood in "the moral and intellectual improvement of the people," but it served to make the boys uncivilized and misdirected in

Burmese interpretation. Proper behavior and morals from the Burmese point of view could not be separated from Buddhism. A system that sought to divide Buddhism from the regulation of proper conduct could only threaten morals, not promote them.

The real problem was not the schools themselves, but what a decline in morals pointed to in larger terms. For those involved with the Buddhist movement, the poor morals and manners of schoolboys were a problem because they signaled the decline of Buddhism, even as Burmese interpretations of the *sāsana* shifted in this period. The Buddhist campaigns for correct behavior, including the conduct of schoolboys, understood the moral practices of individual Buddhists to be tied the state of the *sāsana*. In seeking to revive Buddhist education and return boys to good Buddhist comportment, what was at stake was not the individual karma but the moral community.

THE ASCENDANCY OF VIRTUE

The reform campaigns took Buddhists' morals failings to be both a symptom and a cause of the decline of the *sāsana*. The behavior of Buddhists both represented the declining presence of the Buddha's teachings in the world and simultaneously worked to erode it further. Buddhist associations responded with programs for reform. They organized letters, sermons, pamphlets, articles, and meetings to encourage Buddhist laypeople toward conscious reflection on their behavior and a program of moral self-regulation.

These efforts elevated the Buddhist concept of *sīla,* morality or virtue, to the center of Buddhist practice. Out of the traditional triumvirate of *dāna, sīla,* and *bhāvanā* (giving, morality, and mental cultivation), the new Buddhist journals and lecturers argued that *sīla* was essential for the practice of Buddhism under the particular constraints of the colonial condition, more important than *dāna,* because while Buddhists had been generous in the past, the focus on virtue offered the potential to rescue the *sāsana* from its current peril. They made morality a collective focus and constructed the risks of immorality and the benefits of moral restraint as issues for the community in its responsibility for the *sāsana*.

Whereas *dāna* had operated as the central ritual for the creation of merit and the display of piety, public discussions now sought to supplement it, and at moments to supplant it, with an emphasis on *sīla*. Donations to monks were a customary response to preaching; in this climate, however, Ledi Sayadaw was known to ask his followers to substitute pledges of morality for offerings. The need for morality and its potential benefits had overtaken the karmic benefits of donations, given the threats to the *sāsana*.

U Silacara, a European convert and monk, lecturing to the Buddhist elite at Rangoon College, made the urgency of morality explicit:

> The vehicle that carries a Buddhist eventually to Nibbana has three wheels: . . . Dana, Sila, and Bhavana. For long enough the Burmese have been travelling the Nibbana road . . . upon the one wheel of Dana. But they cannot hope to travel fast or very far on one wheel. It is time now, and high time—for soon it will be too late—to add another wheel of Sila to the Dana wheel, and so they will have a bicycle that will bear them swiftly for many a mile. . . . It is Sila and Sila alone—a firm and steady adherence to Right Conduct as taught by the Lord Buddha—which alone can save Burma from a rapid, fatal degeneration in the days that lie immediately before it.[38]

Morality was central to the future of Buddhism and, without it, not just Buddhists, but Buddhism, would be lost.

This focus on morals did not set Burma apart from its neighbors at the time. Moralist campaigns to regulate behavior were part of the spirit of the age in Southeast Asia and around the Victorian colonial world. European social reformers, colonizers, and indigenous movements across Asia shared an emphasis on conduct and morality. Around the world, both local and colonizing efforts scrutinized individual practice and developed moral regimes as part of broader transformations of society in the name of "modernity" and "progress."

Siam, led by the royal court, was undergoing a major reform of dress and behavior at this time, organized around the ideal of *siwilai,* becoming civilized.[39] The changes implemented there, including changes in wearing shoes and postures of respect that would later be referenced in Burma, sought to transform how Siamese elites viewed themselves and modern authority.[40] As Anne Hansen has demonstrated, similar focus on behavior dominated Buddhist discussions of reform in Cambodia. Where the Burmese focused on memorizing Abhidhamma texts as a means of preserving the *sāsana,* Khmer monks, and later laypeople, were obsessed with the Vinaya rules. The focus on Vinaya began as a means of determining and regulating monastic behavior in an age seen as decadent, but soon gave birth to a wide range of Vinaya-related literature and sermons that sought to transform and regulate the behavior of novices and laypeople.[41] Similarly, in Ceylon, the issue of moral behavior became central, with Anagarika Dharmapala's 1898 *Gihi vinaya,* which cataloged two hundred rules for behavior.[42] This text reflected a broader emphasis on correct behavior, also evidenced in versions of a local Sinhalese text, the *Bauddha ädahilla,* which instructed laypeople in correct ritual and moral performance.[43]

Buddhists' focus on moral performance and behavior operated in a broader context of British colonial discourse and cultural interaction in this period. Some have noted that Dharmapala's *Gihi vinaya* takes many of its cues from Theosophist Col. H. S. Olcott's attempts to reform Singhalese Buddhist behavior a decade earlier, imputing a Protestant origin to this moralizing impulse. However, as Stephen Prothero has argued, the language and types of reforms proposed by Olcott, and later Dharmapala, do not derive from a particularly Protestant worldview or theology, but from the metropolitan gentility that had dominated certain classes of the reform movement in Britain and the United States in the late nineteenth century.[44] Movements for moral and behavioral reform across Buddhist Southeast Asia interacted with European and American movements that had dominated public discourse for much of the century, adapting the language and methods for their local goals.

The nineteenth century had seen the rise of a number of different movements in Britain and the United States that focused on transforming individual moral behavior. Many of these, such as temperance and vegetarianism, began with middle-class members attempting to curb their own behaviors, but soon became interventionist approaches that sought to transform and "civilize" the twin targets of Victorian anxiety—the urban poor underclasses at home and the backward heathen colonial subjects abroad. Bible societies, programs for hygiene, educational schemes, and missionary organizations ventured beyond their middle-class origins to transform the lives of the poor and colonized.[45] This broader civilizing mission, including new social welfare programs, Christian missionizing, and many of the programs of the colonial state, sought to change a range of behaviors labeled "immoral" or "unhealthy." Many of these projects had branches in Burma and saw Burma as a fertile field for such "civilizing" interventions.

European reformers and missionaries understood habit, behavior, and the proper engagement with the material world to have the power to transform the internal state of the potential convert, producing an introspective and self-governing subject with the correct inclination toward salvation.[46] In this way, transforming everyday habits and material minutiae were key not just for missionaries, but for the colonial project generally. It was this transformation of the subject, using changed practices and habits to create a changed orientation and values, that was the core method of the civilizing mission. All of these campaigns, whether instigated by colonizing Europeans or reforming Southeast Asians, sought changed behavior in order to inculcate a set of values and orientations.

Burmese Buddhist efforts were no less interested in the interventionary power of moral reform. Their obsession with the perceived decline of morals and focus on individual behavior was driven by an understanding that behavioral changes had the power to create good Buddhist subjects and a harmonious community to preserve the *sāsana*. Jean and John Comaroff's point that habit and behavior were central to the power of colonialism applies equally to Burmese indigenous campaigns. They argue it is "precisely by means of the residual, naturalized quality of habit that power takes up residence in culture, insinuating itself apparently without agency, in the texture of a life-world. This, we believe, is why recasting mundane, routine practices has been so vital to all manner of social reformers, colonial missionaries among them."[47] The hegemonic nature of colonial power that the Comaroffs describe, its ability to operate below the level of conscious reflection through symbol, culture, and habit, is no less true of the Buddhist projects themselves. The Buddhist associations' campaigns for moral reform sought a transformation in orientation and the internalization of certain values through subtle means. Buddhist interventions in the behavior of boys, against meat eating, drinking, and attending *pwes*, all sought to imperceptibly and gradually transform not just individuals, but ultimately the moral community as a whole—shaping its texture as a "life-world" for the Burmese, one oriented toward self-regulation for the collective benefit of the *sāsana*.

MEAT EATING, MORALITY, AND THE GLORY OF BUDDHISM

Under the threatening conditions of colonialism, even practices long morally acceptable for Burmese Buddhists came to have consequences for the *sāsana*. Although Burmese had regularly eaten meat, including beef, in the first decade of the twentieth century, there were reports from around the colonial province of a movement against meat eating.[48] According to one observer,

In Burma some years ago, on feast days the market was always full of meat, the animals being killed for sale to those persons who feed the hpoongyis [monks]. Owing to the influence of the Ledi Sayadaw (or perhaps owing to a re-action) cow's flesh and the flesh of fowl, etc. is not now eaten on feast days, in order to discourage the meat sellers and others from sacrificing so many lives of animals and birds. We now see that the stalls of the meat sellers are singularly free from beef on feast days, which is a good thing.[49]

Ledi Sayadaw, the famous Abhidhamma scholar and meditation teacher, was well known for his injunction against eating beef. He composed a number of texts on this issue, but he was not the only, or the most prominent, advocate against meat eating at the time.[50] The idea of avoiding meat became quite popular, spawning frequent Burmese newspaper items on the moral advantages of vegetarianism.[51]

Each year, during the rain's retreat, when many Buddhists observed greater piety, pamphlets appeared across Burma exhorting Buddhists to improve their treatment of animals. These petitions were written in the voice of the animals themselves, calling on Buddhists to recognize their mutual plight.[52] In their appeal, the "animals" presented themselves as good Buddhists, albeit karmically inferior to humans as they could not study the scriptures and make merit. Yet, quick to point out the failings of their two legged co-religionists, they cataloged the wrongs they suffered at the hands of humans:

> You can have but a faint idea of our sufferings, not the least of which is our inability to pay our reverence to the memory of the Blessed Buddha and acquire merit which might better our lot in future existences. . . . We have become your most menial slaves, we serve you, and work for you and die for you. Do we ever do anything detrimental to your prosperity and welfare? No! And yet you abuse and beat us, and generally ill-treat us in the most shameful and inhuman manner. More than that you do not hesitate to kill us, and roast, and cook and eat us for the satisfaction of a terrestrial and low appetite.[53]

The petition diverged from the dominant interpretation of the first precept against taking life that allowed that Buddhists were not culpable for the death of animals so long as they did not personally slaughter or request that animals be slaughtered.[54] Here, instead, simply eating the meat of slaughtered animals had karmic consequences. In discussion of pious vegetarianism in colonial Burma, meat eating had become a violation of the first precept and an instance of cruelty. The call for vegetarianism emphasized the karmic commonality of the animals, saying "fruits and vegetables were meant to eat, not we animals who, as well as you, are going on the course of purification and perfection in the ocean of renewed existence."[55] The animals' claimed status as Buddhists gave their memorial greater authority and appeal. The petition continues:

> The waste of life among us is now dreadful, and though most of you are perhaps not guilty of the actual murders, your sin is as great, for by eating that which is killed you become abettors; and your sin will certainly find you out. But there is another still more important reason which should urge you to pity and kindness towards us; and this is the Law of the Buddha and your own future welfare; for those only who fulfill the Law can expect its promises, and its promises are great. Each murder of an animal is a blow to religion and cuts it at the very root; leave this wholesale waste of life and eschew the flesh of animals and you will see Buddhism's glory increase a thousand-fold and illuminate the world.[56]

In this formulation, meat eating was a personal wrong, with detrimental consequences for rebirth; however, as a moral problem it had larger consequences. The petitioners were worried less about the harm those that ate them were doing to their own karma and future rebirths than about the "blow to religion:" the danger their actions posed to the health of the Buddha's *sāsana*.

The collective implications of ethical action adhered because action could shape the state of the *sāsana*. Ethical action and the status of the moral community were embedded in the evolving universalist discourse of *sāsana*. Reformers sought reflection on individual behavior, not for the individual good, but for the greater collective moral endeavor. The animals' petition offers an excellent snapshot of the new discourse of moral reform: Buddhists must refrain from immoral actions not for their own karmic sake, but for the good of the whole *sāsana*.[57]

The Buddhist ethical subject envisioned in these campaigns is similar to the one proposed in colonial Cambodia. Anne Hansen explains that Buddhists promoting "modern Dhamma" in Cambodia sought to create a "purified reinterpretation of Buddhism that would enable individuals to find the right path in the modern world" so that, "as individuals purified their own conduct, they simultaneously purified the religion and the religious community as a whole."[58] The language and techniques of Burmese campaigns against meat eating and other behaviors brought these habits of mind to many across Burmese society.

CONDUCT AND THE HISTORY OF REFORM

Although the Buddhist movements shared much with the colonial reform efforts, they drew on a long-standing local discourse that closely connected behavior, reform, and *sāsana*. The focus on moral behavior and performance as a central concern for the status of the *sāsana* was nothing new.
The history of *sāsana* purification movements over the past three centuries
in Sri Lanka and Southeast Asia had turned on issues of performance and
behavior rather than conflicts over doctrine.

The creation of the new orthodox monastic lineages in the late eighteenth and nineteenth centuries—including the Thudhamma in Burma and
the Mayanikaya in Siam—hinged on claims that previous lineages of monks
were lax in their moral and ritual performance. At each instance, reformers
claimed that the *sāsana* was in decline due to the monk's incorrect behavior.
This, in turn, made these behaviors the key focus of intervention. Claims
that monks were not properly following the rules of the Vinaya, either in
ordination procedures or in rules of dress and daily comportment, led to the
creation of new lineages with stricter adherence and the royal programs to
reordain large groups of monks in a new lineage. Likewise, the mid-nineteenth-
century reformist monastic sects—the Shwegyin and Dwaya lineages in
Burma, the Thammayut in Siam and Cambodia—all staked their claims to
greater purity on even greater fidelity to the rules of behavior, premised on
the understanding that their better ethical and ritual performance would
preserve the *sāsana* where the lax performance of others was allowing it to
decline.[59]

The *sāsana*'s defense relied on correct performance, perhaps nowhere
more urgently than in the eighteenth-century confrontation in Burma over
the proper way to wear monastic robes. In the late eighteenth century, the
Ayoun faction argued that whenever a novice ventured away from the monastery, the upper robe must be draped to cover both shoulders, while the
Atin faction argued that the upper robe should cover only one shoulder,
with the other covered by a separate piece held in place by the chest bind-
ing.[60] In different periods, each faction won the favor of the king, who
would impose restrictions on the other in the name of preserving the *sāsana*.
Such concern for the details of performance had roots in the Vinaya.[61] A
focus on performance dominated reform across the Buddhist networks of
Ceylon and Southeast Asia.[62] In all of these reforms, royal and monastic reformers perceived violations of Vinaya rules of ethical behavior as the signal
of *sāsana* decline, precipitating a reform of the sangha. Nineteenth-century

Burmese monastic debates only increased this focus on behavior, arguing over the correct ritual recitation formulas, the morality of donations to improper monks, and the practices of accused *alajji* monks.[63]

Against this backdrop, Buddhist laypeople at the turn of the twentieth century would have been quite accustomed to examine behavior as a barometer of the status of the *sāsana* and an important site of intervention for its preservation. The *sāsana*'s dependency on ethical performance had been vital to Buddhist reform across Southeast Asia for the past two centuries. This orientation did not disappear with the arrival of colonialism; it merely took on a new object, substituting the lay-dominated moral community for the sangha. The movements at the turn of the twentieth century recontoured the practice of reform; the ethical performance of lay Buddhists was coming to supplant concerns over the performance of the sangha.[64]

Intoxicants and meat eating displaced robes and comportment of earlier reforms, operating as both the sign of *sāsana* decline and the point of necessary intervention. Concerns about the deportment of boys studying at government schools came to replace concerns for the dress of Buddhist novices of earlier generations. In each case, moral performance and behavior held the future of the Buddha's teachings in Burma and thus became the object of public anxiety and debate. Buddhist associations claimed to have inherited the mantle of responsibility for the *sāsana* in the absence of the king, and, at the same time, as much as their reform followed earlier models, their lay members came to occupy the position of the monks as well. These changes not only shifted the practice of preserving the *sāsana*, but contributed to the evolving interpretation of the *sāsana* as a worldview shaped and animated by the colonial encounter.

The anxieties surrounding lay performance in colonial Burma added depth to the developing idea of moral community. The campaigns for reform among the laity, with their focus on the minutiae of behavior and its determining role in the health of the *sāsana*, meant that the laity had come to inhabit the site of the sangha in previous reforms. Their practices did not just take on pseudo-asceticism. The laity of the moral community became the embodiment of the health of the *sāsana*; their performance had to be reformed to save Buddhism. This combination constructed the imagined moral community as both preserver and expression of the *sāsana*: both the collective agent and the collective object of intervention. The changing sense of moral community brought these together into something new, not limited by either archetype.

The purity and performance of the moral community of laypeople now held the key to *sāsana* preservation. Newspaper articles that worried about the moral state of students, and efforts that sought to curtail drinking, gambling, and excess in funerals, jewelry, and pagoda festivals all shared with the projects of the colonial civilizing mission an effort to shape new subjects and reorient values through the regulation of everyday behavior. The Buddhist campaigns brought colonial-era moral reform impulses together with the long-standing interpretation of behavior as central to the state of the *sāsana* to inculcate a sense of belonging within the moral community. The sense of moral community now became coextensive with the health of the *sāsana* in ways that gave each new life.

Anxiety over Buddhists' behavior came to shape the sense of moral community and the contour of *sāsana* reform. The rhetoric and techniques of the movements to transform ethical performance trained Buddhists not only to see themselves as part of the body now responsible for the work of preserving the *sāsana,* but also to regulate their own behavior as the embodiment of the health of the *sāsana*. Projects that sought to imbue individual Buddhists with the power to protect all of Buddhism required a system to train Buddhists to view themselves and their actions in new ways.

FROM PRECEPTS TO PLEDGES

A call to adherence to moral precepts had long been central to lay Buddhist practice. On half- and full-moon Uposatha days, lay Buddhists would gather at the pagodas to recite precepts vowing to adhere to a set of eight moral restraints.[65] This daylong asceticism operated in an economy of merit where self-restraint brought future rewards. Vows deterred actions that would produce demerit harmful to the oath-taker's future existences. The vivid renderings of hells encountered by adulterers, drunks, liars, and thieves that filled Pali literature and Burmese art made the benefits of following precepts clear. The broader system valuing asceticism and detachment meant that the act of ritually keeping precepts would itself produce beneficial merit that could improve one's future existences.[66] Observing precepts, at least on Uposatha days, was a basic act of piety that marked Buddhist identity and determined religious and social status—those who practiced the greatest asceticism were afforded the greatest respect. Thus moral abstention itself was deeply integrated into Buddhist practice and Buddhist identity.

Moreover, in the Burmese worldview, the ability to refrain from certain bad behaviors was understood to produce power that could be harnessed in heterodox ways. As Nicola Tannenbaum has documented for the contemporary Shan, tattoos could ward off harm, even making one impenetrable to bullets and knives, if the tattoo were tied to a special vow to keep one of the precepts.[67] Keeping the precept produced power and afforded protection; if the precept was broken, the power of the tattoo vanished.[68] Tattoos of this sort were popular with many ethnic groups at the time. The Burmese insurgencies against the British after the fall of the Burmese monarchy in 1885 rendered these tattoos particularly advantageous. In the larger Burmese worldview, abstention was understood to produce merit, and sometimes a protective power that could act in the world. Thus, the audiences of the Burmese Buddhist moral campaigns at the turn of the twentieth century would have had an acute understanding of the effectiveness of moral restraint.

Both the protective power of moral action in the contemporary moment and the sense that individual moral action could impact the collective state had precedent for colonial Buddhist audiences, but projects of the colonial era shifted the Burmese view of moral action. These campaigns built upon the commonplace Buddhist ritual of reciting and vowing to keep moral precepts but repurposed the practice to respond to the new concern about colonial decline. Buddhist reformers sought greater reflection and transformation than the traditional precept vows offered and blended Buddhist ritual with European temperance techniques to create a new practice.

The major Buddhist preaching campaigns at the turn of the twentieth century introduced a novel practice—at the end of the sermon the preachers asked their listeners to take a vow to abstain from specific actions. Like other Buddhist rituals, the sermons had begun with ritually reciting the precepts. The innovation was the culminating call to those in attendance to sign a pledge to abstain from behaviors ranging from the use of intoxicants to gambling, eating meat, and attending *pwes*. Although some of these vows overlapped with precepts, their purview was not identical. The behaviors curtailed by the pledges were more concrete and were specific to the problems of the day. Moreover, these vows were publicly acknowledged and recorded, usually in the form of signatures on individual cards or registration books.

The preaching campaigns proved extremely popular. In December 1907, between five thousand and seven thousand people flocked to hear U Wayama preach on the moral decay of the day in the southern port town of Moulmein. At the end, "about five thousand men and women signed the pledge of abstinence from alcoholic drinks and attending *pwes*."[69] In Akyab the next month the newspaper reported: "Thousands of Buddhists, men and women of every grade of society congregate every night under the mammoth mandat, to hear the venerable priest preaching eloquent moral sermons to the people laying stress on avoidance of flesh-eating, drinking spirituous liquors and gambling. More than six thousand Buddhists of this division have taken vows and signed pledges to that effect."[70]

Itinerant monastic preachers brought calls for moral reform to the countryside and drew a broad constituency into the collective discourse over declining morals.[71] The most popular itinerant preachers arrived in towns with fanfare and drew enormous crowds. They took over the largest venues to deliver their sermons for three or four nights. Those trying to hear the sermons would overwhelm all the means of transportation in these towns, creating both brief economic booms and headaches for local colonial officials.[72] There are reports of overfull trains, steamers, bullock carts, and carriages coming to hear preachers. For example, Ledi Sayadaw drew over six thousand people to Akyab in January of 1908.[73]

Preaching events were festive and lavishly prepared despite calls for moderation in other rituals. One observer described Ledi Sayadaw's visit to a Rangoon suburb:

> For days, our little town was enlivened by crowds of people who were flocking to the town from far and wide to assist at the grand preparations. A beautiful archway was made at the entrance to the road leading to the monastery in Zegon quarter. On the archway the picture of the famous preacher was painted. Further on a grand pandal was erected; and a large shed was prepared close to the monastery.... A "waw" or palanquin painted with artistic effects in all the colours of the rainbow was in attendance, and when the Sayadaw entered it a large number of women chanting some sacred Pali verses pulled it along. Crowds of spectators, eager to get a glimpse of the famous preacher, lined the route.... The road up to the monastery was thickly covered with costly garments and wearing apparel which it was deemed would be sanctified by the preacher treading upon them.... The pavilion where upon the dais had been put was effectively decorated with flags and banners. The Sayadaw addressed the gathering and he held them spellbound for over half an hour, after which he retired. Every night he held these sessions. His voice is impressive, and his appearance commanded respect. Every word he uttered was eagerly absorbed by the devotees. The stillness of the night helped the preacher to make his voice clear and distinct.[74]

The sermons at the center of all of this pageantry and emotion addressed a variety of issues, but the most common themes were Buddhist morals and personal reform.[75]

Reformers were not satisfied with appealing to those with exemplary pasts. They took the campaigns into the prisons to appeal to those Burmese who, in their estimation, had been most culpable for the decline of morals. The report of Ledi Sayadaw's sermon in the Bassein Prison in June of 1907 shows the urgency of moral reform. Having preached about the dangers of immoral behavior in this lifetime and the next, the learned monk asked,

> "Were the brethren willing to reform and be absolved?" "Yes" replied the audience. "Then my brethren resolve to give up the eating of meat and flesh and intoxicating drinks. Give charity and spare the lives of all animals especially cattle, fowl, ducks and fish, etc." The Sayadaw said that instead of the numerous customary offerings, from his brethren which they could not give and which he did not want, he would deem it an invaluable present if they would make the offering of a firm resolution to give up intoxicants, killing of animals, eating of flesh, and others sins for any number of years they wished. With one accord the prisoners raised their hand and promised to do so for the rest of their lives.[76]

Ethical practice had changed. No longer was it sufficient to recite and agree to follow the five or eight precepts for the day of the sermon; now new Buddhist moral subjects were asked to vow to adhere to concrete and specific ethical injunctions for far longer. More than this, ritual recitation was no longer sufficient to seal the ethical pledge. The bureaucratic technologies of the day guaranteed adherence not by ritual recitation but with paper and pen. Those shaped by the colonial discipline, no one more than prisoners, knew only too well that in colonial modernity the guarantee of intention and adherence lay in the signature.

Pledges became the ethical technology of the day. As if to reinforce the colonial nature of this new technology, after Ledi Sayadaw's sermon the jailors circulated among the prisoners to collect their pledges. As the *Burma Echo* reported to readers in Rangoon, "The Chief Jailor Mr. S. Ali kindly undertook to make a list of the prisoners who were willing to make the pledge required and the period for which they were willing to take it."[77] The image of a Muslim agent of the British colonial state collecting the ritual vows of Buddhists made at the behest of a monk gives a glimpse of how the ritual of taking precepts had been transformed to respond to the cosmopolitan and colonial world.[78] That this new ritual was repeated across the countryside not in colonial institutions but in the wildly popular public Buddhist preaching events is evidence of how deeply the new hybrid ethical technology was integrated into Burmese Buddhism. Buddhist morals now had new means of enforcement, a system of constraint that could contain the moral intentions of a community coming to be trained in colonial self-regulation. Such campaigns organized massive numbers of Buddhists, registered their abstention, and sealed their vows in this highly bureaucratic fashion.

PRESERVING THE *SĀSANA* BY POLICING THE SELF: NEW ETHICAL SUBJECTS

Buddhists advocating pledges for moral reform likely learned the technique from the temperance movement. Temperance was central to the moral reform movements in Britain and the United States in the nineteenth century and had sent its acolytes around the world with the Christian mission campaigns. By the late nineteenth century the international temperance organizations had branches in all of the major cities of South and Southeast Asia. Their presence inspired a number of indigenous temperance societies as well, which would play a central role in anticolonial politics in Ceylon and across South Asia.

The Anglo-American temperance movement arrived in Burma in the late 1870s and grew as Rangoon became ever more cosmopolitan.[79] These organizations appealed to both Burmese and Europeans to abstain, using the techniques that had dominated the temperance movement in the first half of the nineteenth century. The movement produced countless meetings, tracts, books, sermons, and lectures, but its central technology was the temperance pledge, a written statement to abstain from all alcohol, signed by organizers and new members alike.[80] Those who vowed to completely abstain signed their names in the organization's register. Although the pledge began as a means for the upstanding middle-class organizers to set an example for working-class drinkers, the pledge itself became a ritual of transformation, and soon meetings came to highlight the testimony of reformed drunks.[81] Amanda Claybaugh explains,

> At first these pledges were understood as confirmations, the proof of preexisting statuses; the already temperate signed the pledge to demonstrate that they drank wine only in moderation and drank liquor not at all. But as temperance gave way to teetotalism, to the thoroughgoing rejection in all its forms, the pledge came to be seen as a way of transforming the self. It made the drunk into the sober by setting the will against the body, using the act of signing the pledge to bring a lifetime of repetitive drinking to an end.[82]

In temperance literature on both sides of the Atlantic, the scene of the temperance pledge became the metaphor of personal transformation.[83]

The new sober, rational person created by the pledge in these narratives stood in stark contrast to the ethical subject of traditional Buddhist precept vows. Instead of producing changes in a long karmic cycle, the pledges produced immediate results: new individuals instantaneously free from their sufferings in the here and now.[84] The pledge was about more than just drinking. Through the ritual of the pledge the temperance movement sought to reshape, quickly and radically, not just behavior, but the moral disposition of the inner self, as the convert embraced modern ideals of sober self-discipline and productivity. Buddhists soon made this technology and framework their own.

Burmese campaigns against alcohol came about in a diverse milieu of temperance rhetoric and movements throughout South and Southeast Asia. In addition to the Anglo-American temperance branches in Burma, organizing against alcohol formed an important part of Buddhist rhetoric for revival in Ceylon and Cambodia.[85] Unlike some of these movements, which sought either legal prohibition or community enforcement of values, Burmese reformers sought to turn regulation inward, teaching individuals to police themselves through an understanding of the karmic and community implications of behavior.[86] In this, the rhetoric of the Burmese campaigns created a distinct pedagogy of introspection.

ALCOHOL AND THE ILLS OF THE COMMUNITY

Buddhist movements against intoxicants in Burma appropriated the temperance pledge as a technology of ethical introspection. However, they sought a transformation different from that pursued by Anglo-American temperance advocates. The Burmese Buddhist campaigns depicted alcohol and opium as a threat to the health of their community and to the *sāsana,* using the metaphor of disease to tie personal behavior to broader Buddhist concerns. This meant that rather than allying with European temperance campaigns, Buddhist discourse defined the moral community and its efforts in opposition to outside others.

The prohibition against intoxicants was the fifth of the five precepts laypeople were expected to follow, so Buddhist calls for abstention from alcohol and opium were nothing new. However, through the 1890s and 1900s, more and more propagandists and preachers targeted intoxicants. Burmese print media made the issue a larger concern; newspapers ran articles on the dangers of alcohol, and journals reprinted the reformist preachers' temperance sermons.[87] By 1911, the province-wide Young Men's Buddhist Association (YMBA) took an official stance to promote abstinence.[88]

For the youth educated in the new government-style schools, the appeals were addressed in printed books and special youth associations. U Kyaw Yan wrote his Burmese-language *Thura meraya pakathani kyan* (Treatise on Intoxicating Liquors) in response to appeals from the YMBA and the Burman Youths' Temperance League.[89] U Kyaw Yan, the school inspector turned Buddhist reformer who founded Buddhist Anglo-vernacular schools and associations discussed in Chapter 3, was well versed in both the bureaucratic and scientific cultures and in Buddhist ethics.[90] His writings over his lifetime demonstrate an amazing ability to move back and forth between multiple systems of knowledge, bridging European sciences and Buddhist cosmologies in a way that would have particularly appealed to schoolboys attempting to translate between changing worlds.

His text joined karmic consequences common to precolonial Buddhist moral prescriptions with scientific evidence to persuade the students to abstain.[91] Given the audience trained in the rationalist epistemology of the government's schools, U Kyaw Yan's description of drinking emphasized the problems in the human realm, avoiding the descriptions of hells from Pali sources. He encouraged his young audience to reflect on the consequences of their behaviors, but underscored human consequences in present or future rebirths that would be readily apparent to young students. His topics included "The types of deadly dangers for drinkers," "Three habits that bring ruin in this world," "Four reasons for not being able to establish a married life," "Six destructive ingrained habits," "The sins here in samsara that occur for those who drink," and "The thirty-three benefits of refraining from intoxicants."[92]

The emphasis on habit and worldly consequence was not coincidence; the sixty faults listed in "the sins here in samsara" read like the list of complaints in Burmese newspapers about declining public morals discussed earlier in the chapter, particularly the morals of young Burmese men. Drinkers were said to breach the rules of civility and culture, speak untruths and use rude language, "cause mischief," and "associate with other groups of people, slurp their food and sleep on the ground." They were disrespectful, known to "fight with their parents" and "not follow the advice of elders." They were also destructive to themselves and others in that they "suffer from headaches and diseases"; lose their property, possessions, and inheritance; and even "bring the destruction of villages."[93] U Kyaw Yan's list linked the problems that the letters to Burmese newspapers had identified as symptoms of general decline to a single behavior, the use of alcohol, in order to argue that it was in his young audience's power to change their communal situation. Their resolve not to drink could prevent these greater ills to the community. In his description, the destruction of the Buddhist community and the state of the *sāsana* was the product of specific individual immoral behavior. Young men's choice to drink became the source of the social, financial, and medical ills threatening Buddhists, and they alone held the potential to reverse the situation.

The second half of U Kyaw Yan's text took a different approach, meant to appeal to students training in Western science. It presented studies by doctors in England, Scotland, and America about the health dangers of intoxicants.[94] In translating the medical findings, U Kyaw Yan employed a list form common to Buddhist texts, with the graphic descriptions of stomach ailments, blood, and membranes functioning much like the Pali depictions of hell in other Buddhist texts. The medical studies were taken from European temperance literature and carried the weight of technical knowledge for students being trained to recognize the authority of science.

U Silacara, a European Buddhist convert and monk, offered a similar idea in a lecture to the educated elite of the Rangoon College Buddhist Association. Drawing on new social science data and methods, U Silacara argued that not only could science prove that the increase in disease in Lower Burma correlated to alcohol usage, it would show that use of intoxicants was directly responsible for the perceived recent increase in crime and mental illness. Silacara correlated the increase in problems to the length of colonial contact, contrasting the fate of Lower Burma, British from 1852, with that of Upper Burma, annexed only in 1885. He explained,

> Here in the statistics of crime and mental alienation a notable difference is observable between Lower Burma and Upper Burma. Such differences may have many lesser causes, yet the greatest cause that which contributes most largely to the result, must be admitted to be the spread under the influence of European example, of the habit of drinking intoxicants, together with the increase in the use of narcotic drugs. Lower Burma has been exposed to that—in this respect—pernicious European influence more abundantly and for a greater number of years than Upper Burma.[95]

For this Buddhist and his audience, social scientific enumeration and deduction could prove that communal ills came from immoral behavior and detrimental colonial influence. The solution to the predicament lay not in removing the British or refuting the Christian missionaries, but in reforming the habits of fellow Buddhists and reminding them of their previous temperate ways. By returning Buddhists to moral habits, U Silacara saw the possibility of preserving the teachings in all of their purity. He wrote, "Upon you now before me rests the responsibility as to whether Burma shall present to the world the sad spectacle of yet another people that has adopted all of the vices and none of the virtues of the European; or whether it shall remain the Burma of old."[96] Once again, in this view, the fate of the religion rested on the moral actions of the Buddhists of Burma.

The campaign extended well beyond the large towns and cities. Texts and lectures like these from U Kyaw Yan and U Silacara joined with letters to the newspapers, public debates, and journal articles to appeal to the educated. Preaching campaigns, moreover, took the message to much broader audiences across the colony. Ledi Sayadaw's sermon on intoxicants to a crowd of three thousand in Myaungmya in April of 1908 was typical of these events.[97] The sermon, in its printed version, was in fairly simple Burmese, and his audience was likely drawn from a range of economic and educational backgrounds in this rural area of the Irrawaddy delta.[98] In this sermon he presented an argument on morality that, while embedded within a discourse on longer-term karmic consequences, discussed individual behavior as having direct consequences for contemporary community concerns.

Ledi Sayadaw is most often remembered as the founder of lay mediation movements and as the virtuoso Pali scholar who interpreted Abhidhamma concepts into language comprehensible to the average person, as we saw in the memorization competitions popular with young women discussed in Chapter 2.[99] However, as part of these efforts, he was an extremely popular preacher and understood by many at the turn of the twentieth century as a moral reformer as well. As E. J. Colston explained, "No review of religio-social work would be complete without a mention of the Ledi Sayadaw. His sermons and visitations have a most powerful effect in the country. He has a marvelous influence over young men, and has done much good by preaching on their faults. And he is an able and broad-minded reformer."[100] Ledi Sayadaw's efforts for reform were tied to his Abhidhamma meditation efforts through a concern about the contemporary status of the *sāsana*.

His sermon in Myaungmya in April of 1908 opened with two verses from the *Vipāka Sutta* of the Aṅguttara Nikāya, recited first in Pali and then translated into Burmese.

Surāmerayapānaṃ, bhikkhave, āsevitaṃ nisevitaṃ
　nirayasaṃvattanikaṃ tiracchānayonisaṃvattanikaṃ
　pettivisayasaṃvattanikaṃ.
Yo ca sabbalahuko surāpānassa vipāko, so ummattakasaṃvattaniko.

Using intoxicants leads to rebirth in one of four lower states: rebirth in hell, as an animal, as a *peta* [dissatisfied ghost], or as an *asura* [fallen inferior deity].

The mildest consequence is becoming a lunatic, a half-wit, ruffian, or a rude uncivilized creature.[101]

In the first section of the sermon, Ledi Sayadaw addressed the first verse, stating, "those who indulge in these evil acts without atoning or avoiding them before they die will be reborn in hell."[102] Unlike U Kyaw Yan and U Silacara's appeals to the English-educated elite and schoolboys, Ledi Sayadaw's sermon depicted rebirth in hells in vivid terms, explaining that drinkers will be reborn in the Jālaroruva hell, where they will have "bodies like large and small mountains, and their orifices will burst out of the mountains in rivers and creeks overflowing with molten iron."[103] Opium users will be reborn in the Dhūmaroruva hell, which compounds these tortures further. He admonished hearers to think about these hells before they drank or used opium. Although the discussion of these primary karmic consequences was placed prominently at the beginning of the sermon, where it was sure to catch the attention of those who might be tempted to doze off later, it occupied less than a quarter of the sermon. Its presence was almost a perfunctory introduction to his larger discussion of intoxicants and morals.[104]

Ledi Sayadaw followed with a discussion of the *vipāka,* or fruit of the behaviors. The tone of the sermon changed here, as did his persuasive approach. Moving beyond the initial consequence of rebirth in hell, he dealt with the second verse—the mildest consequences resulting from the action. The preacher explained that those reborn in hells are not immediately thereafter born as good human beings or good gods but either as human beings with social or mental problems or as types of disturbed supernatural beings who cause problems for humanity. Among the human possibilities there were insane people "who are jailed in the government's prisons for the insane"; those who are slightly insane, "who because they are not entirely free from virtue, without really being people are inferior people, more like animals"; rude and violent ruffians, including the inhabitants of the British penal colony in the Andaman islands; and the uncivilized like the ethnic groups of the hill regions of Burma.[105] With this list he translated the long karmic fruits described in the Pali into concrete groups his audience could identify as problems in their midst. As for the disturbed gods who were a product of intoxicants, Ledi Sayadaw explained that they have many names in Burmese, listing a number of locally known malevolent spirits.[106] These beings were the cause of great problems; they liked to feast on the blood and fat of humans and animals and caused a range of diseases. This was a set of natural and supernatural problems that his audience would have known well; plague and cholera were endemic.[107] Burmese understanding related these diseases to supernatural intervention, and villages gathered to beat drums, make loud noises, and chant Pali texts to drive spirits and the diseases away. Ledi Sayadaw himself, while encouraging followers to be vaccinated, visited villages to drive out disease by chanting Abhidhamma texts.[108]

In this discussion, Ledi Sayadaw shifted the focus away from ethics over a course of lifetimes to ethical implications in the here and now. Although technically, intoxicant users would have experienced the secondary fruits in a future rebirth, Ledi Sayadaw's emphasis was on the implications of these actions for the present lives of his hearers. Thus, he subtly conflated the lifetimes'-long cosmological frame of ethics with immediate implications in their contemporary world. In the descriptions of the earthly rebirths of drinkers and opium users, Ledi Sayadaw tied behavior to concrete problems for the community: the presence of those perceived as uncivilized and mentally handicapped in their midst and the diseases that threatened the health of their villages and towns. Whereas the initial consequences of drinking fell onto the drinkers themselves, with rebirth in hell, these further fruits of intoxicants were experienced by the community in the present. Disease operated as a metaphor for decadence in the community, made manifest in specific problems his audience would understand as pressing collective concerns seemingly symptomatic of their colonial condition.

Ledi Sayadaw's calls for moral reform defined the community in opposition to Christians in order to emphasize the potential of good behavior for Buddhists. In Christian ethics, he argued, individual humans could do nothing to change the situation; even Abraham, Isaac, Joseph, and Moses could do nothing more than make offerings and wait for God's intervention.[109] Buddhists, on the other hand, knew well the power of good actions; karma offered the possibility of counteracting the effects of past misdeeds.

> If you memorize and learn the profound teachings of the *rūpa dhamma*, the *nāma dhamma*, the *paticca-samuppāda*, and the Four Noble Truths as stated in the treatises on Abhidhamma and you steadfastly practice the virtue of being free from all intoxicants, if you do these two things, then your previous bad deeds, entailed in being dependent on intoxicants, will disappear, and you will become a virtuous person freed from dependence on intoxicants and the fruits of your previous bad deeds.[110]

Buddhists had the means to correct immoral actions and, in doing so, to rid themselves and their community of the consequences.

Good actions in Ledi Sayadaw's description had positive effects in the world. He argued, "Good deeds are the medicine that can heal the wounds and disease of bad deeds; the medicine that makes bad deeds disappear. And the relevant good deeds can make specific bad deeds disappear."[111] Beyond chanting and banging pots, Ledi Sayadaw's audience now had a prescription for fixing their collective ills. If a lack of morality, evidenced in using intoxicants and other bad behavior, had caused disease in the community, good actions had the potential to heal those diseases and improve the community. The call to sign a pledge against these immoral behaviors offered a prescription for individual intervention to heal the ills of the community and address their greatest collective ailment, the decline of the *sāsana*.

In the Buddhist campaigns against intoxicants, disease operated as a reference to the decline perceived in the colonial condition that appealed in a number of different registers. Whether discussed in scientific terms or as the result of supernatural intervention, the ultimate trajectory of these problems was the decline of the Buddha's teachings in the Burmese community. Just as plague required villagers to come together to drive out evil spirits, the increase in mental illness, crime, and disease from intoxicants required Buddhists to come together and publicly agree to transform their behavior to renew the *sāsana*. Although phrased in different registers, this was fundamentally the same argument put to schoolboys by U Kyaw Yan's text and to Rangoon College students by U Silacara's lecture. Each offered a distinct conception of disease, but sought to internalize a message that individual moral restraint was the key to the health of the *sāsana*. Like the Anglo-American temperance efforts, Buddhist campaigns against intoxicants sought changed behaviors to create changed people, ones who understood themselves as part of an ethical project that went beyond individual karma.

CONCLUSION

If the broader discourse of moral decline imagined a moral community as the site of intervention, the practice of signing pledges sought to train individual Buddhists in a mode of ethical introspection to make them good subjects of this collective identity. The Buddhist moral reform campaigns worked to produce a new kind of ethical introspection. Those admonished by animals' appeals for vegetarianism or Ledi Sayadaw's sermons were to think of themselves and their actions not in terms of their own karmic fate but in terms of their implications for the whole of the *sāsana*. Their actions had clear material civic consequences, seen in the spread of disease or the "destruction of villages." However, these concrete social manifestations, which were the object of the colonizers' reform efforts, were only the first level of the problem from the Buddhist perspective. The social and material effects were a result of the larger soteriological and supernatural problem— the decline of the *sāsana* due to the failings in the members of the moral community.

The Buddhist moral reform campaigns served to reshape subjects and dispositions by changing habit and performance. Manners and behavior had long been central to *sāsana* reform in Burma. Yet, even as Buddhist campaigns claimed a conservative impetus that sought to return Burmese to the good behaviors of a time before colonial corruptions, their intervention was an innovation in Buddhist ethics, a new way of imagining the moral community and forming the layperson as an ethical agent.

This reflection on moral behavior, like the pledges signed at the preaching events, served to produce an individual stake in the collective endeavor. Unlike taking precepts on full-moon days or making a vow with a tattoo, this public agreement operated less to single out the individual for protection or merit than to homogenize the individual within the collective identity and the collective moral project. Signing a pledge, like making a donation recorded in the associations' journals, marked membership in the collective body of Buddhists concerned for the *sāsana*. However, it was not just agreeing to take action to promote the *sāsana* and reform the moral community. To sign acknowledged that the individual's past actions were partially responsible for the fallen state of the *sāsana*. Alcohol, opium, meat eating, and gambling were not simply individual issues that resulted in detrimental rebirth; individual engagement in these practices had precipitated the decline of the *sāsana*. The offer to sign a pledge required the individual to view him- or herself in a new way, not only as a member of the collective dedicated to preserving the *sāsana* but as an ethical actor whose behaviors held the power to threaten or ameliorate the soteriological condition. Signing meant both acknowledging one's partial responsibility for the state of the *sāsana* and simultaneously working for its betterment.

Membership in the moral community responsible for the Buddha's *sāsana* under colonialism gave individual laypeople a new sense of moral agency. They now held in themselves both the responsibility and the power to shape their world in its most important aspect: the soteriological conditions of *sāsana*. The religious project of *sāsana* shaped an ethics of introspection and identity that asked Buddhists to regulate their behavior according to a new purpose. In doing so it offered a new frame of self-understanding to respond to the troubling changes brought by colonialism. Coming to understand oneself, as the animals begged their two-legged brethren to do, as having the power to preserve the *sāsana* with one's everyday actions, created a new way of being for Burmese. Buddhist efforts to restrain and retrain Burmese habits worked to internalize a new conception of the Burmese Buddhist self, one that was strongly constituted by its participation in the moral community and that demanded a new self-discipline as simultaneously patron, agent, and location of *sāsana* reform.

The concept of moral community offered a sense of purpose and mode of identity for Burmese Buddhists, one that was made concrete in the Buddhist associations, which made both the networks between disparate Buddhists and the urgency of their collective endeavor explicit. This growing sense of identity, imagined not through the idea of nation but through a Buddhist worldview and project, was multiplied through the associations' moral reform efforts. Identifying with the moral community offered individual Buddhists immense new importance as patrons and protectors of Buddhism, made manifest not only in their donations, but in the moral choices of their everyday lives. Moreover, this identity required that they now embody a certain type of internal reflection and self-regulation out of concern for the state of the *sāsana*. The concept of moral community took shape in the pages of the association's journals, the projects they undertook, and their donation lists, but it came to life as Buddhists throughout their daily lives came to imagine their moral actions directly united with the future longevity of the Buddha's teaching. A community imaged and made manifest through the collective moral project to preserve the *sāsana* created a new mode of ethical subjectivity for Buddhists in colonial Burma.

5

The Shoe and the *Shikho*

In August of 1899, the stores in Moulmein were over-
whelmed by Burmese and Indian men seeking to buy socks. This sudden
fashion requirement stemmed from a demand by a local European judge
that those appearing before him adhere fully to norms of dress. He ruled
that Burmese men could not enter court wearing both European-style shoes
and a Burmese *gaungbaung* head covering on the principle that mixing Burmese and European attire was disrespectful. Such behavior demonstrated
neither the European respect of removing one's hat nor the Burmese practice
of removing shoes. In his judgment, mixing Burmese and European attire
showed too little deference to the court and the rules of civility. The word
went out that it was no longer acceptable to mix Asian and European customs and, as the local English-language newspaper explained, "counsel having advised that socks are 'de rigueur,' shops are being ransacked to meet
the exigencies of the situation."[1]

While such concern for hosiery seemed laughable even at the time, the
politics of the encounter were anything but. The judge's insistence on the specific demonstrations of respect went to the heart of the European construction of colonial difference and the civilizing mission. Status and the performance of inferiority were worked out through attire and especially gestures
of respect. Such performance of respect stirred controversy in colonial Burma
in part because the rhetoric of mutual respect never convincingly masked the
structures of dominance inherent to colonial power. Demands for respect
offered colonizers a thinly veiled device for reinforcing hierarchies and often
granted the colonized an opening for subversion.

For most of the nineteenth century, colonial authorities expected Burmese to perform culturally specific modes of respect, reinforcing colonial
difference as an unbreachable divide between Europeans and Asians. An
1882 magazine published for Europeans in Rangoon, stressing difference, explained respect in terms of reciprocity.

The Burmese as a people do not use stockings, . . . sandals are in common use and a loose kind of slipper which has no heel to it. On visiting one another and entering houses they divest themselves of these pedal appendages . . . breach of [this] observance is looked upon as impoliteness, and indeed, as evincing that the person who neglects it is one whose breeding has been sadly neglected. We Europeans who wear stockings, socks, boots and shoes, display our politeness in quite a different way. The Burman who removes his feet from his slippers and retains his head covering is only acting up to the custom of his country, the same as the European according to Western usages takes off his hat but retains his shoes, so that when a private Burmese gentlemen calls on a European he acts according to his custom, and the European when he returns the visit removes his hat on entering the house.[2]

The passage implied that the different modes are complementary, equally demonstrating the same respect, albeit reinforcing a distinction between colonializer and colonized.

However, a growing number of Burmese adopting European shoes disrupted this logic of complementary modes of respect. The change in Burmese attire disturbed some colonial officials, a response that belied the assertion that different practices of respect were equal. In reality, such practices were not about equivalencies but about the construction of difference and subordination. In 1867 the Government of India considered changing its policy to allow Asians wearing European style shoes, but not Asian sandals, to retain their shoes in court.[3] Albert Fytche, the chief commissioner of British Burma, objected firmly, protesting that "the mere wearing of a pair of shoes and stockings would enable any Burman to claim the right of walking into our Courts in a fashion dissimilar from anything he does attempt in any other place."[4] The Government of India, unpersuaded by Fytche's protests, allowed Asians to wear shoes in formal gatherings, maintaining that just as the clothes made the man in the refashioning practices of the civilizing mission, they also determined the manners he should practice. For Fytche, however, maintaining authority required a clear distinction between Burmese and Europeans and separate rules of respect for each. For him, colonial difference was central to colonial authority, and being barefoot in court ensured Burmese remained on a lower rung.

These two models of colonial authority—colonial difference and the civilizing mission—came head to head in the courtroom in Moulmein. The judge was forced to concede that, when it came to footwear, Burmese could assimilate to European norms. However, he insisted those norms must be precisely defined, and in all ways distinguished from anything Burmese, lest European civility be tainted with Burmese custom. The situation required he decree what it meant to adopt European modes—down to the stockings. Even the smallest gestures encoded colonial power within this symbolic system.

SYMBOLS, SUBORDINATION, AND RELIGION

Conflicts over dress and modes of demonstrating respect were not unique to Burma in the colonial period. From the British diplomatic missions' refusal to kowtow to the Chinese Imperial Court to Gandhi's insistence on wearing his turban in South African legal courts, dress and respect served as vital symbolic means of inscribing and resisting subordination in colonial relations.[5] At the same time, efforts on the part of Asians to reform sartorial performances and assimilate to European norms served as claims to modernity and equality. In Siam, King Mongkut's decision to allow European shoes and socks at royal courts and Buddhist sites, and the broader adoption of Western dress in King Chulalongkorn's reign, both sought to produce equal status with Europeans through outward appearance.[6] And, as the 2008 incident in which an Iraqi journalist threw his shoe at President Bush demonstrates, footwear continues to convey symbolically charged messages of colonial subordination and its refusal.

Symbols, of course, can work both ways. Burmese became adept at manipulating these symbolic systems. The policy that Burmese remove their shoes where Europeans remove hats demanded that Burmese do what Europeans considered a degrading act—removing their footwear in public. However, the practice could be read quite differently. In the Burmese worldview, the head is considered the highest and most respected part of the body and the feet the lowliest and most degraded. Therefore, some Burmese rakishly interpreted the rule that they must unshoe where Europeans removed their hats to equate Burmese feet with European heads, placing Burmese above their colonizers in the symbolic hierarchy.[7]

Moreover, Burmese found the symbols of respect useful for denoting the limits of colonial authority and their own assimilation. Urban Burmese men's choice of European attire pointed to a larger tendency to "adopt but adapt." Ironic European depictions of these elite Burmese men paint a picture of the limits of their willingness to bend to colonial demands. One English observer wrote:

Neither education nor success leads the Burman astray in dress. Though he attains the dizzy eminence of an Extra Assistant Commissionership, the most he does is to take to himself a gold-topped and silk-tasseled malacca cane, and discard his easy sandals for stockings and shoes. In theory the latter enhance his dignity; in practice they sadly discount it. Garters would overcome the difficulty, but to these the Burman has a rooted antipathy, and official swagger suffers from heavy folds of white cotton stocking about the ankles gathering dust.[8]

While their partial adoption of European dress was a cause of ridicule for the European observer, the incongruity marked quite literally the point to which these Burmese men were willing to accept European sartorial authority and a concomitant shift in subjectivity—to the ankles and no higher.

This chapter wades into a series of these conflicts between Burmese and Europeans over demonstrations of respect that encoded broader issues of subordination and the politics of colonial difference. However, the events are of interest not just for understanding colonial power, but for seeing how Buddhists used the changing definitions of religion to stake claims to autonomy. The ambiguity of the category of religion meant that both Burmese Buddhists and colonial actors could actively contest "religion" as a means of promoting or resisting the power of the state and the cultural projects of colonialism.

As scholars have come to accept, religion is not a natural or inherent category for most of humanity. It is an analytical category advanced by scholars and a European category emerging out of a specific post-Enlightenment Christian context. Recent scholarship on secularism contends that this process in Europe was not the retreat of religion from the otherwise secular social and political life, but the creation of "religion" as a new and separate classification for aspects of social existence. Talal Asad argues that "the secular should not be thought of as the space in which real human life gradually emancipates itself from the controlling power of religion and thus achieves the latter's relocation." Instead, he argues, "Secularism posits a particular conception of the world ('natural' and 'social') and of the problems generated by that world." It is this cosmology that creates "religion" as a separate and bounded category, and empowers a defining and redefining of "religion's competence."[9] Categories and boundaries like this one were central to the colonial project and governmentality, training subjects in proper self-regulation. In some places this effort to limit religion sought to shrink the impact of traditions and render them apolitical.

It would be reductive, however, to assert that colonialism invented Buddhism as a religion or imposed religion where no such idea existed. The Burmese had means of defining what was inside and outside the *sāsana* and the limits to Buddhism's integration in life. Moreover, while it might be easy to characterize the colonial situation by contending that British colonialism imposed the category of religion on the Burmese in order to shape a docile and civilized population, the situation was much more complex. Although a Protestant ideal of religion as primarily a matter of belief and assent to doctrine was in circulation in these debates, it was not the only model of religion promoted by Europeans in colonial Burma. Nor was there a clear dialectic between a bounded European category of religion and a Burmese worldview unlimited by such a distinction. In this period, European actors embraced a variety of definitions of religion, emphasizing more or less its bright distinction with the "secular" or its freedom from state intervention. As we saw with the attempts to bring the monasteries into the government education system, the idea of religion as a means of shaping morally self-regulated subjects held sway for some British officials, a vision that stood at odds with the privatization of religion and official religious neutrality. Others would vociferously defend a model of religion in Protestant form that rejected the significance of ritual, while still insisting on specific (ritualized) performances for a secular practice of respect. When it came to defining religion in this colonial context, the lines were more muddied than the colonial actors or their rhetorics were willing to admit.

Burmese offered up multiple ways of defining religion themselves, producing internal debates as well as lines of skirmish with the colonial state. Far from rejecting religion as a category antithetical to their purposes, as some monks had done in their opposition to government monastery schools, Burmese activists and Buddhist organizers embraced religion strategically, and joined in the game of defining and redefining its substance to respond to different needs. Some embraced sharp boundaries for religion in order to fend off colonial intervention, but insisted in illiberal fashion on the centrality of ritual performance. Others re-centered the debate within the Buddhist community to reexamine the role of internal states, such as karmic intention versus physical performance, in the life and promotion of the *sāsana*. Buddhists became skilled at using the ambiguities of ideas about religion in their twin struggles to resist colonial subordination and preserve the *sāsana*.

Religion was subject to a strategic bricolage, with shifting lines of agreement and divergence. It was shaped through these conflicts to serve a number of different interests, Burmese and European actors alike learning to exploit the limits of colonial secularist discourse. Moreover, it is not clear that the debates were about religion itself, but that defining religion became a central mode of contention. Control of the category and its meaning became an operative mode of power and resistance, adeptly deployed by multiple groups. As we will see, the game of defining religion in colonial Burma was afoot.

RELIGION AND RESPECT: THE *SHIKHO* IN SCHOOLS

Conflicts over respect first became entangled with religion in the protests of high school students against the requirement of a "traditional" salute. As we have seen in Chapters 3 and 4, education and the perceived decline in morals were urgent matters for Buddhists working to protect the *sāsana*. European public opinion expressed in the newspapers tended to agree with the Buddhist leaders that boys educated in the government's schools were losing their respect for authority and their public manners. Although the two groups diverged on the prescribed course of action, there was a consensus that this was one of the most pressing concerns of the day. The Buddhist schoolboy was a key character in discussions of contemporary change and decline. However, as this case will make clear, the schoolboys were neither mute patients nor passive objects of reform, but active as key agents in negotiations of colonial religion and reform.

To help remedy the consensus problem that Buddhist boys were lax in morals, John Van Someren Pope, Director of Public Instruction for Burma, issued a circular in July of 1903 requiring that all students perform a daily salute to their teachers as a demonstration of respect.[10] The required form of salute differed for boys of different ethnicities. Pope had seen the department through most of the conflict over monastery education and the creation of new Buddhist schools, and was the one who had revived the Pali examinations. He perceived himself to be sympathetic to Burmese culture; even when Burmese Buddhists directly opposed him, he felt he was seeking to promote specific cultural practices as against the monolithic colonial impositions demanded by his superiors in Calcutta. Thus he saw the requirement for a culturally specific salute as a compromise to help restore Burmese boys to moral order. In the original version, the requirement for Burmese students was called a salute "in the traditional Burmese form," but it was widely taken to mean a *shikho*—a prostrating bow performed while kneeling on the floor, touching the forehead to the ground.[11] So, while their

Indian, Chinese, and European counterparts were to stand, hands at their sides, or snap a military salute, Burmese students were to prostrate themselves on the ground in front of their mainly European teachers.

The new rule was not well received. Most schools with Burmese headmasters simply refused to enforce it. However, in August, the issue came to a head at the flagship Rangoon Collegiate School.[12] The Burmese students there flatly refused to perform what they felt was an inappropriate salute, refusing to submit their bodies to the demands of "tradition" as described in the department's circular. Their protest was soon joined by students in Akyab and Prome.[13] The requirement, the students argued, was meant to demean them rather than promote appropriate respect for authority. One European master made the politics of the situation explicit, telling Burmese students that in the past they would have been required to kiss his boots.[14] At first, the crisis was averted, when Pope clarified that a *shikho* was not required, but that each community must perform a bow from their own custom, and he offered a clause by which parents could exempt their students from any salute they felt was inappropriate.[15]

However, it soon became clear that neither side was ready to cede any ground. On September 11, an inspector from the Department of Public Instruction arrived at Rangoon Collegiate School and demanded that the boys of the eighth standard perform one of two alternative salutes, stating, despite the lack of serious consultation with the Burmese community, that these were agreed-upon Burmese salutes.[16] The students again refused and, unable to contact their parents for an exemption in the middle of the day, sought to continue classes until the matter could be resolved. The teachers, refusing to teach until they received a modified *shikho* from all students, effectively created a lockout. Since there were no classes, the students of the upper grades left the school at lunch, joined by those in the lower grades in the afternoon.

By the next day, over six hundred students joined the protest. As the *Times of Burma* described the situation: "score of teachers (sixteen masters and four school-mistresses) were employed in . . . admiring the empty rows of benches in the Rangoon Collegiate School, which eloquently proclaimed the utter failure of the attempt that was made of 'fabricating respect' for the teaching staff."[17] The situation escalated, as school officials refused meals to the boarding students and threatened to turn them out onto the streets. Striking students posted a "For Rent" sign on the school gates, expressing their frustration with a school that refused to teach.[18] The students and teachers remained in this standoff for almost a month, with students transferring to other schools in Rangoon and Calcutta that advertised "No *Shikho*."[19] Tempers flared as it became clear that education officials were unwilling to compromise. The students' strike, in their view, only offered further evidence of Burmese boys' unwillingness to submit to authority. The students, in turn, argued that inappropriate *shikho*s served not to demonstrate respect but to demean. They described their situation:

> The young hankerers after education being subjected to this stringent measure, are now at a loss as to what to do; whether to debase themselves by shickhoing . . . or to leave school for good, or to fly to a distant land where pupils are taught without the additional fees of shickhoing; and where . . . they will not be shown the door to leave when the demand for cringing respect is not complied with.[20]

The Burmese students argued that because religion rendered the *shikho* inappropriate for demonstrating respect to secular teachers, they should be allowed to perform the same salute as Europeans. They were being taught to adopt European ideals, and thus *shikho*ing was no longer respectful for them, but degrading. One student who joined the strike from the growing commercial town of Prome, north of Rangoon on the Irrawaddy River, wrote to the local English newspaper there to say,

> We shiko to officials whom we have to fear and to our spiritual teachers to whom the greatest respect is due not only from us, youngsters, but from our parents. Why should the Education Department, which is teaching us all the time to despise anything in the way of servility, now expect us to take up what we have been taught to loathe?[21]

For the secular colonial world of education, the students accepted the premise that the civilizing mission meant they could and should adopt European manners.[22]

The students voiced their objections in the English-language newspapers. They could not *shikho* secular teachers, they argued, because *shikho*ing was a Buddhist practice, reserved for religious objects of respect.[23] According to Pali sources, the five objects worthy of respect are the Three Gems—the Buddha, the Dhamma, and the Sangha—together with parents and teachers. This inclusion of teachers had led Pope to conclude that *shikho*ing teachers was a practice of Burmese tradition that the colonial government could rightly seek to maintain. However, the students wrote:

When a Burman goes to a phoongye, who is a priest or religious spiritual instructor, not a mere teacher of arts and sciences, he bows down on his knees and pays respect. Unlike our teacher he does not demand respect from his visitors or pupils. An old saying is that the gratitude to our "Achariya" i.e. teacher is "Anando" [Pali: *ananta*] (boundless) but these "Achariya" are quite different characters to paid persons as educational instructors.[24]

They argued that the teachers included in the five objects are teachers who teach about the Buddhist doctrine, such as Buddhist monks and lay teachers in the informal village Buddhist schools, but teachers of arts and sciences at a government high school could in no way lay claim to this status.[25] The students' argument was a narrowing of the Pali concept of *ācariya* as teacher, claiming a radical difference between Buddhist and non-Buddhist teachers.

In their protests, the students were part of a long tradition of Burmese resistance to state authority and demands for *shikho*s that required veneration for those to whom no veneration was due.[26] This tradition held that reverence was owed to those who had accumulated *pon,* or merit: monks and other teachers accumulated merit, and thus reverence, by offering Buddhist teachings; parents accumulated merit because they provided life. The requirement to *shikho* a minister of the royal courts (or later a colonial official), on the other hand, had long been a point of controversy. While such precolonial complaints set a precedent, unlike the complaints against *shikho*ing royal ministers or colonial officials, the students did not phrase their objections in English in terms of the amount of merit or due reverence. Instead they relied not on the Buddhist conceptual worldview they sought to defend but on the categories of religious and secular.

European public opinion quickly sided with the students, and even the normally conservative and government-allied *Rangoon Gazette* opposed the *shikho* requirement, arguing, "The Burmese 'shiko' is an anomaly and an incongruity in English schools. In the hpoongyi kyoungs it can be carried out in the orthodox way, and without clashing with the teaching there or with religious ideas of the people, but in an English school it clashes with both."[27] The *Times of Burma* agreed with the boys that this was a religious issue and chided Pope: "It is evident that, if the school boys badly wanted healthy exercise in bowing down to worship, the Shwedagon and the Sule pagodas are sufficient for the purpose; and the parents may be trusted to attend to the religious training of their sons, without the gratuitous intermeddling of secular school teachers."[28] The majority of the nonofficial European community writing to the papers accepted this argument as well. Some Europeans helpfully proposed that if the Director of Public Instruction and his teachers really wanted to be *shikho*ed, they should ordain as Buddhist monks.[29] One European wrote to ask, "Are those, who desire this shikoing, images of the Buddha, Phongyis or Kings? By all means they are not. Yet withal, if they insist on this shikoeing [*sic*] why not then transform them into Phongyis, (as the Irish Phongyi, and a number of other Europeans did lately)?"[30]

As the controversy wore on, its interpretation as a religious concern only spread. An inspector of schools in the far northern outpost of Bhamo insisted that the students *shikho*. When they refused, he surveyed the local parents and was convinced that the Buddhists had a legitimate religious reason for refusing, but then demanded that the Christian converts *shikho*. The Christian missionary headmaster was appalled: "You can well imagine what a struggle was going on in the missionary's mind, when he saw an Englishman debar Christian children from their examinations because they conscientiously refused to follow a heathen custom of worship, from which he had just excused the Buddhists."[31] The Rangoon students' English-language newspaper appeals had succeeded in convincing both the inspector and the missionary at the far end of the colonial province that this was unequivocally a religious practice.

The students' arguments, amplified through the editorials and letters of support in the English-language newspapers, won the day. In the end, with European opinion against him, Pope was forced to resign.[32] Classes returned to session with no salute required. The argument that prevailed had nothing to do with refusing the servile enforcement of colonial authority, but instead focused clearly on the issue of religion. The students argued that the performance of respect and its felicity must be determined not by the ethnic identity of the performer (requiring different salutes from different ethnicities), but by the object of respect, requiring the *shikho* for religious teachers only and other salutes for secular government teachers. In this, the schoolboys introduced a new logic to determine modes of respect. Given that *shikho*s continued to be required for a broad range of elders and superiors in other contexts, the students' argument that *shikho*ing teachers was a religious practice was an innovation. In distinguishing between two categories of teachers, religious and not, the students were introducing a new category into the consideration of *shikho*s, one that does not easily correspond to precolonial practice. Their argument relied on an idea of a religious sphere, one that operates on rules distinct from those of any other aspect of life.

The students' argument that they could not *shikho* teachers because *shikho*ing was a religious practice shrewdly engaged the British policy of noninterference in religious affairs. Since the 1857 mutiny, British policy had held that government could not intercede in matters of religion. The boys educated in English schools had assimilated this norm, and the idea of a bright line between religious and nonreligious issues. If they could succeed in convincing officials and the public that a *shikho,* or at least a *shikho* offered to teachers, was a Buddhist religious practice justified and performed solely in religious terms, they could avoid the humiliation some sought to enforce with the *shikho.*

As we have seen from the conflicts over monastery education, there was significant contention and debate at this time over which practices would count as religion. These questions were part of a broader public negotiation over how aspects of Burmese culture fit into and shaped colonial modernity. Given the wide variety of *shikho*s demanded in official settings, at the outset it was not completely clear that *shikho*ing teachers was a religious practice. The students made a persuasive case that *shikho*s should only be offered to religious teachers and *shikho*ing should be considered religious, but such a classification was not a foregone conclusion. The *shikho* protest brings to the fore that religion and, especially, its conflicted boundaries had become a central battleground for resisting colonial authority and negotiating space for autonomy and self-determination. Not only was religion increasingly being defined as a bounded, separate sphere of social life, but it was becoming understood as a means of claiming space to oppose colonial subordination.

SHOES AT THE PAGODAS

The European practice of wearing shoes at pagodas further highlights the complexity of colonial constructions of religion. From the beginnings of British rule in Burma, Europeans had exempted themselves from the requirement to remove footwear before mounting the steps into Buddhist monuments. This exemption originated from the time the British took the major pagodas in the wars and stationed troops there. Although by the 1890s the local government had relinquished management of the pagodas to Burmese hands, the exemption survived. Until 1916, the elected pagoda trustees acquiesced to the privileged rules for Europeans.

To students of Burmese history, the "shoe question," as it was called, and the controversy that brought an end to the European exemption are well known. Historians have frequently interpreted the events as the opening salvos of the independence movement.[33] In nationalist discourse in the mid-twentieth century, the shoe issue signaled both the beginning and the end of colonial domination. Equating the beginning of the end of Burmese independence with the refusal of the British envoy to the Burmese royal court to remove his shoes, this story took the Burmese victory on the shoe question in 1919 to be the beginning of the end of colonial rule.[34] In this narrative, exemplified in Dr. Khin Maung Nyunt's 1970 "The 'Shoe Question' (or the Loss and Regaining of Our Independence)," the shoe question is fundamentally an issue of the sovereignty of the nation. However, as we will see, the 1916–1919 controversy was only one episode in a longer debate over shoes at pagodas. This debate inextricably linked demonstrations of respect to the status of the moral community responsible for the *sāsana* and the construction of a definition of religion that offered space for Burmese autonomy.

Okpo Sayadaw's Provocation and Mobilizing the Moral Community

In 1892, Okpo Sayadaw, the founder of the Dwaya reformist monastic sect, mounted the covered stairs on the east side of the Sandawshin Pagoda in Prome, shocking the pious worshippers by marching onto the Buddha's reliquary with the dirty soles of his sandals.[35] The action sent a shockwave through the Buddhist community to think that a monk, one highly respected for his strict observation of Vinaya monastic regulations and ritual codes, could engage in behavior that to the average Burmese observer was clearly disrespectful to the Buddha. However, Okpo Sayadaw was trying to make a point. When his actions in Prome failed to provoke the desired public debate and reflection, in 1897 he mounted the Shwemawdaw Pagoda in Pegu with his shoes, and, finally, climbed the elaborate covered walkways of the Shwedagon Pagoda in Rangoon, the most revered Buddhist site in Burma, treading with the soles of his sandals on the most hallowed of Burmese Buddhist spaces.

Why would a highly respected monk engage in this provocative display, which the overwhelming majority understood to be one of the most demeaning and disrespectful acts possible toward the Buddha? And why pose an internal challenge among Buddhists late in his career, when his fame and influence had waned and colonialism seemed to pose such a great external threat to the future of Buddhism? Okpo Sayadaw had been a key figure in the mid-nineteenth-century monastic schisms that had sought to ensure greater asceticism and fidelity to monastic Vinaya rules. In 1855, he founded a reformist monastic sect in Lower Burma, known as the Dwaya, based on a number of critiques of the royally sanctioned Thudhamma monastic lineage. Okpo Sayadaw's decision to challenge one of the most basic and quotidian of Buddhist rituals, one in which the orthodox performance seemed beyond question, harkens back to an earlier moment in his career when he contested another ritual formulation in order to provoke a debate on the correct textual interpretation and the emphasis on mental intention over action.[36] In both cases he sought to shock Buddhists into reforming their practice in order to save the *sāsana* from the laxity of contemporary practice. Okpo Sayadaw hoped to revive the discussion that had propelled him to fame in 1855 and in so doing reform the practice of Buddhism in the colonized and increasingly decadent Lower Burma. However, his action instead instigated a polarizing discourse of defending the Buddha's *sāsana* against the threats of heteropraxis.

Okpo Sayadaw's marches up the stairs in Prome in 1892 and in Pegu and Rangoon in 1897 were provocative challenges, attempts to shock the population into again debating with him about what was really important to preserve the Buddha's *sāsana* in these challenging times. He did indeed provoke debate. There was a very quick and overwhelming public outcry against him, followed by a debate carried out in published treatises, an exchange known as the Zediyingana, or pagoda platform, debates. Okpo Sayadaw defended his actions with both a scholastic interpretation of what constituted the pagoda platform (whether it included the newly cemented platform immediately around the gold base, the stairs leading up to this area, or the whole of the open land surrounding the pagoda) and an emphasis on the intention rather than the action in producing merit. Those shocked by Okpo Sayadaw's actions and by the rationales he offered were quick to mount a reply, insisting on the impropriety of wearing shoes anywhere on stupa grounds, ultimately arguing "with regard to wearing shoes on the pagoda inside the walls on the platform, not only is it a grave disrespect for a person to wear shoes, but it will bring about the destruction of the sāsana."[37]

While Okpo Sayadaw may have succeeded in provoking controversy and debate, he cannot be said to have won. If Okpo Sayadaw wanted a larger debate about scriptural interpretation, the role of intention and action in producing merit, and the correct performance of ritual, what he achieved instead was a galvanized lay majority, set on opposing anything that they could interpret as threatening to the *sāsana*. The debate provoked not a reflection on the issue of intention, action, and Vinaya adherence, but an outburst of emotional sentiment that equated physical postures of respect, especially removing one's shoes, with the preservation of Buddhism under threat. The overwhelming popular majority sided against Okpo Sayadaw and became all the more militant in their views. As it was generally agreed that the Buddha's *sāsana* was under threat, the majority had little interest in the finer points of scriptural interpretation and abstract issues of mental volition and intent. Any action that could be perceived as diminishing the glory of the Buddha had to be vigorously resisted. That the threat came from inside the fold mattered little to the laypeople who now saw themselves as the last hope for preserving Buddhism.

The sentiment rallied by those opposing Okpo Sayadaw spurred the later footwear debates. Less than three years later, as we will see, another popular Buddhist preacher, building on the emotion over Okpo Sayadaw's actions, would publicly object to non-Buddhists wearing shoes at the Shwedagon Pagoda. Yet the response to Okpo Sayadaw's actions in 1897 and the subsequent exchange of treatises was an internal Buddhist argument over the propriety of wearing shoes. While the opposition did not quarrel with Okpo Sayadaw's position that intention held karmic primacy over action, they mobilized to defend the tradition of removing shoes as central to the defense of the status of Buddhism. Although the mid-twentieth-century nationalist narrative would come to read the footwear controversy as a debate with outsiders over sovereignty, such a later Buddhist nationalist position has its origin in an internal Buddhist debate that established the issue as central to the composition of Buddhism as a religion.

Irishmen, Indians, and Respecting Religion

The nationalist narrative has portrayed the 1916–1919 shoe controversy as an issue of national sovereignty and the beginning of the confrontation to end colonial domination. However, the lines of confrontation in the footwear debates did not easily match up with the boundaries of nation. Instead, the conflicts reflect the complicated racial and religious hybrids of colonial Burma. The footwear exemption for Europeans was established on the grounds that Europeans remove their hats where Asians remove their shoes. In 1875, however, the Burmese elders of Rangoon protested that Muslims were wearing shoes at Buddhist pagodas even though Muslims removed their shoes in mosques. The chief commissioner agreed that this was inappropriate and formalized the rule that "those persons, whose creed required them to show respect by taking off their shoes, should take off their shoes on visiting a pagoda."[38] This compromise seems to have satisfied all parties, and there was little mention of the issue of non-Burmese wearing shoes at pagodas for twenty-five years.

The controversy resurfaced in 1901. On March 2, during the March (Taboung) full-moon festival at the Shwedagon Pagoda, U Dhammaloka, the Irish Buddhist convert who had ordained as a monk, confronted an Indian police officer, asking him to remove his shoes. U Dhammaloka had frequently sought confrontation, and his European status emboldened him to confront the officer in a way few Burmese monks would have dared. Authorities had been wary of drunkenness and crime at these festivals, so there were a number of police in attendance. But this man, despite his uniform, was not on duty. As the news reports noted, in line with the 1875 policy, most Indians, including off-duty officers, removed their shoes when walking on the pagoda grounds. This officer, however, took offense at U Dhammaloka's request and filed a report with his European superior officer, who threatened to have U Dhammaloka arrested for sedition.[39]

The event stirred up a storm of letters in the English and Burmese newspapers. Seeking a swift resolution, the government pressured the pagoda trustees to renounce U Dhammaloka and his actions. They sent them a draft resolution stating that U Dhammaloka had disturbed Buddhists worshippers that evening and that if he continued to do so, he would be banned from the pagoda grounds. The resolution sought to bolster the trustees' authority and to reaffirm their willingness to acquiesce to government wishes. However, the plan backfired. At a meeting on March 17, the trustees refused to pass the resolution, and soon even Europeans wrote to the newspapers objecting to government interference.[40]

Although it had been an Irish Buddhist monk confronting an Indian police officer, Europeans were quick to read the controversy as a Burmese Buddhist rejection of Europeans' right to wear shoes on the pagoda. U Dhammaloka's original confrontation not only gained him the sympathy of a large number of Burmese Buddhists, it spurred others to action. In May, an English-speaking Buddhist monk from Ceylon confronted a Eurasian and an Indian at the Shwekyimyin Pagoda in Mandalay, asking them to remove their shoes.[41] And in July, U Dhammaloka returned to the Shwedagon, this time attempting to stop two Europeans from mounting the steps to the pagoda while wearing boots. Despite the European rhetoric that Burmese were seeking to reject Europeans wearing shoes, this was the only time a European had been confronted in the conflict, and until that date no one who identified primarily as Burmese, rather than Irish, Eurasian, Singhalese, or Chinese, had been an antagonist.

Wearing shoes on the pagoda platform held a different significance for differing groups in 1901. British officials were quick to assert that the "shoe question" was not a religious issue. For U Dhammaloka, the issue was clearly the defense of Buddhism. Just before the confrontation, he published a pamphlet entitled "Unity Is Strength," exhorting Buddhists to organize in defense of religion. Building on the interpretation established in opposition to Okpo Sayadaw, this was an issue of defending the *sāsana*. U Dhammaloka's critics were not wrong that, for him, this sentiment was tied to an opposition to colonial rule: the rest of his career would be devoted to a critique of colonialism through the lens of religion.[42]

A different dialogue and debate occurred within the Burmese community. In late May, the *Hanthawaddy Weekly Review,* one of the most popular Burmese newspapers of the day, published an editorial entitled, "Concerning the Issue of Europeans Wearing Shoes at the Shwedagon Pagoda." The editorial held that the behavior of Europeans and others on the grounds of Buddhist monuments was a serious problem that upset many Burmese. "Buddhists do not want to endure people wearing shoes and umbrellas on the pagoda grounds, or spitting, sneezing, selling things, practicing astrology or traditional medicine, dancing, begging with music, talking about sex, using walking sticks or other disrespectful acts."[43] The editorial used a Pali term, *agārava* (translated in English versions as "disrespect"), for its list of actions that should be prohibited, which included many performed by Burmese and Buddhists themselves. The list included a number of practices for which there were clear Pali textual injunctions.[44] In this way, the problem of Europeans and their shoes was located in a larger concern about degrading respect for Buddhism and the decline of the *sāsana.* The editorial acknowledged that religious groups demonstrated respect in different fashions, but this did not change the fact that these particular actions were demeaning to Buddhism. "European English show respect by removing their hats; Pathe Muslims show respect by a salaam with their foreheads and hands; Burman Buddhists remove their shoes and shikho. People of different religions have different gestures. However, the question of whether only Buddhists will be allowed to enter the pagoda grounds has not yet been decided."[45] Subtly elided in the silence between the last two sentences is an understanding that, regardless of intention, English and Muslim customs may actively denigrate Buddhism.

The point of the editorial was to chide the pagoda trustees into doing the right thing to defend the *sāsana,* which the editor felt meant excluding all others from the pagoda grounds, just as, he claimed, Buddhists were excluded from mosques whether or not they wore shoes. Pagoda trustees were morally obligated to enforce this difficult restriction as well as to regulate the longer list of disrespectful acts. The editor appealed to the trustees as "rich, intelligent and brave" guardians who should act "as if parents for the sake of the Buddhist public and the pagoda."[46] He reproached them, saying that despite the fact that Europeans have been allowed to wear shoes for many years, the trustees know that this behavior is not suitable and have only allowed it out of pressure from the government. The internal friction in the Burmese community pitted the editor, and the activist voice on behalf of the *sāsana* he sought to represent, against the historically more conservative and conciliatory pagoda trustees. For now, the conservative position would win out. Despite their earlier resistance, the week after this editorial, the pagoda trustees acquiesced to the government pressure and posted signs informing Buddhists not to interfere with the practices of "those of other nations."[47]

The editor of the *Hanthawaddy* responded with another editorial that expressed dismay with the pagoda trustees' decision, calling it "a cause of great regret."[48] The article demonstrates how shifting and conflicting understandings of religion animated the encounter. The editor politely proposed that both sides were making too much out of a minor issue, when larger matters faced the community. However, this demure attempt to smooth things over and his assertions that Buddhists practice equanimity were accompanied by an equal denial that this was a mere issue of politeness, in which wearing shoes had no consequences.

> In former times, neither the Chinese nor the Burmese Buddhists have raised any cry against Europeans and Englishmen wearing shoes on the Pagoda, nor have they created any disturbance with such visitors on the Pagoda platform. The Buddhists after having made their usual devotions at the Pagoda return home quietly. The Buddhist people seek to have a cool mind, and do not wish to interfere with other people's affairs; they remain in an indifferent state and allow others to bear the sin of their misdeeds, as they know that they will have to bear the sins of their own misdeeds. Besides, Buddhists have never made a distinction of the races; they do not say that foreigners are of our sect. . . . All Buddhists and all other British subjects know that the British government does not interfere with the religions of other people; and not only that but Government gave special assistance for the benefit of Buddhism.[49]

The image of "a cool mind" signals a particular mental state of piety that Buddhists should aspire toward, a religious state of detachment that would preclude becoming entangled in concerns about others' performance. However, this did not mean that others' actions were not "sin." Wearing shoes, whether done by Indians or Irishmen, was a karmic act with karmic consequences. The collective concern for the *sāsana* that had produced an anxiety over individual ethical performance was central. Just because these others were not "of our sect" did not mean that this was not a Buddhist issue. Arguing that bad karma ("sin") accrues whether or not those wearing shoes are of the same "sect" as the Burmese, the editor made clear that this was a matter of religion, not simply in the formal sense falling under the umbrella of religious neutrality, but that universal Buddhist laws applied to such action. While governments and agitators could debate the formal policy and political consequences between human actors, a broader Buddhist metaphysical law would win out. The editor went on to cite religious neutrality, but writing for an audience of Buddhists who could read Burmese, he asserted another, very different definition of religion, one that could not be limited by liberal policy considerations or formal adherence to "our sect."

The editorial gained broader attention, being republished in the Burmese *Friend of Burma* and translated in the English *Times of Burma*, moving the debate beyond the Burmese community. The next week, the editor of the *Times of Burma* responded with a statement that showed how deeply the Burmese editor had confounded habitual liberal colonial thinking. While the *Times of Burma* had been sympathetic to the anti-footwear faction and to U Dhammaloka in particular, the editor showed a different face when the question of religious interpretation came into play.

> We take it that the removal of shoes among Eastern nations is a mark of courtesy that has its equivalent in Europeans "taking off hats," and nothing more. An Atheist (a Kaffir) may remove his hat, or his shoes, when visiting a place of worship, without becoming a religious man (or true believer) and the ceremony of removing his head gear, or foot gear, is nothing more than a display of decent politeness. We are unaware of such a display being considered part of a religious ceremonial.[50]

The *Times of Burma* editor asserted that removing shoes or hats is not a religious practice and, moreover, that performing one or the other observance does not change religious status—making one more or less an atheist, Christian, or Buddhist in the process. These physical rituals were a matter of politeness and manners; religion remained contained in the heart of the "true believer," in internal spiritual states and doctrine. The editor claimed that he did not find removing shoes on the pagoda to be part of any "religious ceremonial" and therefore obligatory, but he implied much more than this: that ritual practices, religious or not, do not transform the person, nor do they mean that any set of religious rules could be understood to apply. Such transformations could only occur as a matter of belief, and it is only to those who have assented to such a belief that the consequences of the performance adhere. Having read in his own pages how little Burmese were concerned about his and his European compatriots' "sins," he sought to prove that no such interpretation could be applied to their performances. Out of this exchange it becomes clear that much more was at stake than whether the issue would fall under the protections of formal religious neutrality. The liberal secularist definition of religion that asserted that religion was mainly about personal, interior belief was quietly held up to scrutiny.

Religion, Autonomy, and the Right to Bare Feet

The final moment of the shoe question began in 1916 when U Thein Maung, a young attorney and member of the pagoda trustees in Prome, decided to remove the phrase "except to Europeans and Americans" on a sign instructing visitors to remove their shoes outside the Toungoo Shwesandaw Pagoda.[51] These events have been recounted and analyzed in multiple places—from popular nationalist accounts by Dr. Khin Maung Nyunt and classic histories by European scholars, to contemporary reflections on Buddhism and popular opposition to the state by Juliane Schober and Donald Seekins—because they are taken to be foundational to the history of Burmese nationalism and the independence movement.[52] However, what is useful for understanding the politics of respect and the history of colonial transformations of religion and identity is less the events themselves than the reasoning that each side used to defend its position.

At first, U Thein Maung's bold change to the footwear exception for Europeans went little noticed. All was well until the viceroy of India proposed to visit Prome on his tour of Burma. The pagoda topped the list of customary tour sites in the town, and local officials were faced with a conundrum. The viceroy would have to honor one convention or the other: either respect European taboos on toes and tread, shod, all over the pagoda trustees' orders and the government's image as respectful of religious difference, or bend to the new Buddhist rules. The authorities leaned on the pagoda trustees, but to no avail. Ultimately, the horror of the Queen's representative appearing barefoot in public was too much, and they excluded the town from the tour. There would be no viceregal feet on the Shwesandaw.

Following this victory, U Thein Maung escalated the campaign. He made an appeal to the increasingly influential Young Men's Buddhist Association (YMBA), which endorsed his position at an emergency meeting in May 1918. The endorsement brought greater publicity to the campaign and sought to repeat the success in Prome by preventing a visit by the governor to the Shwemawdaw Pagoda in Pegu.[53] From then on, trustees at pagodas across the province were under pressure from Buddhist associations to remove the exception for Europeans. A parallel campaign took the issue directly to the government, demanding that they rescind a military directive allowing Europeans to wear shoes. The crusade quickly gained popularity among young urban Burmese agitators and English-educated Buddhist leaders and publishers. Those sympathetic to the British position, particularly reticent pagoda trustees, were ridiculed in letters and cartoons. The "shoe question" became the central rallying point for Burmese Buddhists and was the subject of impassioned calls for reform in the vernacular press.

Government officials took the requirement to remove shoes as a threat to colonial authority. After the May 1918 YMBA meeting, the government sought to censor all further public debate. The chief secretary of the Government of Burma wrote to all newspapers, stating that "It is the government's desire that all discussion in the public press of the question of wearing boots or shoes within the precincts of pagodas should cease forthwith."[54] He instructed them "to see that no further discussion of the question of or correspondence on the subject is published in your newspapers."[55] This public debate, the letter said, would lead to the coercion of pagoda trustees and a breach of the peace between Europeans and Buddhists.

> It has always been the policy of the British government to adopt a neutral attitude upon matters of religious controversy unless intervention has become necessary to secure the maintenance of the peace. It is also, in the opinion of the Local Government, incumbent upon all classes of the community to pay the same respect to the religious edifices of other creeds and denominations as they would pay to those of their own.[56]

The issues raised at the May 1918 YMBA meeting, the letter added, "tend to arouse racial feeling and disturb the harmony. . . . A breach of the harmonious relations which have hitherto prevailed would be deplorable at any time. In the present time of war nothing likely to effect such a breach can be tolerated."[57] The government conceded that the question involved religion, despite rejecting such an interpretation in 1901. But it argued that in a time of war, the threat of civic unrest justified abandoning religious neutrality and invoking formal censorship.

The publication ban did not silence the controversy, and tensions continued to rise over the next year. By October of 1919, the colonial government could no longer ignore the public outcry and was forced to respond to U Thein Maung's petition on behalf of the Buddhist associations. The only official policy granting an exception for Europeans was a military directive, so the government responded with a resolution from the Military Department. In this resolution, the government took pains to argue that not only had the exemption for Europeans endured for decades without protest from the Burmese, but that it was not the policy for Europeans to remove their shoes in either Ceylon or Siam.[58] The government's reference to the Siamese King Mongkut as a Buddhist modernizer who allowed European-style shoes to be worn in pagodas and temples smacked of hypocrisy. When looking for models of Buddhist governance in the past, the government had intentionally overlooked Siamese kings.[59] It was instead Burmese agitators that had appealed to the modernist Thai example of Mongkut when arguing against the policy of requiring *shikhos*.[60]

The resolution offered a long discussion of the background of cross-cultural demonstrations of respect, arguing that for a European to remove his shoes was an act of disrespect, and expressing unconvincing surprise that Buddhists would want Europeans to do them this disrespect.

> The European will remove his hat on entering the hut of the peasant, the court of the Sovereign or the House of God and those of Oriental race who are habituated to the practice of showing respect by going bare-footed will follow the same habit when they enter the hut, the palace or the pagoda. To the Englishman, on the other hand, to enter the presence of others without shoes is a mark not of respect but of lack of courtesy, and it would be strange if Buddhists were to prefer that Europeans should display toward their pagodas not the national signs of respect habituated to them, but an act which to them denotes lack of courtesy.[61]

Ignoring a century of missionary policies, they maintained that European Christians would never require a similar set of rituals from those of another religion.

> He has never desired to intrude where his presence would offend the susceptibilities of the followers of another faith, and in the case of Christian

edifices the European would much prefer that men of another creed who enter the sacred precincts should show the mark of respect which is habitual to their own national custom. If such a man is accustomed to take off his shoes, the European would prefer that he show respect in that way and would not insist upon his baring his head if such an act was contrary to his own social usages. Where however a man of another creed had adopted European practice and European foot apparel, he would never insist upon his going bare-footed, and he would only ask him to bare his head if he were wearing a hat or cap which by his own social usages he would remove in public.[62]

The government's position was that each religious community's own practice should be used to demonstrate respect to monuments of other religions. Requiring a special mode of respect from all toward Buddhist monuments was, in this view, "an unfriendly act, but one to which they have no inherent right to demur."[63] The military resolution ultimately acquiesced, recognizing the right of each set of pagoda trustees to determine the policy for Europeans.

Requiring subjects to follow the practice of respect shown to their own religious sites had offered a pragmatic solution, but one that relied on a curious logic. It assumed that rituals of respect are determined not by the object of respect but by the religious and cultural identity of the person showing respect. But it takes this one step further, implying that not only is the respect accomplished by these differing practices equal but, in the logic of these colonial formulations of religious tolerance, a mosque is the same as a church or a Hindu temple or a Buddhist pagoda. Thus while Buddhists, Hindus, Muslims, and Christians were so fundamentally different they could not adopt each other's practices, pagodas, mosques, churches, and temples were very much the same in the ways they should be treated. Religion was thus a single homogenous container that equated all its contents, but religious people were still irrevocably distinguished by unbreakable divisions of ethnic and colonial difference.

The Burmese argued instead that Buddhist objects require specific rituals of respect regardless of the identity of the person demonstrating respect. For them, religious tolerance required not this equality among religious sites, but recognition of the unique status of Buddhist sites. The means of respecting Buddhism were not interchangeable with other practices of respect—such as removing one's hat—and could not be appropriated for other purposes—such as showing respect to secular teachers.

In arguing that Europeans should be allowed to wear their shoes but remove their hats when visiting pagodas, the military resolution asserted that respect was the representation of an internal state whose outward expression should be determined by the rules of colonial difference. Retaining European shoes and removing a hat was equivalent to removing Asian slippers and retaining head coverings because both reflect an identical internal state, but one that required external forms that reproduced the radical distinction between colonizer and colonized. In the logic of this position, Buddhism only deserved respect because it participated in the category "religion." Buddhism was due respect from Europeans only to the extent that it conformed to the unspoken ideals of what constituted a religion. Adapting properly to the category "religion" made the sacred space of the pagoda an equal to churches, mosques, and temples. It was not the particularity of the tradition or the site that produced respect. In fact, to gain respect, Buddhism must deemphasize its particularity, such that Buddhism's commonalities with Christianity (and nominally Islam, Hinduism, and others) were prominent enough to justify its status as a religion. The military resolution was explicit about the qualities of Buddhism that earned it status in the category "religion." It claimed that Buddhism "has gained the respect of all Englishmen on account of the purity and selflessness of its tenets and the toleration and kindness that its followers extend to those who profess different religion," and that "Christians of all degree recognise and admire in the founder of the Buddhist religion one of the greatest Teachers of humanity that the world has produced."[64] Buddhism, as a religion, resided in its tenets and teachings of the founder, not in its contemporary practices and pagodas.

The military resolution, ordered by the lieutenant governor, proposed a model of religion as a homogeneous class, one in which the specific content of any given religion was overshadowed by respect for religion as a universal category. Colonial recognition required that traditions were equated in the category "religion." The importance of religion resided only in interiorized belief or doctrine, not external practices. To be respected in this system, Buddhism must assimilate to the universal language of religion in European thought. As Tomoko Masuzawa has argued, the emerging discourse of world religions in the nineteenth century traded the formal primacy of Christianity as the best and only universal religion for a pluralist discourse that allowed for a diversity of traditions, but required that those traditions conform to its criteria for religion. She writes, "The new discourse of pluralism and diversity of religions . . . neither replaced nor disabled the logic of European hegemony—formerly couched in the language of the universality of Christianity—but in a way, gave it a new lease."[65] European dominance survived in this liberal pluralist model of religion by setting the terms of inclusion and by equating and homogenizing traditions. A universal category of religion was due respect from everyone, but this did not mean that those offering respect were equal. In this model of religion, Buddhism had to shed its claims to the universal applicability of ritual performances in order to be a member of the inviolate category "religion." And Europeans could tread all over the pagoda, because respect for Buddhism could only require the same performance as Christian respect.

Yet the formal policy of noninterference forced the colonial government to admit the possibility of another model of religion. Burmese staked their claim on a model in which the special and protected status of religion was premised on its specificity and difference. By 1919, the anti-footwear proponents, who made up the majority of the Buddhist associations, rejected the government's way of defining religion. In their argument that Buddhist pagodas required specific modes of respect from all actors, they rejected the equivalence and spiritualization of religions. The Burmese insisted that respect for the Buddha and his *sāsana* could not be achieved by substituting alternative rituals of respect. In so doing they affirmed that each religion's content and practices are unique. Not only did the physical postures of respect matter, but Buddhism, as a religion, was unique in its logic and could not be equated with other religions. These Burmese sought the protections of the government's policy of noninterference because the *sāsana*, not religion, was in decline. The footwear debate since 1897 had been framed in terms of the defense of the *sāsana*.[66] The specific Buddhist nature of the *sāsana* and the status of the moral community now responsible for the *sāsana* justified challenging the state. They asserted that the necessity of religious noninterference came not from the universality that framed liberal secularism but from the distinct nature of each religion. Moreover, they implied that performance and ritual were not merely symbolic and secondary but that the felicity of respect and the state of the *sāsana* relied on specific performances from all. On its face, this assertion does not sit well with the Buddhist philosophical tradition that emphasizes that intention, not performance, has karmic effect, as Okpo Sayadaw had earlier argued. But since Okpo Sayadaw's 1897 confrontational march up the stairs, most members of the Buddhist associations had come to a pragmatic interpretation that stressed the conformity of performance for the defense of the *sāsana*.

CONCLUSION

Burmese lay Buddhists won a victory in 1919 because they mobilized the British colonial policy of noninterference in religious affairs. This was not simply a case of shrewdly manipulating colonial policy against colonial interests. Their success was the result of their longer and subtler negotiation of how the category "religion" would be constructed in their colonial context. To assert that, whatever the intent or setting, certain practices were religious, as was the case in the debate with the *shikho* in schools, was to claim that religion adhered to practices, not just to beliefs and intentions. It meant that anywhere a practice could be interpreted as religious, colonial policy could be restrained. The education department's earlier attempt to limit religion to content, to set religion off from the rest of education in monasteries, had failed. Beyond this, now even in the most secular flagship colonial school, the religious nature of certain practices could now hem policy. Moreover, the 1901 claim in the *Friend of Burma* that Europeans' choice to wear shoes was a "sin" and fell within the laws of Buddhist karma, not those of secular politeness, quietly asserted that the category "religion" must take seriously the claims to universal applicability of karma. Religious laws applied to everyone, not only to those who believed, as European public opinion had asserted. A breach of those laws, Burmese Buddhists claimed in 1916, constituted a threat to Buddhism, one that the policy of noninterference must deter. The colonial government proposed an alternative model in 1919, but by then it had lost too much ground. Forced to grant that religion resided in performances of all people, regardless of their beliefs, it had to cede control to the trustees and hope these allies were sufficiently indoctrinated to promote the government's liberal definition of religion over that of the Buddhist popular majority. But this was not to be. Anti-footwear candidates were elected as new pagoda trustees, and even the older trustees were forced to cede to the growing Buddhist and nationalist interpretations.[67]

Debates over the practices of respect were about authority, subordination, and autonomy, concerns that were only ever thinly veiled in the public discussions. Such practices became symbolic means of working out colonial relations, negotiated through shifting definitions of what would be considered religious. Buddhism was central to the Burmese experience of colonialism that saw transformations in the evolving discourse of *sāsana* and the new modes of identity enabled by participation in the moral community. What stands out, however, is not just the role of religion in the colonial encounter but how the process of defining religion was itself a technique of power. The ambiguity of the category meant that Burmese Buddhists and colonial actors alike could actively contest "religion" as a means of promoting and renegotiating the power of the state and the cultural projects of colonialism. In this back and forth, religion became a powerful taxonomy whose contents could be leveraged for a variety of goals. What would count as religion became a site of contention where the status of the moral community and its autonomy could be worked out.

Religion was an excellent means of repelling unwanted intrusions of colonial dominance, allowing Burmese Buddhists to legitimately refuse a demeaning *shikho* or a shoe-clad European because these fell in religion's bounds. Religion was much more fluid than a liberal discourse that naturalized "religion and the secular" as absolute and opposing categories let on. Religion, in this sense, was an artifact of colonialism. Not that the colonizers invented religion out of whole cloth, but that the meaning and defining characteristics of the category were the product of power and negotiation in a colonial context. Attention to the propositions about the nature of religion entailed in conflicts over shoes and *shikhos* offers the potential to understand the complexities and multiplicities of religion in the colonial context. Shifting our focus in this way exposes the indeterminacy of what are too often taken for analytical categories, reminding us to pay attention to the places where the concepts that we take for granted were fluid, undergoing a process of definition and redefinition through the colonial encounter.

6

Conclusion

At the turn of the twentieth century, the need to preserve the *sāsana* under the changing times of colonialism motivated Buddhist organizing. Understanding the contemporary situations in terms of *sāsana* decline allowed Buddhists to draw on the long history of reform in Burma and the repertoire of techniques for preservation. The *sāsana*—the Buddha's teachings and dispensation, impermanent like everything else—was always in decline, and always the most precious and defining element in a Buddhist society. And yet, viewed historically, the meaning of *sāsana* was never fixed or singular. It was fluid, reinflected, and reinvented with each new instance of *sāsana* reform. The idea of *sāsana* proved dynamic, shaped by those who sought to preserve it, and flexible enough to respond to the new conditions of the colonial era.

Burmese Buddhists, organized in the new Buddhist associations, approached the work of preserving the *sāsana* in a syncretic fashion. They drew on past techniques but creatively united these with new technologies gleaned from colonial sources. The concept of *sāsana* and the projects for its preservation proved fertile enough to weave together the old and the new in useful hybrids. For as much as the rhetoric of *sāsana* reform called for a restoration of past soteriological conditions, the practice of *sāsana* reform was, as it had ever been, an engine of change in Burmese society, realigning values and hierarchies, inflecting orientations, and creating new ways forward.

Burmese dedicated to preserving the *sāsana* were themselves changed. Coming together to preserve Buddhism worked to shape a new identity for many. The Buddhist associations offered a means for masses of otherwise lowly Buddhists to become patrons of the teachings and in the process to see themselves and their connections with each other in a new light. Their common moral project fostered a sense of moral community, a network of connections that allowed individuals to reimagine the impact of their actions.

No longer could they consider moral decisions in terms of personal karma alone; now their own moral action had impact on the whole of the community. The moral community offered a new sense of collective belonging and importance but required that Buddhists learn to regulate themselves and their actions in relation to the larger community project. In this, the Buddhist associations combined technologies of imagining from European social reform and Buddhist thought to create new blends.

As much as the efforts of the Buddhist associations and Buddhists' means of understanding themselves were shaped by their colonial conditions, they also resisted the pull of colonial forces. They were happy to "adopt but adapt" colonial ideas, desires, and projects, but they rarely made colonial goals their own. This produced not just hybrids but at times stark miscommunications and clashes across the colonial divide. Buddhists often appropriated techniques originally designed to create docile and modern colonial subjects and repurposed them to work to preserve the Buddha's teachings. Burmese Buddhists at the turn of the twentieth century were influenced by the larger goals of British colonialism and the worldview it sought to foster, but they resisted its disciplinary forces and categories, at times turning colonialism's terms and techniques back upon itself.

In all of this, Buddhists in colonial Burma proved active and adept bricoleurs, gathering elements from past Burmese practice and colonial interventions while rejecting and resisting any effort understood as counter to their purpose of preserving the Buddha's teachings in Burma. The three decades in which the Buddhist associations flourished and dominated public discourse set the stage for future transformations. Yet in the end, the Buddhist associations had not only succeeded in keeping *sāsana* at the center of Burmese thinking and communal life for that period, they had reshaped how the idea of *sāsana* and communal identity unfolded in Burmese history.

THE YEAR 1920 AND BEYOND: THE NATION AND ITS SHADOWS

With the 1919 victory in the shoe controversy there was a shift in Burmese organizing. Buddhist associations remained prominent in the towns and villages, and over the next decade their membership and activity would grow. However, new voices within these organizations suggested that preserving the *sāsana* was only one part of a different, larger project—the preservation of national sovereignty. The work the Buddhist associations had done at the turn of the century set the stage for these nationalist discourses and shaped how Burma would be imagined as a nation. Nationalist efforts reinterpreted, at times liberally rewrote, the history of the Buddhist associations to subsume the project of saving the *sāsana* into a telos of national liberation. Nonetheless, the necessity of preserving the *sāsana* and of belonging to a moral community lived on as a separate, if temporarily subordinated, trajectory.

By 1920, the place of Buddhism in colonial conflicts had changed. The years from 1918 to 1920 were a time of upheaval. The "shoe question" came to center stage with the May 1918 Young Men's Buddhist Association (YMBA) general meeting, and would not be resolved until the government withdrew its opposition in October of 1919. In the meantime, an important division arose in the YMBA. At the end of 1918, a younger faction split with the older members over Burma's exclusion from the Montagu-Chemsford reforms toward greater self-rule for India and the much weaker Craddock scheme offered in their place. The older generation shied away from explicitly political matters, while the younger faction sought more direct political confrontation. By the March 1920 general convention, the younger faction had taken over and reorganized as the General Council of Burmese Associations, with explicit goals of greater national sovereignty.[1] The change from "Buddhist Association(s)" to "Burmese Associations" marked a significant shift in orientation. The change announced that ethnicity or nation was to be the pivotal term, and the group set out to convince itself, and others, that perhaps this had been true all along. The minutes of the 1920 conference attempted an explicit rewriting of the history of the Buddhist associations that stripped them of any higher purpose than nation and excluded much of the work and complexity I have discussed in the past five chapters.[2] The choice by the rising faction to rename themselves in terms of Burmese, and not Buddhist, identity speaks volumes about the shift in their priorities and their interpretation of religion and its limited role in public life.[3]

The *shikho* and shoe controversies flowed almost seamlessly into the 1920 Rangoon University Strike. The spirit of reform and political engagement was in the air. In December of that year, Burmese students from colleges and high schools throughout Burma launched a boycott of the government education system to protest the Rangoon University Act. The creation of a university in Burma had been long awaited, and the students took it as a slap in the face when they found elements in its founding documents that continued to promote Burmese exclusion and subordination.[4] The student boycott was massive in its impact: by the government's estimate, at its height almost twelve thousand primary and secondary students participated.[5] The strike fostered a system of "national education" as an alternative to the boycotted government schools and earned a formative place in the development of the independence movement.

The students organizing the boycott made prominent use of Buddhist symbols and institutions. The first call for a boycott was held on the Shwedagon Pagoda platform, and the strikers' camp, where the students lived in fabled asceticism for six months, was on the grounds of U Ariya's monastery in Bahan quarter near the pagoda.[6] Many of the schools and teachers for the national school system came directly out of the Buddhist associations' schools and their two decades of educational work. However, the tone and the goals of the national school movement were different from those of the earlier Buddhist associations: *sāsana* did not provide the same clear motivation or sense of identity to these young leaders. Instead, the language of nation came more readily to their lips. Even in their engagement with Buddhism, something significant had changed.

These young nationalists no longer turned to religion for their arguments against colonial imposition and injustice. However much they literally inhabited the space of Buddhism as a place of safety and consolidation, moving into monasteries or occupying Buddhist schools, religion was no longer the site of conflict. For much of their work, Buddhism was tucked away as separate from secular life—the place of Burmese identity and autonomy but no longer a means of responding to change and tyranny. Religion served as a set of symbols that could motivate people, not an explanation of history or a discourse that could contest current conditions. The new activists were no longer trying to preserve the soteriological conditions of Buddhism, only a sovereign national community where they understood it to reside.

Buddhism came to assume an instrumental rather than an ordering role for those who sought the political independence of the imagined nation. It became an adjunct to the nationalist project, no longer the project itself. Buddhism and nationalism would become deeply intertwined over the course of the twentieth century and remain so to this day, but in the public discourse of the nationalists and the governments that succeeded them, Buddhism became an essential element of a national identity and a means of mobilization to national ends.[7] An article entitled "Preaching Freedom," published in 1922 in the nationalist *Freedom Journal: For the Freedom and Welfare of the Burmans*, featured an illustration that depicted a rapt congregation listening to a monk preach the truths of freedom from colonial rule.[8] Buddhism had become a means to achieve a different, higher end. Buddhism might become inextricable from the Burmese nation, as in the axiomatic "To be Burmese is to be Buddhist," but for many, Burma as nation became the dominant and ordering partner in the pair.[9]

The shift had been coming slowly. The *Thuriya* (Sun) newspaper was founded in 1911, and while at the outset it resembled other Burmese-language newspapers—like the *Maha-Bodhi News* or the *Hanthawaddy Weekly Review*—that had been key vehicles for the Buddhist associations, it quickly shifted to a more nationalist tone. Likewise, the language of the "official *shikho*" debate from 1910 to 1913 that contested the requirement of a *shikho* from junior Burmese staff in business and government offices began to offer a different image of community and purpose of solidarity.[10] Multiple discourses of identity were operative in this period, and Burmese were partially shaped by more than one.

The political and nationalist turn did not preclude Buddhist organizing or the sense of responsibility for the *sāsana* that participation in the moral community engendered. Buddhist associations carried on with many of the projects that had defined their first three decades. Even as the nation became the dominant public concern for many Burmese, the ideals and projects of protecting the *sāsana* remained an important undercurrent.

In Burmese discourse and thinking outside of the anticolonial nationalist movement, concern for the decline of the *sāsana* and the moral community continued. Throughout the twentieth and into the twenty-first century, certain groups continued to orient their efforts in relation to *sāsana* as the ultimate concern, creating new incarnations of the moral community along the way. *Sāsana*, and reform to prevent its decline, remained a potent orientation for implementing change and identity, one that stood alongside nation but offered a distinct cosmology and motivation.

A community organized for the defense of *sāsana* emerged in varied modes—orthodox and esoteric—through the twentieth century. Lay meditation became popular in the years following independence, and the occasion of the 2,500th anniversary of the end of the Buddha's teaching life and his final *parinibbāna* inspired a clear public moral project to preserve and promote *sāsana*. As Ingrid Jordt has documented, lay meditators understood themselves to have the power to transform Burmese society and the world.[11] Inheriting the mantle from the colonial Buddhist associations, they were the self-appointed patrons and defenders of the *sāsana*, and they understood themselves to have the power to enact great transformations.

Whereas the Buddhist associations in colonial Burma were focused on moral behavior, the meditators now felt that mental concentration held the power to save Buddhism and transform society. They had moved from *dāna* (donation), through *sīla* (morality), and on to *bhāvanā* (meditation) as the key technique for preserving *sāsana* in the world. And with this shift in technique there was a shift in ethical subjectivity as well—the ideal person was defined not by regulating action but by introspection and development of inner states.

This sense of mission on behalf of *sāsana* had multiple incarnations responding to different political turns. Hiroko Kawanami reports that monks who organized in opposition to President U Nu and in support of Ne Win's military coup in the early 1960s claimed that their support was based on a need to preserve the Buddha's teachings—and that the moral failings and religious policies of U Nu threated the future of *sāsana*.[12] This sense that defense of the *sāsana* required political change was recurrent, although, by the end of the twentieth century, few would have associated it with support of the Ne Win regime.

In the middle of the twentieth century, underground groups gathered arms to battle for the future of the *sāsana* in heterodox ways as well. *Weikza* cults, and in particular the Ariya-Weikza organization studied by Niklas Foxeus, identified a number of threats to the *sāsana* and organized themselves into bands of initiates under the supernatural leadership of the now deceased founder who was understood to be both Setya Min—a mythical world emperor—and a *weikza*—a person who has accumulated sufficient supernatural powers to defy death and achieve near immortality.[13] The members continue to be initiated through a series of rituals into a community dedicated to the defense of the *sāsana,* appropriating the symbols and language of Burmese royalty. These organizations have an elaborate understanding of the threats to Buddhism, ranging from colonial powers to Islam, as well as a clear royal and militaristic system for its defense. Members dedicate themselves to the production of symbolic and ritual weapons for the upcoming spiritual war. As Foxeus' and others' work makes clear, much of the work of the organization is to produce a sense of belonging among the members attached to their spiritual founder.

The most vivid image of the moral community incarnate and its defense of *sāsana* remains the 2007 protests popularly referred to as the Saffron Revolution. In the early days, laypeople flooded the streets to form human chains around the lines of marching monks—hand in hand surrounding and protecting the sangha. These laypeople understood the monks to be under grave threat from the government, who had beaten protesting monks in the monastic university town of Pakkokhu. The monks were the face of the *sāsana* in that moment, and violence against individual monks was taken to be violence against the *sāsana* itself. The defense of *sāsana* took on an embodied mode. As the scale of the protests evidenced, the need to defend Buddhism against perceived threats engendered a sense of belonging in a massive communal moral project.[14] Like the technologies of Victorian reform employed by colonial-era Buddhist associations, posters of the Buddha, Buddhist flags, clandestine cell-phone videos, and Internet video servers all became new technologies to preserve the Buddha's teachings from the contemporary threat. Some of this mobilization carried forward in the local response to Cyclone Nargis a few months later. Visions of community and its moral responsibility motivated Burmese to gather donations for those devastated by the storm in the delta, organized most often by monks and done in the name of *sāsana*.

The defense of the Buddha's *sāsana* is a strong undercurrent in much more destructive mobilization as well. The ugly complement to the current liberalization and optimism in Myanmar is a turn toward violent religious and racial hatred. The rhetoric of the defense of the *sāsana* that fueled the inspiring events of 2007 also underlies the recent attacks on Muslims, and particularly the Rohingya ethnic minority.[15] The current popular insistence that there cannot be any indigenous Muslims in the historic territory of Burma/Myanmar—the imagined cultural and geographic boundaries of nation—reprises both the military government's divisive nationalist rhetoric that scapegoated Muslims to distract from its abuses, and British colonial policy for India that used the census and early anthropology to construct racial and national categories largely on the basis of religion. However, the current "969 movement" for Buddhist chauvinism and the murderous drives to avenge imagined harms to Buddhism are no less motivated by an interpretation of the moral defense of *sāsana* than were the early twentieth-century Buddhist associations or the protests of 2007.

My point here is not to highlight the similarities of these cases or to propose the perennial resurgence of the defending of the *sāsana* as a trope in Burmese history. Instead, I note the divergences between these different instances and their methods. The diverse projects of the Buddhist associations at the turn of the twentieth century demonstrated that Buddhism was both syncretic and dynamic. These later twentieth- and twenty-first-century examples underscore how fertile and productive fear of *sāsana* decline and the ideal of moral community remain. Although these efforts were all united by a motivation to protect the teachings, each of them created very different types of ethical subjectivity and visions for transforming the world out of the contingent historical interactions. While Burmese claims to preserve the *sāsana* may appear to have been a conservative impulse, each individual reform effort held the potential to reshape society, its priorities and aspirations.

The fluidity and invented nature of identity are, perhaps, the most useful and hopeful insights that emerge from this historic perspective. Regardless of how much any given project has sought to claim to be restoring a pristine past, the past and future of *sāsana,* moral community, or nation are never fixed or immutable, but continually reinvented and shaped. Burmese have the power to shape their community and the *sāsana* through renewed moral vision. In many ways, these later incarnations of *sāsana* reform, with their varied trajectories, not only highlight the ways in which Buddhists combined the history of preserving the *sāsana* with new techniques and technologies, but emphasize the continuing transformation of the three discourses set in motion by the colonial encounter. *Sāsana,* identity, and religion all continue to change and adapt in postcolonial Burma/Myanmar, but are deeply shaped by the interactions, miscommunications, and hybrids of the Buddhist movements of the turn of the twentieth century.

SĀSANA CHANGES

Sāsana reform, as a practice, proved a useful means of transforming society. Moreover, the meaning of *sāsana* was shaped in the process of reform. Concern for the *sāsana* was not a static structure but a mechanism for change that was fluid enough to incorporate new technologies and face new challenges. *Sāsana* proved much more fluid than the rhetoric of preserving the pure teachings implies. To defend the *sāsana* was to claim to return to a single purified past. However, the *sāsana,* even, or perhaps especially, as it was seen to slip away, was not one thing, but a vessel for a variety of aspirations, priorities, and innovations.

What constituted the core of the *sāsana* in need of preservation—the knowledge of the texts, the morals of the laity, or the welfare of the sangha— could shift with the times. Its meaning altered with the different mechanisms for its preservation. While new efforts might share with the eighteenth- and early nineteenth-century monastic reforms a focus on *pariyatti* knowledge, the *sāsana* meant something slightly different if its essence could be memorized by young women in a single poem or learned by students in a half hour a day in a government school. It was not the same thing that was at peril if novices wore their robes covering one shoulder in the late eighteenth century or young men drank alcohol at *pwe*s in the early twentieth century. Buddhists had the power to reinflect and reinvent Buddhism through their efforts to save it.

Buddhism—itself a changeling—was useful for making changes in priorities and values, and for shaping subjects. Work to preserve the *sāsana,* given the potency of the discourses it invoked, had the power to create broader transformations and orientations across Burmese society. As the meaning of *sāsana* shifted, its momentum shaped social priorities and goals, revealing a world in which the *sāsana* was much more active and integral to society than certain colonial interpretations of religion would allow. *Sāsana* reform was fundamental to creating Burmese subjects, their motivations, and orientations. Buddhism proved not a fixed truth to be preserved or a hegemonic conservative force but a pragmatic and fluid means of resisting other impositions and inventing new Burmese realities. It proved a fair way of sidestepping the colonial forces that were coming to impinge on Burmese lives, but more than that it created means for Burmese to continually reimagine and reinvent their world.

MORAL COMMUNITY AND IDENTITY

Working to save Buddhism transformed not only Burmese politics, but Buddhists as well. The need to preserve the *sāsana* offered a moral project that motivated Burmese and shaped how they viewed themselves. The absence of the king as chief patron had created a space for lay Buddhists to reinvent themselves as collective patrons and defenders of the teachings. The urgency and the moral necessity of this project brought Burmese together into a new collective body, one that was imagined in ways similar to the concept of nation as Benedict Anderson has described it, but imagined instead in moral, soteriological, and supernatural terms.[16] The need to save the Buddha's teachings was a compelling motivation that engendered a sense of connection with thousands of other unseen, unknown Burmese Buddhists, and a feeling that the potential to meet the challenges posed by the current colonial condition resided in collective, not individual, efforts.

Membership subscriptions, letters in the newspapers, and massive preaching events all gave individual Buddhists a purpose and means of locating themselves inside the broader body of Buddhists. It was a sense of belonging with a long history in Buddhist thought, but one reimagined through new technologies and in response to new challenges. The Buddhist associations and the sense of belonging they created offered a democratized and homogenized Buddhist identity that leveled out some of the hierarchies. These new ways of being Buddhist valued the chanting of young women alongside that of senior male monks and raised clerks to the level of grand patrons by requiring the contributions of all members for the collective project. Moral acts on behalf of Buddhism gained significance not from their individual karmic merit but from being one of thousands of identical acts (donations to an association, verses memorized, pledges to abstain) that collectively achieved the goal. This change in perspective homogenized moral actions and Buddhist moral actors at the same time as it elevated the lowly individual Buddhist to the status of defender of the *sāsana*.

The associations transformed individual identity and position in society. Leadership in a Buddhist association became a means to prominence for those with otherwise modest roles in colonial society. Teachers and clerks gained stature and built social and economic connections as they were elevated to the authoritative status of vice-president, recording secretary, or treasurer. The associations helped foster a sense of middle-class status for low-level government servants and businessmen and quickly produced a new elite—English-educated university graduates and attorneys who found themselves at the top of associations and their broader networks. The projects of the Buddhist associations helped to elevate some more plebeian voices as well. The efforts of those who came from the countryside gained greater significance for the center: projects in small towns were important enough to be reported in newspapers and journals across the colonial province. And anyone who could write gained a voice in the letters-to-the-editor and contributors' sections of newspapers and journals.

The idea of moral community operated at a deeper level as well. The community worked to shape individual Burmese desires, aspirations, and visions for the future as it offered interpretations of the present. Buddhist reformers not only identified the decline of the *sāsana* as an urgent calamity, they located the origin of the problem in the moral actions of the members of the collective. The community served not simply as a proxy royal patron for the *sāsana*, but as the moral locus of its rise and fall. This was a much more weighty responsibility, one that required a new type of ethical subject. To preserve the *sāsana* in this case required individual members to look inside themselves and to regulate their moral actions, not just in line with individual karma, but as implicated in the future of the Buddha's teachings. The pledges against alcohol and meat eating and other campaigns for moral reform discussed in Chapter 4 trained Buddhists to view themselves and regulate their actions in relation to the larger moral project.

The projects of the Buddhist associations actively constructed and reconstructed the sense of moral community felt by the members, revealing the indeterminacy and imagined nature of Burmese identity. Buddhist associations produced a community of belonging, one that would later be appropriated for nationalism, but it was not the same as national or ethnic identity. The moral community, in the incarnation actively produced in the colonial situation, reveals an alternate mode of imagining belonging in Burma. Examined in this light, the nation is denied its monolithic and universal claims on identity. The colonial Buddhist moral community allows us to see identity as indeterminate and molded through the processes of competition and collective moral endeavor. Ethical subjectivity, racial makeup, and national orientation prove fluid as well, open to definition and redefinition. Efforts under the rubric of *sāsana* reform offered the potential to invent and reinvent belonging and purpose. Investigating the multiple historical inventions of Burmese identity in terms other than nation works to undo scholarly and popular unconscious assumptions of nation as the subject of history, offering the potential to hear a greater diversity of voices in the present.

RELIGION AND COLONIALISM

Buddhism had shaped subjects and societies in Burma for centuries using techniques similar to those proposed by the colonial civilizing mission. It was this power to shape how people understood and regulated themselves that made Buddhism and Buddhist projects particularly attractive to those colonial administrators who thought to make Buddhism an adjunct to their civilizing efforts. Yet there was ambivalence among Europeans. Was Buddhism part of a backward local tradition, full of lazy monks, meaningless chants, and idolatrous displays of conspicuous donations, to be resisted in favor of civilizing modernity? Or was it a set of local tools that could be adapted for achieving colonial ends? Was state entanglement with Buddhism a threat to rational secularism as the bedrock of modernity? Or was it a creative pragmatic response that elevated Buddhism as a rational scientific religion in the midst of an otherwise decadent Asian culture? Europeans in Burma offered a conflicting hodgepodge of answers. They proved that colonialism was never as absolute or as systematized as it tried to present itself.

It was the same power of religion to shape social worlds and identity that made it useful in the hands of Burmese grappling with their changing conditions. Buddhism had never been one thing—it had always changed and adapted to the problems of the day. The language of preservation of the singular and pure teachings had an ironic potential to create change. Reform required restructuring the ideas and practices that were understood to constitute the core of the *sāsana,* reshaping Buddhist practice and society in its wake. In the hands of the leaders of the new Buddhist associations, *sāsana* reform became a way of both responding to colonial changes and restructuring their world in their own terms.

The official and unofficial agents of colonialism—education officials, missionaries, European temperance advocates—were not wrong that Buddhist interventions shared with the civilizing mission the ability to move men and women to new actions, desires, and worldviews. Just as some aspects of Buddhism were attractive to colonial agents, the methods of colonial cultural interventions were equally susceptible to imitation and later subversion for Buddhist ends. Technologies like the subscription association, the temperance pledge, and the modern school were as useful for preserving the *sāsana* and engendering a sense of moral community as they were for creating modern docile colonial subjects. Unconsciously deploying skillful means, Buddhists actively redeployed the technologies that were meant to make them modern, civilized, and self-regulated to create a new future for the *sāsana.* Buddhists and Buddhism in Burma were undoubtedly shaped toward colonial ends, but they were able to orient and interpret the frameworks of the changes in local terms and goals.

Both Burmese and British interventions were syncretic, drawing from local and cosmopolitan efforts to suit the moment. Monastery pedagogy, *shikhos,* and moral textbooks were part of the same bag of tricks used both by colonial officials looking to train disciplined colonial subjects and by Buddhists, who also embraced print journals, student strikes, and letters to the editor as convenient means to preserve the Buddha's teachings. Both colonizer and colonized were equally internally diverse. Preserving the *sāsana* meant different things to different Buddhists. Preserving the teachings meant something slightly different to young women chanting Pali Abhidhamma verse in a village and English-educated male scholars debating the morality of *pwes* at the Rangoon College Buddhist Association. Europeans were no more likely than Burmese to agree on the desired outcomes of their colonial interventions in Burma: education officials had to face scathing criticism of their vision of the "moral and intellectual improvement" of Burmese students from other Europeans in the newspapers and at the same time dodge very different visions of state secularism from higher-ups in Calcutta and London. Colonial modernity was as plural in the minds of its agents as Buddhism was for the Burmese.

COLONIAL WAYS OF ORDERING THE WORLD AND THEIR LIMITS

British colonialism operated through culture, symbols, and ideas. Its modes of power included not just the coercive apparatuses of violence and economic and material might but the power to reshape desires, ideas, and aspirations, limiting worldviews and orientations. As colonialism opened doors, it also closed them. One part of this project was promoting cultural modes and values—encouraging desires for Western clothes or schools with printed books and desks, as advocates of the Victorian reform efforts explicitly sought to do. But such overt cultural impositions could be, and often were, easily rejected. Moreover, colonial power was rarely so rigid or omnipotent; it did not mechanically reproduce societies around the globe in its own image.[17]

Colonial power in its cultural modes operated on a much more fundamental level as well, by shaping the conditions of local cultural adaptation and innovation. This was achieved, as Talal Asad explains, as

> social and cultural variety everywhere increasingly responds to and is managed by categories brought into play by modern forces. If as some anthropologists now put it, culture is always invented ... if invention always opens up the possibilities for difference, then it should also be clear that the conditions of invention are no longer what they once were. ... More precisely, even if it is true that new cultural forms are being continuously invented in different societies, these societies now live in a single, shared world, a world brought into being by European conquest.[18]

The categories imposed by colonial rule were perhaps the most insidious intervention because they limited the types of possible questions and visions by dividing and constraining different modes of thought and practice—granting or denying their potency in certain aspects of life. Some categories, like "public" and "private," are perhaps easier to see and diagnose, but others were quickly taken as obvious, inherent, and universal—projected into the past in ways that obscured their novelty and power in the present. As Asad explains, it is through these categories that "new possibilities are constructed and old ones are destroyed" such that "only new (i.e. modern) choices can be made."[19] Imposing these categories "involve[s] the reformation of subjectivities and the reorganization of social fields in which subjects act and are acted upon."[20]

It is often difficult for us to recognize religion as one of these fundamentally ordering and constraining categories, a testament to its ability to become naturalized, presumed universal and unchanging. Defining religion as an aspect both fundamentally different and necessarily separate from the rest of communal life was essential to the operation of colonial administration. It allowed colonizers to limit religion's supernatural claims on their colonial subjects and to regulate all aspects of life deemed outside religion's purview. Such categorization is no less foundational for scholars in the humanities and social sciences—we define fields of study and limit the impact of discourses that refuse to conform to our secularist epistemologies. Dividing off religion in this way is so foundational for these efforts that the division appears natural and universal. However, "religion" in its current form is an invention of relatively recent origin in Europe, coming out of a specific history of sectarian conflict, and a key export and tool of colonial power.

Religion was limited and bounded as a domain by the recognition of the secular social world as the universal state of common existence and interaction. Discussing the transition to this model of religion in Europe, Asad argues that

> the very essence of religion was differently defined—that is to say, in each of the historical moments different conditions of religion's existence were in play. What we now retrospectively call "the social," that all-inclusive secular space that we distinguish conceptually from variables like "religion," "state," "national economy," and on which the latter can be constructed, reformed, and replotted, did not exist prior to the nineteenth century. Yet it was precisely the emergence of *society* as an organized secular body that made it possible for the state to oversee and facilitate an original task by redefining religion's competence: the unceasing material and moral transformation of its entire national population regardless of their diverse "religious" allegiances.[21]

The invention of society, and imbuing it with a secular nature, spawned religion. In Burma, an idea of religion as the product of the creation of a secular "social" could only be created by the colonial state. No precolonial Burmese monarch or local authority needed an undistinguished secular society to justify intervention. The *sāsana* and its constructions of justice, morality, and polity justified all number of interventions in realms now labeled political, economic, and social. Colonial officials brought this construction of the secular social and of bounded religion to Burma and required that Burmese rethink and respond in these terms. The result was that a number of Buddhist projects had to be reconceptualized in these terms. Colonial requirements necessitated adapting and shaping other categorical distinctions like *sāsana* to mesh with European religion.[22] "Religion," as Asad argues, for all such categories, changed the conditions for cultural innovation and imagining. In Burma, for example, as we have seen in Chapter 3, it required rethinking the place and purpose of education and conceding scope and legitimacy to the state in matters like literacy, now defined as social welfare.

However, religion was never a singular or universally defined boundary in European thought. As Tomoko Masuzawa and others have demonstrated, Europeans spent much of the nineteenth century debating and redefining the meaning of religion and its capacities. Forced to consider religious worlds outside of Christianity, European thinkers had slowly come to define religion less in terms of a single universal (Christian) worldview and more and more in terms of universalized forms and modes. This approach increasingly reinscribed and required European forms even as it particularized Christianity as one religion among many.[23] The developing definitions of religion worked to limit the material, social, and political impact of religion, making it increasingly about ideas, the voluntary assent of belief, and symbolic intervention in ways that imprinted European norms and superiority. Even as a plurality of religions was recognized, the traditions were defanged—made impotent in terms of having a serious impact on the material and political world.

Burmese had to come to terms with the invasive creep of definitions of religion that allowed Buddhism an ever-smaller impact in their world. Accepting that Buddhism could be located only in the content of the teachings, rather than the entirety of the practice of pedagogy, for instance, was a major concession that reined in the impact of the teachings. By defining Buddhism in this way, Buddhists conceded the universal applicability of the *sāsana* as the defining feature of Burmese lives. Such a concession bought them a space of potential autonomy from state intervention inside the propositional boundaries of religion. The cost for this space was high in the ways it otherwise limited Buddhism and the impact of *sāsana*.

However, the limiting and disciplinary march of "religion" is not the whole story. Burmese Buddhists conceded the universal nature of religious and secular as defining categories for public life, but they continued to contest the nature and capacity of religion. Despite the hegemonic insistence built into colonial policy that religion was a single clear and recognizable entity, what did, and did not, count as religion was a key point of contention in colonial Burma. Arguing that one could refuse to *shikho* to a European teacher because the *shikho* was a religious practice put the question of religion in the center of conflicts with the colonial state. Contending, as did the Burmese newspaper editor described in Chapter 5, that European shoes on pagodas were not just cultural insults and tactics of subordination, but "sin," and a threat to the Buddha's teachings, challenged a definition of religion as private and individual, claiming instead a universal and ultimate reach for its claims. Contesting what counted as religion was not just a flexible tactic for creating autonomy and resisting specific interventions—be it teaching in Buddhist schools or students' *shikhos*—it was also a way of disputing the disciplinary nature of the broader categories themselves. It was a means to reject the whole range of categories that the British sought to impose on Burmese lives. The hegemonic classification was never absolute.

Asad is correct that categories—broad frameworks for understanding the world, such as "religious" and "secular"—orient thought and practice in specific and unseen ways, and limit questions and interventions. However, the practice of definition was never simple or straightforward. For all the constraints, Burmese Buddhists challenged the categories Europeans proposed. They questioned and rejected some of the cultural products and the ways in which the construction of religion and the definition of its capacities constrained their imagination and vision of their communal future. Definitions of religion were more contested and more malleable than either our academic analysis or colonial officials were comfortable with. Religion proved to be, if less fluid than *sāsana* and identity, still a place of active dispute, invention, and redefinition. Buddhists in colonial Burma worked these things out pragmatically—with their shoes off.

In *The Nation and Its Fragments,* his classic study of anticolonial nationalism, Partha Chatterjee proposed that formulating resistance to colonialism through culture and religion was a key technique that preceded political nationalist struggles across Asia.[24] He argued that despite adopting or assimilating to the colonial mode of thinking in the nation-state, anticolonial nationalists offered their own tactic for circumventing total assimilation by inventing an internal division to facilitate resistance. He writes:

By my reading, anti-colonial nationalism creates its own domain of sovereignty within colonial society well before it begins its political struggles with imperial power. It does this by dividing the world of social institutions and practices into two domains—the material and the spiritual. The material is the domain of the "outside," of the economy and of statecraft, of science and technology, a domain where the West had proved its superiority and the East had succumbed. . . . The spiritual on the other hand is the "inner" domain bearing the "essential" marks of cultural identity.[25]

The spiritual domain became the primary site of activity for early nationalists, in Chatterjee's analysis, constructing a national identity and essence separate from colonial power. "This inner domain of culture is declared the sovereign territory of the nation where the colonial state is not allowed entry, even as the outer domain remains surrendered to colonial power."[26]

Chatterjee's frame provides unconscious logic for many who wish to explain the prominence of religious movements in colonial Asia, as well as later nationalists who sought to subsume the religious efforts of earlier eras under the aegis of preparatory steps for the later political struggles, claiming that they were equally organized under the universal logic of nation. It is striking not only how much Chatterjee's description replicates nationalists' depictions of their own histories—absorbing earlier cultural movements into their later political struggles—but how the division of spiritual and material that Chatterjee attributes to anticolonial nationalists resembles the division of religion and secular that Asad identifies as a key mode of colonial power. Chatterjee's typology and his understanding of resistance to colonialism does not account for how much "spiritual" and "material" themselves were products and techniques of the colonial intervention. His account ignores the extent to which the imagined "spiritual" domain was already enmeshed in the European colonial project of differentiation and classification that produced religion as a separate category. His analysis does not take into account the formative and limiting aspects of these categories or the multiple ways that the colonized resisted, subverted, and redefined them, as Buddhists consistently did in colonial Burma.

The "spiritual" project to preserve the *sāsana* and forge a moral community in Burma was not an anticipatory, consolidating move in a larger struggle for "material" national independence. The Buddhists active in this period did not necessarily take such categories for granted. To assume as much is to accept both the framework of colonial power and the concept of nation as its adjunct and substitute a nationalist teleology for historical analysis.

Instead, Buddhist movements in Burma sought to contest, in certain ways, the framework as a whole and the universality of its goals. Efforts to preserve the *sāsana* made concessions to the limitations of the definition of religion but agitated against its constraints. More than this, Burmese Buddhists rejected the universality of the material goals of colonial modernity—keeping the goal of preserving the *sāsana,* however fluidly defined, ahead of creating modern colonial or national subjects.

However, Chatterjee's last point in *The Nation and Its Fragments* offers some insights into the Burmese case. He argues that the cultural projects in the spiritual domain allowed colonized people the potential of formulating identity outside the disciplined limits of colonial subjectivity (and, he implies, limiting forms of national subjectivity) in a mode of identity organized around community. Community as an alternative mode of identity is the hopeful potential he sees in nationalism, too quickly squandered when the new nation-state inherited the projects of the colonial state. While I disagree with his need to read these projects through the lens of nation, it does seem that the Buddhist movements at the turn of the twentieth century offered the potential to be formed by a subjectivity and moral project outside of the limits of colonial discipline or its nationalist incarnations. They offered modes of imagining that at times defied the interventions of colonial governmentality and proved that not all identity within modernity must be limited by secular, colonial, national, or ethnic formations.

Scholars of religion have long been aware of the invented and imagined nature of religion as a category. Much of the theorizing in the study of religion over the past few decades has focused on the problems of defining religion as an analytical exercise and the power of these definitions to marginalize, exclude, and elevate different modes of communal life. Slowly the history of religions as a field has come to grips with the implications of our classificatory acts. Anticipating the more recent critiques about the implications of "religion," Jonathan Z. Smith warned over two decades ago that,

> if we have understood the archaeological and textual record correctly, man has had his entire history in which to imagine deities and modes of interaction with them. But man, more precisely western man, has had only the last few centuries in which to imagine religion. It is this act of second order, reflective imagination which must be the central preoccupation of any student of religion. . . . Religion is solely the creation of the scholar's study. It is created for the scholar's analytic purposes by his imaginative acts of

comparison and generalization. Religion has no independent existence apart from the academy. For this reason, the student of religion, most particularly the historian of religion, must be relentlessly self-conscious. Indeed, this self-consciousness constitutes his primary expertise, his foremost object of study.[27]

The events in Burma would contest Smith's assertion that only scholars imagine and invent religion or imbue it with classificatory and disciplinary power. Not to deny the ways in which scholarship was enmeshed with the colonial project, but it seems clear that many other parties had a stake in the definition and redefinition of religion in colonial Burma.[28] Whether as a limitation on state authority, a potential medium for colonial governmentality, or resistance to state interventions, Burmese and Europeans alike were invested in the messy work of defining and contesting religion in its local manifestations.

However, it seems to me that careful observation of the Burmese conflicts and confrontations and their strategies for defining and at times defying religion could provide good training for the relentless self-consciousness that Smith requires of us as scholars of religion. Noting not just that religion was not fixed or universal, but how definitions shifted and were critiqued in practice, and what was at stake in these maneuvers, tells us something more about the careful and fraught game we play when we set out to study phenomena we label "religious." This can, and should, inform our own approach. Furthermore, this approach should remind us of the power of defining religion, whether it is done with the pen in a scholar's study or by schoolboys refusing to bow down to authority.

BUDDHIST BRICOLEURS AND THE POWER OF INCHOATE AWARENESS

The Buddhist associations did not plan to resist British colonialism or to save the Burmese nation. They were not conceived as a means to resist colonial hegemony, reshape Burmese modernity, or consciously reshape Buddhism and Burmese identity. They arose as independent and contingent responses to locally perceived problems and a general unease with what was going on in their world. Concern that boys were not properly trained, or that monks would have to go without royal donations of rice, coalesced into a broader effort to improve their collective condition. Coming together to sponsor, and later take, Pali examinations or to confront the scourge of alcohol on their villages was not a quiet or convenient cover for nationalist aspirations or a cultural insurgency against colonialism. These were simply specific responses to a general disconcerting feeling that something fundamental to Burmese life was changing. The world was shifting, and the evidence seemed to be both everywhere and nowhere in particular. The explanation that made sense of all of this inarticulable drift was the broader soteriological frame of *sāsana* and its inevitable decline. The framework of *sāsana* brought with it not just order and intelligibility but a range of symbolic and moral recipes for intervention—something to *do* to counter this uneasy feeling. It was an opportunity that inspired a new set of Buddhist bricoleurs to borrow liberally from the symbols, language, and techniques of previous incarnations of *sāsana* reform and from the technologies of the European acolytes of the civilizing mission and their cosmopolitan cousins from across Asia who were busy inventing their own modernities. The problem of *sāsana* decline and its mandate for intervention became itself a mechanism for broader social change—ushering in new priorities, new leadership, and new ways of understanding oneself as a moral individual and as part of a community.

The appeal to *sāsana,* with its powerful symbols and meaning-making frame, opened up the indeterminacy of the colonial encounter for the Burmese in ways that insurgencies and political confrontations could never achieve. As Jean and John Comaroff explain, the potential for change and resistance lay in a realm below direct confrontation.

> Between the conscious and the unconscious lies the most critical domain of all for historical anthropology and especially for the analysis of colonialism and resistance. It is the realm of partial recognition, of inchoate awareness, of ambiguous perception, and, sometimes, of creative tension: that liminal space of human experience in which people discern acts and facts but cannot or do not order them in narrative descriptions or even into articulate conceptions of the world; in which signs and events are observed, but in a hazy and translucent light; in which individuals or groups know something is happening to them but find it difficult to put their fingers on quite what it is. It is from this realm, we suggest, that silent signifiers and unmarked practices may rise to the level of explicit consciousness, of ideological assertion, and become the subject of overt political and social contestation—or from which they may recede into the hegemonic to languish there unremarked for the time being. As we shall see, it is also the

realm from which emanate the poetics of history, the innovative impulses of the bricoleur and the organic intellectual, the novel imagery called upon to bear the content of symbolic struggles.[29]

Sāsana, at this moment in colonial Burma, carried the weight of symbolic struggle. The misrecognition and multiple inventions of religion and *sāsana* offered a creative tension. Organizing to preserve the *sāsana* intervened in the structures that colonialism sought to impose—deflecting and inflecting some of the impact of colonial modernity on Burmese laypeople. It did something about the changes Burmese could see and feel around them. The effort to preserve the *sāsana* negotiated the imposition of colonial categories and colonial efforts to turn Burmese Buddhists into docile subjects, and it subordinated these within a larger Buddhist frame of meaning. At the same time, it produced new ethical subjectivities of its own, shaping Buddhist priorities with the shifting meanings of *sāsana* and identity within the belonging of the moral community.

The Buddhist movements were a symbolic means of responding to what were experienced as fundamental changes in the Burmese world. The focus on the *sāsana* became a means of bringing these intuitions closer to the level of conscious reflection and action. Movements that drew their purpose from the preservation of the *sāsana* could articulate the sense of decadence. It allowed them to think explicitly about alterations in worldview and diminished future prospects even while they were unable to explain what it was colonialism wanted out of them. They operated in a space between conscious reflection and fixed presumptions that allowed them a broad flexibility—an ability to effect change and contest the presumptions that colonial efforts sought to make hegemonic and unquestionable. They worked at the level of the most fundamental symbols in Buddhism—the life of the teachings—but inflected their meaning and implications in ways that transformed how Burmese saw themselves and their world.

NOTES

NOTE ON TRANSLITERATION

1. When writing about the contemporary period, I opt for the contemporary naming systems, including the name "Myanmar."
2. On the history of Burmese transliteration and transcription, see John Okell, *A Guide to the Romanization of Burmese* (London: The Royal Asiatic Society of Great Britain and Ireland, 1971).
3. I follow the version of the Okell system laid out in John Okell, with Saw Tun and Daw Khin Mya Swe, *Burmese: An Introduction to the Script* (Dekalb: Northern Illinois University, Center for Southeast Asian Studies, 1994), appendix 3. My thanks to Chris Clark for aid in transliterating and checking my transliterations.

CHAPTER 1: INTRODUCTION

1. Prasenjit Duara, *Rescuing History from the Nation: Questioning Narratives of Modern China* (Chicago: University of Chicago Press, 1995).
2. Anne M. Blackburn, *Buddhist Learning and Textual Practice in Eighteenth-Century Lankan Monastic Culture* (Princeton, NJ: Princeton University Press, 2001); Michael Charney, *Powerful Learning: Buddhist Literati and the Throne in Burma's Last Dynasty* (Ann Arbor: Center for South and Southeast Asian Studies, University of Michigan, 2006); Patrick Pranke, "The 'Treatise on the Lineage of Elders' (Vaṃsadīpanī): Monastic Reform and the Writing of Buddhist History in Eighteenth-Century Burma" (PhD diss., University of Michigan, 2004); Craig J. Reynolds, "The Buddhist Monkhood in Nineteenth Century Thailand" (PhD diss., Cornell University, 1972).
3. Richard Gombrich and Gananath Obeyesekere, *Buddhism Transformed: Religious Change in Sri Lanka* (Princeton, NJ: Princeton University Press, 1988); Kitsiri Malalgoda, *Buddhism in Sinhalese Society, 1750–1900: A Study of Religious Revival and Change* (Berkeley: University of California Press, 1976).
4. Blackburn, *Buddhist Learning*, 8.
5. Anne M. Blackburn, *Locations of Buddhism: Colonialism and Modernity in Sri Lanka* (Chicago: University of Chicago Press, 2010), 201.
6. Thomas Borchert, "Worry for the Dai Nation: Sipsongpannā Chinese Modernity, and the Problems of Buddhist Modernism," *Journal of Asian Studies* 67, no. 1 (2008): 112.

7. Anne Ruth Hansen, *How to Behave: Buddhism and Modernity in Colonial Cambodia, 1860–1930,* Southeast Asia—Politics, Meaning, Memory (Honolulu: University of Hawai'i Press, 2007).

8. Benedict R. Anderson, *Imagined Communities: Reflections on the Origin and Spread of Nationalism,* rev. and ext. ed. (London: Verso, 1991).

9. Penny Edwards, *Cambodge: The Cultivation of a Nation, 1860–1945,* Southeast Asia—Politics, Meaning, Memory (Honolulu: University of Hawai'i Press, 2007); Thongchai Winichakul, *Siam Mapped: A History of the Geo-Body of a Nation* (Honolulu: University of Hawai'i Press, 1994). In a similar vein, see Tamara Lynn Loos, *Subject Siam: Family, Law, and Colonial Modernity in Thailand* (Ithaca, NY: Cornell University Press, 2006); Maurizio Peleggi, *Lords of Things: The Fashioning of the Siamese Monarchy's Modern Image* (Honolulu: University of Hawai'i Press, 2002).

10. Stephen Berkwitz, "History and Gratitude in Theravada Buddhism," *Journal of the American Academy of Religion* 71, no. 3 (2003): 597.

11. Ibid., 599.

12. Talal Asad, "The Construction of Religion as an Anthropological Category," in *Genealogies of Religion: Discipline and Reasons of Power in Christianity and Islam* (Baltimore, MD: Johns Hopkins University Press, 1993), 27–54; Talal Asad, "Religion, Nation-State, Secularism," in *Nation and Religion: Perspectives on Europe and Asia,* ed. Peter van der Veer and Harmut Lehmann (Princeton, NJ: Princeton University Press, 1999), 178–93; Tomoko Masuzawa, *The Invention of World Religions, or, How European Universalism Was Preserved in the Language of Pluralism* (Chicago: University of Chicago Press, 2005).

13. For a good overview and introduction to this body of scholarship, see Markus Dressler and Arvind-Pal S. Mandair, "Introduction: Modernity, Religion-Making and the Postsecular," in *Secularism and Religion-Making,* ed. Markus Dressler and Arvind-Pal S. Mandair (New York: Oxford University Press, 2011), 1–36.

14. "Thathanabaing Burmese Archbishop," 1887, Series 1/1/(A), Accession 2574, File 21P, Myanmar National Archives, Yangon, Myanmar; Sir Herbert Thirkell White, *A Civil Servant in Burma* (London: Edward Arnold, 1913), 189–90.

15. "Thathanabaing Burmese Archbishop," 1887, Myanmar National Archives. Note that later the claim was that the Thathanabaing's authority only extended to Upper Burma.

16. Ibid.

17. Alexey Kirichenko, "'The Last of the Mohicans': Taunggwin Hsayadaw and the Transformation of Monastic Hierarchies in Colonial Burma" (paper presented at the Conference on Theravada Buddhism under Colonialism: Adaptation and Response, Narlanda Sriwijaya Centre, Institute for Southeast Asian Studies, Singapore, May 24, 2010).

18. Donald M. Seekins, *State and Society in Modern Rangoon* (New York: Routledge, 2011), 26–27.

19. Htin Aung, trans., *Burmese Monk's Tales* (New York: Columbia University Press, 1966), 144–45.

20. This idea of intervention for the welfare of the people was used to provide imperialism with a moral purpose. John S. Furnivall, *Colonial Policy and Practice: A Comparative Study of Burma and Netherlands India* (New York: New York University Press, 1956), 62–63. There is evidence that Arthur Phayre sought to turn the province toward a social interventionist policy a decade earlier. See Chapter 3.

21. Although there had been judicial, police, and forestry systems, and some road construction since the 1830s, these had limited impact on the daily lives of the majority of Burmese. Ibid., 72–73.

22. Graham Burchell, Colin Gordon, and Peter Miller, *The Foucault Effect: Studies in Governmentality* (Chicago: University of Chicago Press, 1991).

23. Gauri Viswanathan, *Masks of Conquest: Literary Study and British Rule in India* (New York: Columbia University Press, 1989).

24. Telegram from Viceroy to Chief Commissioner, January 16, 1886, "Appointment of Thathanabaing Headship of the Buddhist Church," 1886, Series 1/1/ (A), Accession 1778, File 18, Myanmar National Archives, Yangon, Myanmar. The concern turned out to be unjustified, and most Burmese responded that the relation to the Chinese emperor was trivial.

25. Telegram from Viceroy to Chief Commissioner, January 18, 1886, "Appointment of Thathanabaing Headship of the Buddhist Church," 1886, Myanmar National Archives.

26. Telegram from Chief Commissioner to Viceroy, January 20, 1886, "Appointment of Thathanabaing Headship of the Buddhist Church," 1886, Myanmar National Archives.

27. Telegram from Viceroy to Chief Commissioner, January 21, 1886, "Appointment of Thathanabaing Headship of the Buddhist Church," 1886, Myanmar National Archives.

28. Head of Buddhist Religion in Burma, Meeting Minutes, February 2, 1886, Government House, "Appointment of Thathanabaing Headship of the Buddhist Church," 1886, Myanmar National Archives.

29. Ibid.

30. "Thathanabaing Burmese Archbishop," 1887, Myanmar National Archives, Yangon, Myanmar.

31. "Editorial," *Burmah Herald,* February 3, 1886. The translation is from the colonial government's archival files. Unfortunately, no original copies of the Burmese language *Burmah Herald* for this period survive. "Appointment of Thathanabaing Headship of the Buddhist Church," 1886, Myanmar National Archives.

32. "On Sāsana Affairs," *Burmah Herald,* February 4, 1886. Translation in "Appointment of Thathanabaing Headship of the Buddhist Church," 1886, Myanmar National Archives.

33. W. R. Winston, *Four Years in Upper Burma* (London: C. H. Kelly, 1892), 33–41.

34. For instance, meetings and public lectures for Buddhist associations were often held at the (Tamil) Maduray Pillay School, which served as an alternative public locale to the YMCA building.

35. Penny Edwards, "Relocating the Interlocutor: Taw Sein Ko (1864–1930) and the Itinerancy of Knowledge in British Burma," *South East Asia Research* 12, no. 3 (2004): 277–335; Penny Edwards, "Adventure Capital: Political Enterprise in Colonial Southeast Asia" (paper presented at the Association of Asian Studies, Honolulu, Hawaii, April 2, 2011); Su Lin Lewis, "Asian Urbanites and Cosmopolitan Cultures in Bangkok, Penang, and Rangoon 1910–1940" (PhD diss., University of Cambridge, 2010).

36. "Sagaing and Ywataung," *Times of Burma,* February 4, 1899, 5; *Burma Echo,* February 29, 1908, 10; "Freethinkers in Rangoon," *Burma Echo,* October 12, 1907, 12.

37. Alicia Turner, "The Irish Pongyi in Colonial Burma: The Confrontations and Challenges of U Dhammaloka," *Contemporary Buddhism* 11, no. 2 (2010): 149–71; Alicia Turner, Laurence Cox, and Brian Bocking, "Beachcombing, Going Native and Freethinking: Rewriting the History of Early Western Buddhist Monastics," *Contemporary Buddhism* 11, no. 2 (2010): 125–47; John L. Crow, "The White Knight in the Yellow Robe: Allan Bennett's Search for Truth" (master's thesis, University of Amsterdam, 2009); Elizabeth Harris, *Ananda Metteyya: The First British Emissary of Buddhism,* Wheel Publication No. 420/422 (Kandy, Sri Lanka: Buddhist Publication Society, 1998).

38. The YMBA is perhaps the best known of these organizations due to later nationalist narratives, but it was not the dominant or even the most prominent association until the late 1910s.

39. Naoko Kumada, "Rethinking Dana in Burma: The Art of Giving" (paper presented at the Buddhism and the Spirit Cult Revisited Conference, Stanford University, May 22–23, 2004).

40. My main source for these printed materials was the extensive collections of the Universities Central Library at Yangon University, supplemented by the collections of the British Library; the School of Oriental and African Studies (SOAS) Library, University of London; and the Donn V. Hart Southeast Asia Collection at Northern Illinois University. In addition, numerous private collections throughout Myanmar proved treasure troves of rare surviving periodicals, books, and records.

41. Manuscript colonial records cited here came from the Myanmar National Archives in Yangon and the India Office of the British Library. Among printed

records, the *Reports on the Administration of Burma,* the *Catalogue of Books and Pamphlets Published in Burma,* and the *Report on Public Instruction in Burma* were especially useful.

42. The Buddhist associations included people from a wide range of ethnic groups represented in Burma, including Mons, Shans, Arakanese, and Chinese, but ethnicity was rarely discussed in their literature.

43. Records survive for Buddhist associations and schools in Moulmein, but I was unable to locate any records from those in Akyab, despite the fact that there are indications of vibrant and diverse Buddhist activities there in this period. Likewise, to the best of my knowledge, no copies of the newspapers published in Moulmein, Akyab, Bassein, or Pegu prior to 1920 have survived.

44. Erik Braun, *The Birth of Insight: Meditation, Modern Buddhism and the Burmese Monk Ledi Sayadaw,* Buddhism and Modernity (Chicago: University of Chicago Press, 2013).

CHAPTER 2: *SĀSANA* DECLINE AND TRADITIONS OF REFORM

Epigraph: Ivan Pavlovich Minayeff, *Travels in and Diaries of India and Burma,* trans. Hirendranath Sanyal (Calcutta: Eastern Trading Co., 1956), 168.

1. Ibid., 130.

2. Ibid., 129–30.

3. Ibid., 129.

4. Ibid., 127.

5. Anne M. Blackburn, *Buddhist Learning and Textual Practice in Eighteenth-Century Lankan Monastic Culture* (Princeton, NJ: Princeton University Press, 2001), 8.

6. Taw Sein Ko, ed., *The Kalyani Inscriptions Erected by King Dhammaceti at Pegu in 1476 AD, Text and Translation* (Rangoon: Superintendent, Government Printing, Burma, 1892), 44.

7. Edward Michael Mendelson, *Sangha and State in Burma: A Study of Monastic Sectarianism and Leadership,* ed. John P. Ferguson (Ithaca, NY: Cornell University Press, 1975).

8. Jan Nattier, *Once Upon a Future Time: Studies in a Buddhist Prophecy of Decline* (Berkeley, CA: Asian Humanities Press, 1991), chap. 3.

9. See V. Trenckner, Dines Anderson, and Helmer Smith, eds., *A Critical Pāli Dictionary* (Copenhagen: A. F. Høst and Søn, 1924–), "antaradhāna"; *The Questions of King Milinda,* trans. T. W. Rhys Davids (New York: Dover Publications, 1963), 1:185–90.

10. John Strong, *Relics of the Buddha* (Princeton, NJ: Princeton University Press, 2004), 221–24; *Chaṭṭhana Saṅgāyana,* CD-ROM, 3rd ed. (Dhammagiri: Vipassana Research Institute, 2003).

11. Blackburn, *Buddhist Learning*, 77–90.

12. Jason Carbine, "Shwegyin Sāsana: Continuity, Rupture, and Traditionalism in a Buddhist Tradition," in *Historicizing "Tradition" in the Study of Religion*, ed. Steven Engler and Gregory Grieve (Berlin: Walter de Gruyter, 2005), 146–52.

13. Patrick Pranke, "'Bodawpaya's Madness': Monastic Accounts of King Bodawpaya's Conflict with the Burmese Sangha," *Journal of Burma Studies* 12 (2008): 1–28; Patrick Pranke, "History and Eschatology in Burmese Buddhist Chronicles" (paper presented at the Association of Asian Studies, San Diego, CA, March 23, 2013).

14. Personal communication, Alexey Kirichenko, October 2008 and July 2011. My thanks to both Kirichenko and Pranke for their ever-insightful discussions of this issue.

15. Patrick Pranke, personal communication, October 2008 and July 2011.

16. Mahādhamma saṅkram, *Sāsanālaṅkara cā taṃ': [Thathanalankara sadan]* (Rangoon: Hanthawaddy, 1956), 115–17.

17. Ibid., 234–41. The *Thathanalankara sadan (Sāsanālaṅkara cā taṃ':)* and *Sārasaṅgaha* both list the *antaradhāna*s as *pariyatti, paṭipatti, paṭivedha, liṅga,* and *dhātu,* substituting *paṭivedha* for *adhigama* from the *Manoratha pūraṇī,* and promoting *pariyatti* to the first element to be lost. Genjun Sasaki, ed., *Sārasaṅgaha* (Oxford: Pali Text Society, 1992), 27–37.

18. Mabel Haynes Bode, ed., *Sāsanavaṃsa,* Pali Text Society Publications 121 (London: H. Frowde, 1897), 73–74. The tradition of interest in the decline of the *sāsana* continues with Ledi Sayadaw's 1919 *Thathanawithodhani (Sāsanavisodhanī),* which includes extensive discussions of stages and signs of decline. Ledi Sayadaw, *Sāsanavisodhanī [Thathanawithodhani]* (Rangoon: Hanthawaddy, 1954 [1919]), 1:46–56.

19. Ivan Pavlovich Minayeff, "Anāgata-Vaṃsa," *Journal of the Pali Text Society* (1886): 33–53.

20. Steven Collins, *Nirvana and Other Buddhist Felicities: Utopias of the Pali Imaginaire,* Cambridge Studies in Religious Traditions 12 (Cambridge: Cambridge University Press, 1998), 359–75; Jacqueline Filliozat, "The Commentaries to the Anāgatavamsa in the Pali Manuscripts of the Paris Collections," *Journal of the Pali Text Society* 19 (1993): 43–63; Udaya Maddegama and John Holt, *Anāgatavamsa Desana: The Sermon of the Chronicle-to-Be,* Buddhist Tradition Series (Delhi: Motilal Banarsidass Publishers, 1993); K. R. Norman, "The Anāgatavaṃsa Revisited," *Journal of the Pali Text Society* 28 (2006): 1–37.

21. The fourth manuscript was an unrelated text discussing the history of the next ten Buddhas. This theme is picked up in some twentieth-century Burmese commentaries with the *Anāgata* title as well.

22. There is a reference to a copy of the *Anāgata vaṃsa* in a Pagan inscription from 1442. Mabel Haynes Bode, *The Pali Literature of Burma* (London: Royal Asi-

atic Society of Great Britain and Ireland, 1909), 105. Bechert et al. list multiple manuscript copies, including a *nissaya* version dated to 1842. Heinz Bechert et al., *Burmese Manuscripts*, vol. 1, Verzeichnis Der Orientalischen Handschriften in Deutschland Bd. 23 (Wiesbaden: Steiner, 1979). A further manuscript copy is currently housed at the Universities Central Library of Rangoon University. My thanks to U Thaw Kaung for allowing me access to a handwritten copy of this manuscript.

23. "Burma," *Pioneer*, January 23, 1895, 4.

24. "The Late Maung Hpo Hmyin," *Rangoon Gazette and Weekly Budget*, January 26, 1895, 5.

25. Henry Steele Olcott, *Old Diary Leaves: The History of the Theosophical Society*, vol. 4, 1887–1892 (Adyar: Theosophical Publishing House, 1910).

26. Anagarika Dharmapala, "Moung Hpo Myin, KSM," *Journal of the Maha-Bodhi Society* 3, no. 10–11 (1895): 86; "Personal Items," *Journal of the Maha-Bodhi Society* 1, no. 10 (1893): 3; "Personal Items, March," *Journal of the Maha-Bodhi Society* 1, no. 11 (1893): 5.

27. Tragically it seems that Maung Hpo Hmyin also suffered from severe mental illness. He entered the Rangoon Lunatic Asylum in 1895, where he committed suicide. Dharmapala, "Moung Hpo Myin, KSM," 86; "The Late Maung Hpo Hmyin," *Rangoon Gazette and Weekly Budget*, January 26, 1895, 5.

28. *Anāgata buddhavaṃsa katha kyam': [Anāgata buddhavamsa katha kyan]* (Rangoon: Hanthawaddy 1902); *Anāgatavan' kyam': yan'mhion' [Anagatawin kyan yinmhaung: The Future Buddhas]*, ed. Ma Thein Tin (Rangoon: Zabu Mingala Press, 1904); *Anāgatavan' kyam': [Anagatavan kyan]* (Rangoon: Tuin Ok Bha Ma, 1907; Rangoon: Kawimyakmhan, 1924; Rangoon: Ledi Mandaing, 1956); *Anāgatavan' vatthu [Anagatavan wuttu]* (Rangoon: Hanthawaddy, 1928). The 1904, 1907, and 1924 volumes are listed by the titles in brackets in Kenneth Whitbread, *Catalogue of Burmese Printed Books in the India Office Library* (London: Her Majesty's Stationery Office, 1969). My thanks to Bo Bo Lasin and San San May for helping me consult these versions. The rest I either obtained from private libraries in Rangoon or found in the *Catalogue of Books and Pamphlets Published in Burma* (Rangoon: Superintendent, Government Printing, Burma).

29. *Catalogue of Books and Pamphlets Published in Burma*, 1st quarter 1908. Burmese currency in this era was divided such that there were four *pya* in one *anna* and sixteen *anna*s in one *rupee*.

30. It is at many points a verbatim copy of the *Manoratha pūraṇī* Pali commentary, changing only the verb tenses in order to make it read as a set of predictions from the Buddha to Sariputta. A Burmese edition of the *Manoratha pūraṇī* was also published in 1898. Kyithe Sayadaw, *Manorathapūraṇī kyam': [Manorathapurani kyan]* (Rangoon: Ma E Me, 1898), found in *Catalogue of Books and Pamphlets Published in Burma*, 1st quarter 1898.

31. It lists the five stages as "(1) the disappearance of analytical insight (*patisambhidā*), (2) the disappearance of the Path and Fruition States, (3) the disappearance of the practice (*paṭipatti*), (4) the disappearance of the texts (*pariyatti*), and (5) the disappearance of the Sangha." This translation appears in Chit Tin and William Pruitt, *The Coming Buddha Ariya Metteyya*, 2nd ed., the Wheel Publication No. 381/383 (Kandy, Sri Lanka: Buddhist Publication Society, 1992), 27–28.

32. Minayeff, "Anāgata-Vaṃsa," 34–35.

33. Anagarika Dharmapala, *Report of the Maha Bodhi Society, from 1891 to 1915* (Calcutta: Maha Bodhi Society, 1915); Buddhist Community of Burma, *Buddha Gaya* (Calcutta: Maha Bodhi Society, 1907).

34. Minayeff, *Travels in and Diaries of India and Burma*, 168.

35. While the other *antaradhāna*s receive only minimal treatment in some versions, the description of the decline of *pariyatti* learning is reproduced in detail in all of the contemporary sources: the *Sārasaṅgaha*, the *Thathanalankara sadan (Sāsanālaṅkara cā tam':)*, the Maung Hpo Hmyin version of the *Anāgata vaṃsa,* and the *Anagatawin kyan (Anāgatavan' kyam':)*.

36. Translation in I. B. Horner, "The Buddhist Apocalypse," in *Buddhist Texts through the Ages,* ed. Edward Conze et al. (New York: Harper & Row, 1954), 35.

37. The Sutta Piṭaka will be lost starting with the Aṅguttara Nikāya through the Khuddaka Nikāya. Paradoxically, the Jātakas will be preserved after the loss of the Khuddaka Nikāya. The loss of the Jātakas is described in a separate section between the loss of the Sutta and Vinaya, beginning with the Vessantara Jātaka. Minayeff, "Anāgata-Vaṃsa," 35. The *Manoratha pūraṇī* also includes this curious separation of the Jātakas from the Sutta Piṭaka.

38. Horner, "The Buddhist Apocalypse," 35–36.

39. Nattier, *Once Upon a Future Time,* 119.

40. See, for example, "Mantale: mrui. Pariyattisāsanāhita asañ': akroñ':" [About the Mandalay Pariyatti Thathanhita Society], *Maha-Bodhi News,* March 23, 1902, 18; "Paṭhama pran' cā me pvai: akroñ':," *Maha-Bodhi News,* July 4, 1902, 84.

41. Khammai Dhammasami, "Between Idealism and Pragmatism: A Study of Monastic Education in Burma and Thailand from the Seventeenth Century to the Present" (PhD diss., University of Oxford, 2004), 64–73.

42. Ibid., 86–88.

43. Myo Myint, "The Politics of Survival in Burma: Diplomacy and Statecraft in the Reign of King Mindon 1853–1871" (PhD diss., Cornell University, 1987), 164.

44. Ibid., 164–65; Francois Tainturier, "The Foundation of Mandalay by King Mindon" (PhD diss., School of Oriental and African Studies, University of London, 2010).

45. "To His Excellency the Right Honourable George Nathaniel Lord Curzon, Baron of Keddleston," *Maha-Bodhi and the United Buddhist World* 10, no. 10 (1902): 98–99.

46. "Alhū Dāna Sataṅ':," *Maha-Bodhi News,* March 1, 1902, 1; "Vattukaṃ ṅve paṅ' ṅve raṅ':," *Mandalay Pariyatti Thathanahita Society Monthly Journal* (1908); Mandalay Pariyatti Thathanahita, *Nhac' tac' rā praññ'. samuiṅ:* (Mandalay: Sukhavatīpiṭaka, 1998).

47. On the Pakhan Sayadaw and the Minekhine Sayadaw, who write strongly against monastic participation in government projects, see Chapter 3 of this volume. Sin': Chve Ū:, "Kuiluinī khet' buddhasāsanā (1885–1938)" (master's thesis, University of Mandalay, 1994), 64; Rhve Kuiṅ': Sā, *Anhac' 100 praññ'. mantale:* (Mandalay: Krī: pvā: re: puṃ nhip' tuik', 1959), 285.

48. "To His Excellency the Right Honourable George Nathaniel Lord Curzon, Baron of Keddleston," 98–99.

49. "Pariyatti Thathanahita Society, Mandalay, U.B., the Objects of the Society," *Mandalay Pariyatti Thathanahita Society Monthly Journal* (1908).

50. "Mantale: mrui. Pariyattisāsanāhita asaṅ': akroṅ': [About the Mandalay Pariyatti Thathanahita Society]," *Maha-Bodhi News,* March 23, 1902, 18.

51. Win Mar, "The Role of the Malunze Rice Offering Society in Propagating the Buddha Sasana" (master's thesis, Mandalay University, 1996); Mandalay Malunze Rice Donating Society, *Mantale: mrui. ma lvan' jhe: chan' lhū asaṅ': krī: nhac'-100-praññ'. cā coṅ'* (Mandalay: Ma lvan' jhe: chan' lhū asaṅ':, 1996).

52. Dhammasami, "Between Idealism and Pragmatism," 137.

53. Sin': Chve Ū:, "Kuiluinī khet' buddhasāsanā (1885–1938)," 67.

54. 'E: Krū, *Britishya mran'mā khet' cā kraññ'. tuik' myā: akhre ane 1826–1947* (Yangon: Universities Press, 1979), 113; "A New Library," *Burman Buddhist* 2, no. 5 (1909): 97–98.

55. John Minus, "The Bernard Free Library," in *Annual Report of the Burma Educational Syndicate for the Year 1914–1915* (Rangoon: Office of the Superintendent, Government Printing, Burma, 1915), 5–6. This library remains on the grounds of the Shwedagon Pagoda.

56. *Report on Public Instruction in Burma for the Year 1892–93* (Rangoon: Superintendent, Government Printing, Burma, 1893), Upper Burma, 1; *First Quinquennial Report on Public Instruction in Burma for the Years 1892–93—1896–97* (Rangoon: Superintendent, Government Printing, Burma, 1897), 63–64. The *Report on Public Instruction in Burma* is abbreviated in repeated citations as *RPI.*

57. Donald Eugene Smith, *Religion and Politics in Burma* (Princeton, NJ: Princeton University Press, 1965), 69.

58. *First Quinquennial RPI 1892–93—1896–97,* 63; *Report on Public Instruction in Burma for the Year 1905–06* (Rangoon: Superintendent, Government Printing, Burma, 1907), 9.

59. *Report on Public Instruction in Burma for the Year 1897–98* (Rangoon: Superintendent, Government Printing, Burma, 1898), 5.

60. "Paṭhama pran' cā me: pvai: sabhaṅ' kyaṅ': pa pru lup' saññ'. akroṅ':," *Maha-Bodhi News,* June 28, 1902, 75–76; "Mran'mā nuiṅ' ṅaṃ toṅ' paṭhama pran' pvai oṅ' mraṅ' sū tui akroṅ':," *Hanthawaddy Weekly Review,* October 4, 1905, 711; "Paṭhama pran' pvai nhuik' vaṅ' rok' pran' chui oṅ' mraṅ' sū tui. akroṅ':," *Hanthawaddy Weekly Review,* August 10, 1901, 669.

61. "Education: Pali Examination to Be Held in Mandalay for Monks and Laymen," 1892, Series 1/15(E), Accession 11225, File 2E-12, Myanmar National Archives, Yangon, Myanmar.

62. "Piṭakat' paṭhama pran' pvai krī: chaṅ' yaṅ' kyaṅ': pa maññ' akroṅ':," *Hanthawaddy Weekly Review,* May 26, 1900, 158.

63. "Mantale: mrui. buddhabhāsāsāsanā pru asaṅ': mha paṭhama kyo' pran' chui oṅ' mraṅ' sū ā: piṭakat' suṃ puṃ cā up' myā: lhū dān': ran' praṭṭhān': khraṅ': akroṅ':," *Hanthawaddy Weekly Review,* October 4, 1901, 711.

64. "Paṭhama pran' cā me pvai: akroṅ':," *Maha-Bodhi News,* July 4, 1902, 84; "Paṭhama pran' dāyakā dhammāruṃ asaṅ': amhu choṅ' ko'mītī lū krī: myā:" *Hanthawaddy Weekly Review,* March 7, 1906, 265.

65. Nuns were first allowed to sit for the examinations in 1901. The first time a nun won the *Patamakyaw* was 1926. Sin': Chve Ū:, "Kuiluinī khet' buddhasāsanā (1885–1938)," 46.

66. The awards from the Pariyatti Thathanahita and the Zediyingana became the most prestigious monastic titles, and their exam lists came to dominate monastic curriculum, so much so, Dhammasami argues, that by the late twentieth century, monastic learning was focused on studying almost exclusively for these examinations. Dhammasami, "Between Idealism and Pragmatism," 7–8, 145.

67. A 1954 pamphlet described ten of the most famous examinations that had been founded since 1896, but noted that "there are many similar Pariyatti examinations held at different parts of Burma under the auspices of various Buddhist organizations." Union Buddha Sasana Council, *Report on the Situation of Buddhism in Burma* (Rangoon: Union Buddha Sasana Council, 2498 [1954]), 17.

68. "Yeanangyoung," *Burma Echo,* September 7, 1907, 11.

69. "Modern Preaching," *Burman Buddhist* 1, no. 3 (1908).

70. Erik Braun in his work on Ledi Sayadaw discusses these associations in detail. Erik Braun, *The Birth of Insight: Meditation, Modern Buddhism and the Burmese Monk Ledi Sayadaw,* Buddhism and Modernity (Chicago: University of Chicago Press, 2013), 119–21.

71. Ledi Sayadaw, *Paramattha samkhip' kyam':* [*Paramattha thankheip kyan*] (Rangoon: Hanthawaddy, 1956 [1903]).

72. This only includes those editions that were registered with the government. See *Catalogue of Books and Pamphlets Published in Burma, 1904–1907.*

73. Histories of Ledi Sayadaw's work largely deny the gendered nature of these associations. See, for example, Htay Htay Lwin, "History of the Maha Ledi

Sasana" (master's thesis, Mandalay University, 1998), 59. However, all of the contemporary accounts of the Paramattha Thankheip associations I found in newspapers, both Burmese and English, indicate that their membership was largely, if not entirely, female. One colonial source says that Ledi Sayadaw preferred to promote Abhidhamma education for women because as mothers they could teach their children. K. M. Ward, "Right Conduct," in *A Compilation of Lectures,* ed. The Rangoon College Buddhist Association (Rangoon: Sun Press, 1914), 13.

74. "Praññ' mrui. satañ': / Rhve: chaṃ to' bhurā: krī: cetīyaṅgaṇa upāsakā asañ': ka paramatta saṃkhip' cā pran' pvai pru lup' kyañ': pa maññ'. akroñ':," *Hanthawaddy Weekly Review,* March 17, 1906, 345; "Ledi Sayadaw," *Burman Buddhist* 1, no. 2 (1908) 27–28.

75. "Insein," *Burma Echo,* December 7, 1907, 11.

76. "Moulmein," *Burma Echo,* December 7, 1907, 10.

CHAPTER 3: BUDDHIST EDUCATION

Epigraph: Peter Hordern, "Buddhist Schools in Burmah," *Fraser's Magazine* 16, no. 95 (1877): 627.

1. *First Quinquennial Report on Public Instruction in Burma for the Years 1892–93—1896–97* (Rangoon: Superintendent, Government Printing, Burma, 1897), 18; Sir James George Scott, *The Burman, His Life and Notions* (New York: Norton & Co., 1963 [1882]), chap. 2. The *Report on Public Instruction in Burma* is abbreviated in repeated citations as *RPI.*

2. Michael Symes, *An Account of an Embassy to the Kingdom of Ava: Sent by the Governor-General of India, in the Year 1795* (London: W. Bulmer and Co, 1800), 123.

3. The earliest report on Burmese education was from Ralph Fitch in the 1580s. John Horton Ryley, *Ralph Fitch, England's Pioneer to India and Burma: His Companions and Contemporaries, with His Remarkable Narrative Told in His Own Words* (London: T. Fisher Unwin, 1899), 168–70.

4. Father Sangermano, *A Description of the Burmese Empire,* trans. William Tandy (Rome: Oriental Translation Fund of Great Britain and Ireland, 1833), 121. *Talapoin* is a word used originally by the Portuguese to refer to Buddhist monks.

5. Alice Marion Rowlands Hart, *Picturesque Burma, Past & Present* (London: J. M. Dent & Co., 1897); R. Talbot Kelly, *Burma,* 2nd ed. (London: A&C Black, Ltd, 1933 [1905]); George W. Bird, *Wanderings in Burma,* 2nd ed. (London: Simpkin, Marshall, Hamilton, Kent and Co., 1897); Charles J. F. Smith Forbes, *British Burma and Its People: Being Sketches of Native Manners, Customs and Religion* (London: Murray, 1878).

6. Scott, *The Burman, His Life and Notions,* chap. 2; H. Fielding Hall, *The Soul of a People,* 4th ed. (London: Macmillan and Co., 1913 [1898]), chap. 11; John Nisbet, *Burma under British Rule—and Before* (Westminster: A. Constable, 1901), 1:251–56; Albert Fytche, *Burma Past and Present,* vol. 2 (London: C. K. Paul & Co., 1878), app. G; W. R. Winston, *Four Years in Upper Burma* (London: C. H. Kelly, 1892), 122–26; George E. R. Grant Brown, *Burma as I Saw It, 1889–1917, with a Chapter on Recent Events* (New York: Frederick A. Stokes Company, 1925).

7. Hordern, "Buddhist Schools in Burmah," 626–34; "Foreign Literary Notes," *Eclectic Magazine of Foreign Literature* 47, no. 2 (1888): 286; Ernest G. Harmer, "The Transformation of Burma," *London Quarterly Review* 7, no. 1 (1902): 53.

8. Ivan Pavlovich Minayeff, *Travels in and Diaries of India and Burma,* trans. Hirendranath Sanyal (Calcutta: Eastern Trading Co., 1956), 128, 30, 32–34.

9. Bernard S. Cohn, *Colonialism and Its Forms of Knowledge: The British in India* (Princeton, NJ: Princeton University Press, 1996).

10. *Report on the Census of British Burma Taken in August 1872* (Rangoon: Government Press, 1875), 24–25.

11. Part of the perceived discrepancy with these figures may be due to the fact that the census covered only Lower (British) Burma, which had a larger migrant and agricultural population.

12. Kenneth J. Saunders, *Buddhism in the Modern World* (London: Society for Promoting Christian Knowledge, 1922), 3–4.

13. The 1891 census, with a renewed faith in its methods, included a chart comparing the literacy rates of men and women in Burma with those of a number of other British colonies and provinces, as well as with a number of European countries. The numbers were higher than in any British territory in Asia, with the exception of Australia, and higher than those of Italy in Europe. The chart is reproduced in Sir James George Scott and J. P. Hardiman, eds., *Gazetteer of Upper Burma and Shan States,* vol. 2 of pt. 1 (Rangoon: Superintendent, Government Printing, Burma, 1900), 540. These statistics initiated a string of European comparisons. Jardine placed Burmese literacy rates between those of Belgium and Austria. Justice Jardine, "University for Burma at Rangoon," *Asiatic Quarterly Review* 7, no. 13 (1894): 72. Max and Bertha Ferrars placed literacy rates in Burma "midway between those of Ireland and Austria on the one hand and Italy and Spain on the other." Max Ferrars and Bertha Ferrars, *Burma,* 2nd ed. (London: Sampson, Low, Marston and Company, 1901), 11–12.

14. Henry Gouger, *Two Years Imprisonment in Burma (1824–26),* ed. Guy Lubeigt, Burma Historical Reprint Series (Bangkok: White Lotus, 2002 [1860]), 22. Bigandet argues that because of literacy, Burmese Buddhists knew more about their religion than poor Europeans knew about theirs: "Most of them are possessed of a certain amount of more or less limited information concerning

Buddha and his law. In this respect they are perhaps ahead of many nominal Christians in several countries of Europe who dwell in large manufacturing towns and remote country districts and belong to the lower classes, and who live without even a slight acquaintance with the essential tenets of the Christian creed." Paul Bigandet, *The Life or Legend of Gaudama, the Buddha of the Burmese, with Annotations,* 4th ed. (London: Kegan Paul, Trench, Trübner & Co., 1911 [1858]), 2:301.

15. John S. Furnivall, *An Introduction to the Political Economy of Burma* (Rangoon: Burma Book Club Ltd., 1931), x.

16. Scott and Hardiman, *Gazetteer of Upper Burma and Shan States,* 540–41.

17. Phillip McCann, "Popular Education, Socialization and Social Control: Spitalfields 1812–1824," in *Popular Education and Socialization in the Nineteenth Century,* ed. Phillip McCann (London: Methuen & Co., 1977), 1–40; W. B. Stephens, *Education in Britain, 1750–1914* (New York: St. Martin's Press, 1998), chap. 1.

18. Graham Burchell, Colin Gordon, and Peter Miller, eds., *The Foucault Effect: Studies in Governmentality* (Chicago: University of Chicago Press, 1991).

19. Brown, *Burma as I Saw It,* 90.

20. For a discussion of the ways that Burma seemed like English civilization to the British, in contrast to India, see Peter Hordern, "An Episode in Burmese History: Being a Contribution to the History of Indigenous Oriental Education," *Asiatic Quarterly Review* 4, no. 7 (1892): 30–32.

21. I use the term "monastery education" to refer to the initial education of lay boys before they were ordained as novices. This is not to be confused with "monastic education," i.e., the training of ordained novices and monks that was the object of reform in the eighteenth and nineteenth centuries.

22. There are a few reports of young girls taught in monasteries, although their presence was always the exception to the rule. See Edward Michael Mendelson, *Sangha and State in Burma: A Study of Monastic Sectarianism and Leadership,* ed. John P. Ferguson (Ithaca, NY: Cornell University Press, 1975), 152.

23. One of the most detailed early descriptions of monastery education is found in Bigandet, *Life or Legend of Gaudama,* 289–302. For other accounts of monastery education, see Kaung, "A Survey of the History of Education in Burma before the British Conquest and After," *Journal of the Burma Research Society* 46, no. 2 (1963): 9–23; San': Thvat', Mran'mā nuiṅ' ṅam phun' to' krī: kyoṅ': paññā re: samuiṅ: (Yangon: 'Un': paṅ' puṃ nhip' tuik', 1980); Hordern, "Buddhist Schools in Burmah"; Paul Richmond Hackett, "Religious Education of Burman Buddhists" (master's thesis, University of Chicago, 1921); Scott, *The Burman, His Life and Notions,* chap. 2; Ono Toro, "The Development of Education in Burma," *East Asian Cultural Studies* 20, nos. 1–4 (1981): 107–33.

24. The *Lokaniti* prescribed the best days for instruction and consequences for learning on inauspicious days, specifying that learning is best begun on a

Thursday, while beginning one's education on either a Tuesday or Saturday would have disastrous consequences. Likewise, it set out the proper diet for a student. James Gray, ed., *Ancient Proverbs and Maxims from the Burmese Sources: The Nīti Literature of Burma* (London: Trubner & Co., 1886), 34 v. 153.

25. Mendelson, *Sangha and State in Burma,* 152.

26. Bigandet, *Life or Legend of Gaudama,* 299.

27. For examples of the content of *thinbongyi* texts, see Krī: Phe, "Saṅ' puṃ krī: mha saṅ' pun': krī: sui. proṅ': sa lo," in *Mran'mā. cvay cuṃ kyam': cā pe bimān' ey' rup' pya bahusuta bhaṇ'* (Yangon: Cā pe bimān' puṃ nhip' tuik', 1973). L. E. Bagshawe notes that there were fifty thousand copies of *thinbongyi* texts published between 1880 and 1885, creating "something like a revolution in teaching methods . . . a rapid movement in Burmese schools from the traditional oral learning to learning from the book." Leonard Evans Bagshawe, "A Literature of School Books: A Study of the Burmese Books Approved for Use in Schools by the Education Department in 1885, and of Their Place in the Developing Educational System in British Burma" (master's thesis, School of Oriental and African Studies, University of London, 1976), 155. While it is clear that many of the texts in the monastery school curriculum had early printed editions, accounts from former students that they were rarely allowed to use books, and school inspectors' complaints that books were not used, somewhat mitigate the claim of a "revolution."

28. Kaung, "History of Education in Burma," 29.

29. Mendelson, *Sangha and State in Burma,* 154.

30. Kaung, "History of Education in Burma," 29.

31. Jeffrey Samuels, "Toward an Action-Oriented Pedagogy: Buddhist Texts and Monastic Education in Contemporary Sri Lanka," *Journal of the American Academy of Religion* 72, no. 4 (2004): 956.

32. Mendelson, *Sangha and State in Burma,* 154.

33. Samuels, "Toward an Action-Oriented Pedagogy."

34. On this type of Pali *nissaya* and its use in Burma, see Patrick Pranke, "The 'Treatise on the Lineage of Elders' (Vaṃsadīpanī): Monastic Reform and the Writing of Buddhist History in Eighteenth-Century Burma" (PhD diss., University of Michigan, 2004). On the pedagogical uses of *nissaya* in northern Thailand and Laos, see Justin McDaniel, *Gathering Leaves and Lifting Words* (Seattle: University of Washington Press, 2008).

35. Mendelson, *Sangha and State in Burma,* 154.

36. Heinz Bechert and Heinz Braun, eds., *Pāli Nīti Texts of Burma: Dhammanīti, Lokanīti, Maharahanīti, Rajanīti,* Pali Text Society Text Series 171 (London: Pali Text Society, 1981), 171:31. "Buddharūpaṃ" can be translated as referring to the body of the Buddha, his relics, or images. Likewise, the Burmese word likely used to translate the Pali refers to the Buddha, pagodas with his relics, or images of the Buddha and monks. James Gray translates it as "Each letter is the

image of Buddha." Gray, *Ancient Proverbs and Maxims from the Burmese Sources,* 113. The student's translation is found in Mendelson, *Sangha and State in Burma,* 154.

37. Howard Malcom, *Travels in the Burman Empire* (Edinburgh: William and Robert Chambers, 1840), 59.

38. Reverence for education has a long history, evidenced in the *Dhammanīti* composed in the late fourteenth to early fifteenth centuries. The *Lokanīti,* composed sometime between the mid-fifteenth and mid-eighteenth centuries, gives specific ritual prescriptions for the commencement of education. Bechert and Braun, *Pāli Nīti Texts of Burma,* xlix–li, lv–lvi. The *Puttovada son ma sa,* composed in the mid-eighteenth century, prescribes a specific curriculum for young boys, starting with a *thinbongyi* and the *Maṅgala Sutta* (Burmese *Mingala*) through the last ten Jātakas, that is strikingly similar to the one recorded in the late nineteenth century. 'Oṅ' Sin':, ed., *Haṃsāvatī chuṃ ma cā poṅ': khyup'* (Rangoon: Haṃsāvatī puṃ nhip' tuik', 1960), 127–59; San': Thvat', *Mran'mā nuiṅ' ṅaṃ bhun' to' krī: kyoṅ': paññā re: samuiṅ:,* 109–14.

39. For comparisons with the educational system in Siam and Laos, see Daniel M. Veidlinger, *Spreading the Dhamma: Writing, Orality, and Textual Transmission in Buddhist Northern Thailand,* Southeast Asia—Politics, Meaning, Memory (Honolulu: University of Hawai'i Press, 2006); McDaniel, *Gathering Leaves;* David K. Wyatt, *The Politics of Reform in Thailand: Education in the Reign of King Chulalongkorn,* Yale Southeast Asia Studies (New Haven, CT: Yale University Press, 1969). On Sri Lanka, see Anne M. Blackburn, *Buddhist Learning and Textual Practice in Eighteenth-Century Lankan Monastic Culture* (Princeton, NJ: Princeton University Press, 2001), 55–56; Elizabeth Bopearachchi, *L'éducation Bouddhique dans la société traditionnelle au Sri Lanka: Les formes ee pensée et les formes de socialisation,* Recherches Asiatiques (Paris: Harmattan, 1994), 39–47. On the comparison between Burmese and Sri Lankan educational systems, see Heinz Bechert, "Über Sanskrit-Bildung und Schulsystem in Birma und Ceylon," *Wiener Zeitschrift für die Kund Süd- und Ostasiens un Archiv für Indiche Philosophie* 7 (1963): 1–12; Bechert and Braun, *Pāli Nīti Texts of Burma,* xxxvii–xl.

40. Victor Lieberman, *Strange Parallels: Southeast Asia in Global Context c. 800–1830, Integration on the Mainland* (New York: Cambridge University Press, 2003), 1:188–92; Pranke, "Lineage of Elders," 316–18.

41. Pranke, "Lineage of Elders," 317–18; Blackburn, *Buddhist Learning.*

42. Michael Charney, *Powerful Learning: Buddhist Literati and the Throne in Burma's Last Dynasty* (Ann Arbor: Center for South and Southeast Asian Studies, University of Michigan, 2006), 43–44; Pranke, "Lineage of Elders," 27–30.

43. Khammai Dhammasami, "Between Idealism and Pragmatism: A Study of Monastic Education in Burma and Thailand from the Seventeenth Century to the Present" (PhD diss., University of Oxford, 2004).

44. Pranke, "Lineage of Elders," 5.
45. Kaung, "History of Education in Burma," 73–75; Hordern, "An Episode in Burmese History," 34–35.
46. Arthur Purves Phayre, "Memorandum on Vernacular Education for British Burma," 1865, reprinted in Kaung, "History of Education in Burma," 89.
47. His plan included the appointment of a Director of Public Instruction, Mr. G. H. Hough, who had extensive personal relationships with influential monks. Unfortunately, Hough died after less than a year in office. His first replacement lasted less than a year as well. The next Director of Public Instruction, Peter Hordern, had experience in the Indian Educational Service, but never replicated Hough's intimacy with the monks or knowledge of Burmese culture. Kaung, "History of Education in Burma," 80; Leonard Evans Bagshawe, "The 'Moral and Intellectual Improvement of the People': Western Education in Burma to 1880," in *Études Birmanes: En hommage à Denise Bernot,* ed. Pierre Pichard and François Robinne, Etudes Thématiques, 9 (Paris: Ecole Française d'Extrême-Orient, 1998), 276.
48. *Report on Public Instruction in Burma for the Year 1891–92* (Rangoon: Superintendent, Government Printing, Burma, 1892), Report on Upper Burma, 71.
49. Kaung, "History of Education in Burma," 33–35; Charney, *Powerful Learning,* 54–57.
50. Furnivall finds this antithetical to Phayre's plan. "This was tantamount to the reversal of Phayre's plan as he had insisted on the *gradual* development of monastic schools *without* alternative vernacular facilities." John S. Furnivall, "Material for Studying the Social and Economic Evolution of Burma" (unpublished manuscript, Cornell University Library, John M. Echols Collection, n.d.), part 2: British Period 1826 to 1941, vol 2: Extracts and Notes Preliminary, 12.
51. *Third Quinquennial Report on Public Instruction in Burma for the Years 1902– 03—1906–07* (Rangoon: Superintendent, Government Printing, Burma, 1908), Resolution 3–4.
52. The Director of Public Instruction tried offering visiting circuit teachers, itinerant teachers, and government-trained lay teachers at no expense to the monasteries. Albert Fytche, *Burma Past and Present* (London: C. K. Paul & Co., 1878), 2:207–8; *RPI 1891–92,* 24; *First Quinquennial RPI 1892–93—1896– 97,* 2. They offered normal school training to monks and set up special exam competitions in mathematics for monks to encourage expanding the curriculum. *Report on Public Instruction in Burma for the Year 1914–15* (Rangoon: Superintendent, Government Printing, Burma, 1915), 16. They also sought to entice the monks into the system with the Pali examinations. Donald Eugene Smith, *Religion and Politics in Burma* (Princeton, NJ: Princeton University Press, 1965), 46; *Report on Public Instruction in Burma for the Year 1897–98* (Rangoon: Superintendent, Government Printing, Burma, 1898), 3, 89. When

these efforts failed, the colonial government recognized a new Thathanabaing on the condition that he support the work of the department. D. H. R. Twomey, "Thathanabaing, Head of Burmese Monks in Burma," *Asiatic Quarterly Review* 17, no. 34 (1904): 326. Finally, they adjusted the rules for monastery schools, allowing them to substitute Pali for math in the curriculum, creating a substitute lower set of standards for monastery education. *Report on Public Instruction in Burma for the Year 1904–05* (Rangoon: Superintendent, Government Printing, Burma, 1905), 15.

53. *Report on Public Instruction in Burma for the Year 1912–13* (Rangoon: Superintendent, Government Printing, Burma, 1913), 8.

54. Smith, *Buddhism and Politics in Burma,* 64–65. It is difficult to offer reliable statistics to demonstrate this decline because there was never any thorough survey of the monastic schools outside the government system. The shift can be seen in the numbers of the monastery schools that did participate in the government's system, listed below. Monastery schools had substantially fewer pupils per school, meaning the shift in numbers of schools represented an even larger shift in the population of students. Note also that the overall numbers of monastery schools decline, even when the monastic heartland of Upper Burma is added in the 1898 figure. These numbers cannot directly represent the influence of the monastery schools, given the monastic resistance to the government system, but they demonstrate the basic trend. Source: Education Department, *Report of the Vernacular and Vocational Education Reorganization Committee* (Rangoon: Superintendent, Government Printing and Stationery, 1936), 136–37.

Year	Monastery Schools	Lay Schools
1878 (Lower Burma only)	2,626	337
1888	3,685	657
1898 (all of Burma)	2,975	1,280
1906	2,369	2,899
1919	2,648	4,993
1928	1,080	4,930
1933	928	4,967

55. Bagshawe, "Moral and Intellectual Improvement," 279–80.

56. See, for example, *Report on Public Instruction in Burma for the Year 1894–95* (Rangoon: Superintendent, Government Printing, Burma, 1895), Resolution 4.

57. *Second Quinquennial Report on Public Instruction in Burma for the Years 1897–98—1901–02* (Rangoon: Superintendent, Government Printing, Burma, 1902), 41; *Report on Public Instruction in Burma for the Year 1902–03* (Rangoon: Superintendent, Government Printing, Burma, 1903), 3; *Report on Public Instruction in Burma for the Year 1895–96* (Rangoon: Superintendent,

Government Printing, Burma, 1896), Resolution 4; *RPI 1891–92*, Report on Lower Burma 58.

58. See, for example, *RPI 1891–92*, Report on Upper Burma 4–5; *RPI 1895–96*, Resolution 3–4.

59. Kaung, "History of Education in Burma"; Education Department, *1936 Report on Vernacular and Vocational Education*, 127–44.

60. John S. Furnivall, *Colonial Policy and Practice: A Comparative Study of Burma and Netherlands India* (New York: New York University Press, 1956), 283.

61. Chief Commissioner of British Burma Lt. Col. Arthur Purves Phayre to Officiating Secretary to the Government of India Hon. R. N. Cust, Rangoon, 1864, "Home Department: Education," reprinted in Kaung, "History of Education in Burma," 83–86.

62. Compare Anne Blackburn's discussion of colonial officials' mistaken understanding of their "common cause" with Hikkaḍuvē Sumaṅgala at the Vidyodaya Pirivena. Anne M. Blackburn, *Locations of Buddhism: Colonialism and Modernity in Sri Lanka* (Chicago: University of Chicago Press, 2010), 69–78.

63. Blackburn, *Locations of Buddhism;* Arthur Purves Phayre, "Memorandum on Vernacular Education for British Burma," 1865, reprinted in Kaung, "History of Education in Burma," 89.

64. The quotation is from the 1858 Dispatch on Education, quoted in Bagshawe, "Moral and Intellectual Improvement."

65. Bagshawe, "Moral and Intellectual Improvement." On the Protestant ethic in colonial and educational settings, see Jean Comaroff and John L. Comaroff, *Of Revelation and Revolution: The Dialectics of Modernity on a South African Frontier,* vol. 2 (Chicago: University of Chicago Press, 1997); Max Weber, *The Protestant Ethic and the Spirit of Capitalism,* 2nd ed. (New York: Scribner, 1976); W. B. Stephens, *Education in Britain: 1750–1914* (New York: St. Martin's Press, 1998).

66. Quoted in John Lawson and Harold Silver, *A Social History of Education in England* (London: Methuen & Co., 1973), 243.

67. *Fourth Quinquennial Report on Public Instruction in Burma for the Years 1907–08—1911–12* (Rangoon: Superintendent, Government Printing, Burma, 1912), 3; *Report on Public Instruction in Burma for the Year 1899–1900* (Rangoon: Superintendent, Government Printing, Burma, 1900).

68. *RPI 1891–92*, Report on Upper Burma 5; *RPI 1895–96*, Resolution 4.

69. *Report on Public Instruction in Burma for the Year 1908–09* (Rangoon: Superintendent, Government Printing, Burma, 1909), 23.

70. *RPI 1908–09*, 22–23; *Third Quinquennial RPI 1902–03—1906–07*, 33; *First Quinquennial RPI 1892–93—1896–97*, 15.

71. The timing of this resistance corresponds to the beginning of colonial rule in Upper Burma, and the resistance of groups of monks, often led by the Pakhan Sayadaw, to any aspect of colonial intervention. This position was endorsed by

the Thathanabaing in a statement in 1891. Smith, *Buddhism and Politics in Burma*, 59.

72. *RPI 1891–92*, Report on Upper Burma, 25; Taw Sein Ko, "Minutes of a Meeting Held on the 13th August 1911 in the Thathanabaing's Monastery to Discuss the Question of Primary Education in Monastic Schools," in *Burmese Sketches*, vol. 1 (Rangoon: British Burma Press, 1913), 266; *RPI 1902–1903*, 3.

73. "Sāsanā puiñ' myā:," in *Mran'mā. cvay cum kyam': cā pe bimān' ey' rup' pra bahusuta bhaṇ'* (Rangoon: Mran'mā nuiñ' ṅam bhāsā pran' cā pe asañ':, 1972).

74. John P. Ferguson, "The Symbolic Dimensions of the Burmese Sangha" (PhD diss., Cornell University, 1975), 231.

75. Mendelson, *Sangha and State in Burma*, 114–15.

76. Twomey, "Thathanabaing, Head of Burmese Monks in Burma," 328.

77. Taw Sein Ko, "A Buddhist Archbishop for Burma," in *Burmese Sketches*, vol. 1 (Rangoon: British Burma Press, 1913); Taw Sein Ko, "The Thathanabaing," in *Burmese Sketches*, vol. 1 (Rangoon: British Burma Press, 1913).

78. *RPI 1891–92*, Report on Upper Burma, 2.

79. Minekhine Sayadaw, "Lokāyatādivinicchaya," in *Lokāyatādivinicchaya*, ed. Bhurā: Phrū Charā to' (Rangoon: Dī: dut' satañ': cā pum nhip' tuik', 1929 [1913]). I would like to thank Alexey Kirichenko for bringing this text to my attention and providing me with a copy.

80. This was the Burmese-language newspaper called in English *Maha-Bodhi News*, not the *Journal of the Maha-Bodhi Society*. I have not been able to obtain copies of the originals, but it was republished in a pamphlet in 1929.

81. Juliane Schober, "Colonial Knowledge and Buddhist Education in Burma," in *Buddhism, Power and Political Order*, ed. Ian Charles Harris (New York: Routledge, 2007), 62.

82. Smith, *Buddhism and Politics in Burma*, 59, 63.

83. As we will see in Chapter 4, these boys and their supposed unruliness became the subject of great public anxiety as well, and the focus of attention for education officials, Burmese parents, and other Europeans.

84. *Times of Burma*, January 14, 1899, 7.

85. Taw Sein Ko [Rambler, pseud.], "Education in Burma: From a Native Point of View," *Our Monthly: A Magazine of General Literature* 2, no. 5 (1883): 167–69.

86. "Buddhist Schools," *Burman Buddhist* 1, no. 1 (1908): 18.

87. Tilawka, *Buddhasāsanānuggahanaya cā tam':* (Mandalay: Mran'mā. tā rā satañ': cā pum nuip' tuik', 1901), 8–9.

88. Ananda Metteyya, *On Religious Education in Burma*, Publications of the Buddhasasana Samagama 2 (Rangoon: Hanthawaddy, 2446 [1903]), 5.

89. May Oung, "Education," *Times of Burma*, September 12, 1900, 5.

90. *Who's Who in Burma, under the Distinquished Patronage of H.E. Sir Harcourt Butler, Governor of Burma: A Biographical Record of Prominent Residents of Burma with Photographs & Illustrations* (Calcutta & Rangoon: Indo-Burma

Publishing Agency, 1927), 172; Moṅ' Jeyyā, *Mran'mā lū kyo' 100*, vol. 1 (Rangoon: Unity, 2010).

91. May Oung, "A Suggestion," *Times of Burma*, August 8, 1900, 5; May Oung, "Education," *Times of Burma*, August 18, 1900, 5; May Oung, "Educational Horror," *Times of Burma*, September 5, 1900, 5; May Oung, "Education," *Times of Burma*, September 12, 1900, 5.

92. May Oung and John S. Furnivall, "The Dawn of Nationalism in Burma: The Modern Burman," *Journal of the Burma Research Society* 33, no. 1 (1950): 4.

93. These concerns were expressed in ways that mirrored colonial officials' complaints against monastic teaching methods—they derided them for focusing on mere chanting without understanding. Sir James George Scott, "Buddhists and Buddhism in Burma," *Cornhill Magazine* 42, no. 252 (1880): 730; *Report on Public Instruction in Burma for the Year 1907–08* (Rangoon: Superintendent, Government Printing, Burma, 1908), Resolution 6. This is not surprising, given the fact that some of the most prominent leaders of the Buddhist associations had been employed by the Department of Public Instruction. U May Oung taught in Moulmein and was later appointed to the Educational Syndicate. U Mon, like U Kyaw Yan, was an inspector of schools and later authored textbooks for the department. While their worries paralleled European dismissals of monastery education, they were not opposed to memorization per se, given the reliance on memorization of both the respected European Classical education and the British pedagogical methods of the day.

94. Taw Sein Ko, "Moral Education in Burma [1883]," in *Burmese Sketches*, vol 1, (Rangoon: British Burma Press, 1913), 229. For more on Taw Sein Ko and his unique interstitial position in Burmese society, see Penny Edwards, "Relocating the Interlocutor: Taw Sein Ko (1864–1930) and the Itinerancy of Knowledge in British Burma," *South East Asia Research* 12, no. 3 (2004): 277–335.

95. "Mrs. M. M. Hla Oung," *Buddhist Review* 2, no. 4 (1910); Co Muṃ Ññaṅ':, *Bamā amyui: sa mi:* (Yangon: Sīha puṃ nhip' tuik', 1976).

96. "Burma Round Table Conference Representation of Women Urged by Various Women's Organisations; Miss May Oung Appointed," 1931, BL IOR/L/PO/9/3 India Office Records Collection, British Library.

97. Ananda Metteyya, "Buddhist Activities," *Buddhism: An Illustrated Quarterly Review* 1, no. 1 (September 1903): 174.

98. "Buddhist Schools," 19.

99. "Advertisement," *Buddhism: An Illustrated Quarterly Review* 1, no. 1 (1902).

100. This was also known as the Sam Buddhaghosa School. Ananda Metteyya, "Buddhist Activities," *Buddhism: An Illustrated Quarterly Review* 1, no. 3 (March 1904): 527; Ngwe Thein, ed., *A Guide to the Pagodas on Moulmein Ridge with Notes on Buddhism and References about Moulmein, Burma* (Moulmein: Mingala Sa Pone Hnep Taik, 1961), 14; Bha San':, *Yakhaṅ' yakhu*

mo'lamruiṅ' samuiṅ': (Moulmein: Ū: Cin' Raṃ aṅ' chan': cā puṃ nhip' tuik', 1949), 137–52; "Buddhasāsanā // Aṅgalip' Mran'mā: 2 bhāsā cā saṅ' kyoṅ': krī: takhu tañ ñ' thoṅ' pru cu ran' lū lrī: lū loṅ': tui. tuiṅ' paṅ' chve: nve: kroṅ':," *Maha-Bodhi News,* March 1, 1902, 8.

101. Bha San':, *Yakhaṅ' yakhu molamruiṅ' samuiṅ':,* 151; Ananda Metteyya, "Buddhist Activities" (1904): 527.

102. For more on U Kyaw Yan, his varied interests, and his nationalist career, see Alicia Turner, "Narratives of Nation, Questions of Community: Examining Burmese Sources without the Lens of Nation," *Journal of Burma Studies* 15, no. 2 (2011): 263–82.

103. Maung Maung Pye, *Burma in the Crucible* (Rangoon: Khittaya Publishing House, 1952); C. P. Khin Maung, *Buddhabhāsā mran'mā msaṅ': myā: ey' aṭṭhuppatti cā taṃ':* (Mandalay: Kū bhan': roṅ': vay: re: cā puṃ nuip' tuik', 1920). Maung Maung Pye and later secondary sources refer to the association as the Buddha Kalyana Metta Association, but their 1897 rules refer to the Kalyanathingaha Society. Kyaw Yan, *Rules of the Kalyanathingaha Society, Myingyan* (Mandalay: Mandalay Times Press, 1897). The *Rules* themselves have not survived, but we have reference to them in *Catalogue of Books and Pamphlets Published in Burma* (Rangoon: Superintendent, Government Printing, Burma).

104. "Myingyan," *Times of Burma,* July 29, 1899, 9.

105. "Wanted: Two Teachers for the Anglo Vernacular School, Myingyan," *Times of Burma,* October 7, 1903, 7; A Sympathizer, "Myingyan," *Burma Echo,* February 29, 1908, 8.

106. Their association took as its patrons Ledi Sayadaw and his associate U Tilawka.

107. Tilawka, *Buddhasāsanānuggahanaya cā taṃ':,* 16–17.

108. See, for example, Kyaw Yan, *Sīla adippāy' laka'svai [Thila Adeikbe Letswe, Handbook on Buddhist precepts]* (Mandalay: Irrawaddy Press, 1901), of which 23,000 copies were published by 1903; Kyaw Yan, *Mhat' krī: tarā rhac' luṃ:* [One hundred and eight things to remember] (Mandalay: Indian Press, 1903). Turner, "Narratives of Nation."

109. "Buddhist Free Schools in Burma," *Mran'mā alaṅ': maggajaṅ':* 3, no. 1 (1914): 125–32. Despite the English title, the article is in Burmese.

110. Ananda Metteyya, "Buddhist Activities" (1903), 168.

111. "Edu: Anglo-Vernacular Boys' School Pyapon," 1910, Series 1/15(E), Accession 3340, File 2E-6(a), Myanmar National Archives, Yangon, Myanmar.

112. At St. Patrick's Catholic School in Moulmein, students organized a Buddhist association and printed a special book for Buddhist students. U Ledi Keikti, *A Book of Instructions for the Religious Guidance of Boys* (Moulmein: Burma Times Press, 1908), found in *Catalogue of Books and Pamphlets Published in Burma,* first quarter of 1909.

113. Colston claims that every neighborhood association with a building ran a free Buddhist school for the children who could not afford another school. E. J.

Colston, "Some Recent Social Movements in Burma," *Asiatic Quarterly Review* 29, no. 57 (1910): 75. It would take more research into these schools to understand their relationship to the precolonial lay house schools and the new Buddhist Anglo-vernacular schools, however it seems clear that they are part of the trend toward seeking Buddhist education outside monasteries.

114. While little has been written about Buddhist schools in this period, the role they played should not be underestimated. Many early nationalists got their start as Buddhist schoolteachers, and students from these schools went on to be nationalist leaders. When students boycotted government and missionary schools during the Rangoon University Strike of 1920, they gravitated toward Buddhist schools as alternatives. This had precedent in earlier school strikes— boys striking at St. John's College in 1907 instead attended Empress Victoria Buddhist Boys' School and the Theosophical School. As striking university students in 1920 established an alternative education system, these Buddhist schools were transformed into the first national schools. Where the Buddhist Anglo-vernacular schools' buildings are still standing today, for instance, the Shin Buddhaghosa School in Moulmein, they are state B.E.H.S. (Basic Education High Schools), a legacy of their status as national schools.

115. The pamphlet was frequently quoted and reprinted, but was predated by very similar and likely more influential calls published in Burmese. Ananda Metteyya, *On Religious Education in Burma*, 2.

116. Tilawka, *Buddhasāsanānuggahanaya cā tam':*.

117. On the fear of moral decline, see Chapter 4 in this volume. The Director of Public Instruction called for a return of religion into education in 1899. "A University for Burma," *Times of Burma*, July 29, 1899, 6.

118. Taw Sein Ko, "Moral Education in Burma [1883]," 227–33; Taw Sein Ko, "Education in Burma: From a Native Point of View," 167–69.

119. F. R. Nethersole, President Pegu Municipality, "Translation of Entries for the Week Ending 15th August 1902 Made in the Register of Preaching in the Municipal Anglo-Vernacular School at Pegu and Copy of Deputy Commissioner's Remarks Thereon, Dated the 18th August 1902, Forwarded for Information with the Suggestion That Identical or Similar Arrangements Might Be Made Throughout Burma in Similar Schools," in *On Religious Education in Burma*, ed. Ananda Metteyya, Publications of the Buddhasasana Samagama 2 (Rangoon: Hanthawaddy, 1902), 18–25.

120. "Introduction of Religious Instruction into Government Vernacular Schools," 1907, Series 1/15(E), Accession 2922, File 2E-6, Myanmar National Archives, Yangon, Myanmar.

121. Smith, *Buddhism and Politics in Burma*, 71.

122. *Report on Public Instruction in Burma for the Year 1909–10* (Rangoon: Superintendent, Government Printing, Burma, 1910), 25.

123. Smith, *Buddhism and Politics in Burma*, 74; "Religious Instruction," *Burman Buddhist* 2, no. 5 (1909): 101–2.

124. *RPI 1909–10,* 1.
125. Smith, *Buddhism and Politics in Burma,* 74. By 1931, religious instruction was actively required by the department for all government and lay schools.
126. Tilawka, *Buddhasāsanānuggahanaya cā tam':.* The annual exams were much in keeping with the contemporary trend toward Pali exams.
127. Minna G. Cowan, *The Education of the Women of India* (London: Oliphant, Anderson & Ferrier, 1912), 234–35. This may have been related to Col. H. S. Olcott's *Buddhist Catechism;* there is not enough in the quotation to compare. Olcott's *Buddhist Catechism;* was first published in Burmese in 1886. Henry Steele Olcott, *Buddhabhāsā ame: aphra kyam':* (Rangoon: Maung Po O, 1886).
128. Saya Wa's curriculum substitutes a life of the Buddha for the second standard and puts the qualities of the Three Gems and the *awkatha* in the third standard and the Five Precepts in the fourth standard. Wa, *Buddhabhāsā san' khan': cā dutiya tan': mha catuttha tan':* (Rangoon: Superintendent, Government Printing and Stationery, 1939). U Mon was retired from the Department of Public Instruction and a supporter of the Rangoon College Buddhist Association. His textbook does not specify a grade level, but covers many of the same topics. Mon, *Buddhabhāsāmūla akhre pra kyam': cā,* 4th ed. (Rangoon: British Burma Press, 1915). *Teacher's Handbook on Buddhist Religious Instruction High Department* (Rangoon: Superintendent, Government Printing and Stationery Burma, 1934); Nethersole, "Preaching in the School at Pegu"; Kyaw Dun, *Report of the Committee Appointed to Consider and Report upon Buddhist Religious Instruction for Buddhist Pupils in Vernacular Lay Schools under Buddhist Management 1928–29* (Rangoon: Superintendent, Government Printing and Stationery, Burma, 1931).
129. Many of those who were leaders in the efforts to create Buddhist Anglo-vernacular schools had worked for the Department of Public Instruction themselves and were well versed in both its methods and its failings.
130. H. Fielding Hall, *A People at School* (London: Macmillan and Co., 1906), 251–52.

CHAPTER 4: MORALS, CONDUCT, AND COMMUNITY

1. "Rangoon Institutions," *Our Monthly: A Magazine of General Literature* 2, no. 1 (1883).
2. "Meiktila," *Times of Burma,* July 25, 1900, 6.
3. E. J. Colston, "Some Recent Social Movements in Burma," *Journal of the Burma Society* 1, no. 1 (1910): 43.
4. Benedict R. Anderson, *Imagined Communities: Reflections on the Origin and Spread of Nationalism,* rev. and ext. ed. (London: Verso, 1991).
5. "Meiktila," *Times of Burma,* July 25, 1900, 6.

6. Ibid. For a broader discussion of similar organizations, including those in Prome and Thonze, see Colston, "Some Recent Social Movements in Burma," 43–44.

7. A Correspondent, "Minbu," *Times of Burma,* September 4, 1901, 6.

8. "Buddhist Revival in Burma," *Times of India,* April 9, 1907, 9.

9. Win Mar, "The Role of the Malunze Rice Offering Society in Propagating the Buddha Sasana" (master's thesis, Mandalay University, 1996); Mandalay Malunze Rice Donating Society, *Mantale: mrui. ma lvan' jhe: chan' lhū asaṅ': krī: nhac'-100-praññ'. cā coṅ'* (Mandalay: Ma lvan' jhe: chan' lhū asaṅ':, 1996).

10. Ananda Metteyya, "Buddhist Activities," *Buddhism: An Illustrated Quarterly Review* 1, no. 1 (September 1903); "Mandalay," *Times of Burma,* August 4, 1900, 6.

11. These preachers could explain philosophical concepts to the laity in simplified Burmese. Whereas preaching had previously been dominated by recitation with the face of the preacher obscured behind a fan, associations like the Dhammathawana promoted preachers as orators who were able to charismatically hold the interest of large groups, "bringing home the truths of the law to their minds in plain, earnest language." "Modern Preaching," *Burman Buddhist* 1, no. 3 (1908).

12. Ibid. For a comparative perspective on the history of Buddhist preaching, see Mahinda Deegalle, *Popularizing Buddhism: Preaching as Performance in Sri Lanka* (Albany: SUNY Press, 2006).

13. A Buddhist, "Selarakkheta Society," *Times of Burma,* March 20, 1901, 6.

14. Colston, "Some Recent Social Movements in Burma," 44.

15. *Catalogue of Books and Pamphlets Published in Burma* (Rangoon: Superintendent, Government Printing, Burma, 1902–3), 1st quarter 1902, 2nd quarter 1903.

16. The only former member of the royal court listed as influencing the Buddhist associations was the Kinwun Mingyi, and even this was a limited role, acting as host to negotiations on the recognition of the Thathanabaing.

17. The overarching emphasis was on male leadership and male behavior, but a few women rose to prominence, and others created separate organizations for women. Daw Mya May was the patron and treasurer of the Buddhasasana Samagama (International Buddhist Society). *Revised Prospectus of the Buddhasasana Samagama,* Publications of the Buddhasasana Samagama, 1a (Rangoon: Hanthawaddy Press, 1903). There are a few reports of separate women's Buddhist associations prior to 1920. The earliest of these was a Ladies' Auxiliary of the Arakan Maha-Bodhi Society in Akyab founded in 1893. "Ladies Branch of the Maha Bodhi Society," *Journal of the Maha-Bodhi Society* 1, no. 9 (1893). There are scattered reports like those of nuns teaching Buddhist girls in 1906: "Mran'mā lū myui: min' ma kale: tui. buddhabhāsā cā saṅ' kyoṅ': nhaṅ'. cap' lyaññ': so akroṅ':," *Hanthawaddy Weekly Review,* December 22, 1906, 615. The earliest report of a Paramattha Kummari or Young Women's Buddhist Association (YWBA) is in Rangoon in 1907. *Burma Echo,* June 8, 1907, 9. Very lit-

tle has survived on the earliest history of the YWBA and related associations. On gender in colonial Burma generally, see Chie Ikeya, *Refiguring Women, Colonialism, and Modernity in Burma,* Southeast Asia—Politics, Meaning, Memory (Honolulu: University of Hawai'i Press, 2011).

18. The boom in Buddhist associations started a decade before the Japanese victory over the Russians, but Colston's comments capture the sense that this was a Burmese incarnation of a broader spirit of the age. Colston, "Some Recent Social Movements in Burma," 43.

19. While the loss of the king, and royal financial patronage, did constitute a material loss for Buddhism, historians would be hard pressed to identify a decline in lay or monastic enthusiasm, activity, or daily practice in this period to match the claims of Buddhism in despair. In fact, as I hope to demonstrate, quite the opposite was true.

20. The technology of the membership association allowed Buddhists to imagine otherwise unseen connections in much the same way as Benedict Anderson has described the role of print media. On the role of publishing in the formation of nationalist identities, see Anderson, *Imagined Communities.*

21. See, for example, Taw Sein Ko, ed., *The Kalyani Inscriptions Erected by King Dhammaceti at Pegu in 1476 AD, Text and Translation* (Rangoon: Superintendent, Government Printing, Burma, 1892), 44.

22. To put the importance of the names of subscribers and donors in perspective, the names of the monks themselves were not listed, only the number of monks per named monastery.

23. "Vattukaṃ nve pañ' ñve rañ':," *Mandalay Pariyatti Thathanahita Society Monthly Journal* (1908): 13–20.

24. Their first issue listed 103 members, taking up one-third of the total pages. "Asañ': lū krī: myā: rañ':," *Dhammadesanā tarā: satañ': cā* 1, no. 1 (1909): 17–24. *Thila shin* (lay nuns) were included in this list of female donors; monks were listed only as recipients.

25. The Buddhasasana Samagama (International Buddhist Society) listed the amount collected at the Buddhist Girls' School. *Revised Prospectus of the Buddhasasana Samagama,* 1a, xiv.

26. On the census as colonial technology, see Bernard S. Cohn, *Colonialism and Its Forms of Knowledge: The British in India* (Princeton, NJ: Princeton University Press, 1996); Nicholas B. Dirks, *Castes of Mind: Colonialism and the Making of Modern India* (Princeton, NJ: Princeton University Press, 2001), chap. 10. On the panopticon, see Michel Foucault, *Discipline and Punish: The Birth of the Prison,* 2nd Vintage Books ed. (New York: Vintage Books, 1995).

27. Mary Poovey, *Making a Social Body: British Cultural Formation, 1830–1864* (Chicago: University of Chicago Press, 1995).

28. Charles J. F. Smith Forbes, *British Burma and Its People: Being Sketches of Native Manners, Customs and Religion* (London: Murray, 1878), 45–46.

29. Taw Sein Ko, "Moral Education in Burma [1883]," in *Burmese Sketches*, vol. 1 (Rangoon: British Burma Press, 1913).

30. "Im' rhe. uparājāvela maṅ': sā: smī: to' tui. akroṅ': nhaṅ' mān' māna thoṅ' lhvā: rwe. mhā: yvaṅ': so mran'mā lū myui: tui ey' ayū vāda akroṅ':," *Hanthawaddy Weekly Review,* June 2, 1900, 162.

31. "Laṅ' yokyā: tui. ey' kyaṅ'. vat' ma myā: min': ma tui. kyaṅ': vat' myā: akroṅ':," *Hanthawaddy Weekly Review,* April 6, 1901, 523; "Se raññ' se rak' kui sok' cā pai khraṅ': mha pa pyok' ran' akroṅ':," *Maha-Bodhi News,* June 28, 1902, 74–75; "Kui: kvay saññ' bhāsā tui: tak' ran' kram rvay khraṅ': Propagation of Religion," *Hanthawaddy Weekly Review,* April 5, 1905, 878.

32. Ian Brown has written on the relationship between this perception and reality. Official government discourse labeled Burma as the most criminal province in the empire, and the Burmese dacoit became the image of savage criminality in the British imaginary. As Brown has noted, seeing Burma as the most criminal province, a discourse supported by the fact that the British imprisoned a greater percentage of the population in Burma than anywhere else, was not far removed from seeing the Burmese as the most criminal race in the empire. However, prison officials tended to resist this racialist interpretation in favor of schemes that explained Burmese criminality in terms of circumstances. Ian Brown, "A Commissioner Calls: Alexander Paterson and Colonial Burma's Prisons," *Journal of Southeast Asian Studies* 38, no. 2 (2007): 293–308. Any discussion of an increase in crime should take into account the classification of violent resistance to colonial rule that persisted despite British "pacification" campaigns.

33. Taw Sein Ko, "Moral Education in Burma [1883]."

34. Taw Sein Ko [Rambler, pseud.], "Education in Burma: From a Native Point of View," *Our Monthly: A Magazine of General Literature* 2, no. 5 (1883): 167–68. On peashooters, see *Times of Burma,* September 16, 1899, 9.

35. Drunkenness and arrests: A Sympathizer, "Myingyan," *Burma Echo,* February 29, 1908, 8; Gambling arrests: "Pokukku," *Burma Echo,* January 18, 1908, 11.

36. Morals, "The Educational Horror," *Times of Burma,* November 21, 1900, 5.

37. Morals, "The Educational Horror," *Times of Burma,* January 5, 1901, 5.

38. Silacara and G. R. T. Ross, *The Fifth Precept and Social Service,* Rangoon College Buddhist Association Publications (Rangoon: Sun Press, 1912), 12–13.

39. Maurizio Peleggi, "Refashioning Civilization: Dress and Bodily Practice in Thai Nation-Building," in *The Politics of Dress in Asia and America,* ed. Mina Roces and Louise Edwards (Brighton: Sussex Academic Press, 2009), 65–80; Thongchai Winichakul, "The Quest for 'Siwilai': A Geographical Discourse of Civilizational Thinking in the Late Nineteenth and Early Twentieth-Century Siam," *Journal of Asian Studies* 59, no. 3 (2000).

40. Maurizio Peleggi, *Lords of Things: The Fashioning of the Siamese Monarchy's Modern Image* (Honolulu: University of Hawai'i Press, 2002), 3; Craig J.

Reynolds, "Thai Manual Knowledge: Theory and Practice," in *Seditious Histories: Contesting Thai and Southeast Asian Pasts* (Seattle: University of Washington Press, 2006), 235–39.

41. Penny Edwards, *Cambodge: The Cultivation of a Nation, 1860–1945,* Southeast Asia—Politics, Meaning, Memory (Honolulu: University of Hawai'i Press, 2007), 114–21; Anne Ruth Hansen, *How to Behave: Buddhism and Modernity in Colonial Cambodia, 1860–1930,* Southeast Asia—Politics, Meaning, Memory (Honolulu: University of Hawai'i Press, 2007), chaps. 3 and 5.

42. Richard Gombrich and Gananath Obeyesekere, *Buddhism Transformed: Religious Change in Sri Lanka* (Princeton, NJ: Princeton University Press, 1988), 213–15.

43. Carol Anderson, " 'For Those Who Are Ignorant:' A Study of the *Bauddha Ādahilla*," in *Consituting Communities: Theravāda Buddhism and the Religious Cultures of South and Southeast Asia,* ed. John Holt and Jacob Kinnard (Albany: SUNY Press, 2003), 171–88.

44. Stephen Prothero, "Henry Steel Olcott and 'Protestant Buddhism,'" *Journal of the American Academy of Religion* 63, no. 2 (1995): 296–99.

45. Poovey, *Making a Social Body,* chaps. 1 and 2.

46. Jean Comaroff and John L. Comaroff, *Of Revelation and Revolution: The Dialectics of Modernity on a South African Frontier,* vol. 2 (Chicago: University of Chicago Press, 1997).

47. Ibid., 2:31.

48. On Buddhist complaints about serving meat to monks in the 1880s, see Taw Sein Ko [Rambler, pseud.], "My Visit to the Kyoungs on the Day of the Thadingyoot Festival," *Our Monthly: A Magazine of General Literature* 2, no. 11 (1883).

49. "Akyab," *Burma Echo,* November 2, 1907, 11.

50. An 1894 text by the Maha Withuddhayon Sayadaw, entitled *Gonamātikā ovādakathā kyam'ː,* was republished six times between 1900 and 1907, and was likely equally influential. Mahāvisuddhārum charā to' burā: krī:, *Gonamātikā ovādakathā kyam'ː* (Rangoon: Amyui: sā: cā pum nhip' tuik', 1907). For the frequent reprint history, see *Catalogue of Books and Pamphlets Published in Burma.* Ledi Sayadaw produced at least three texts on the issue in this period. In addition to the 1885 letter, he published the *Ahaya dīpanī kyam'ː* [Diet as treated from a religious point of view] in 1903 and the *Gonasura dīpanī kyam'ː* [Protest against cow slaughter and consumption of intoxicating liquors] in 1907.

51. See, for example, this 1901 article in the Burmese-language *Hanthawaddy* newspaper: "Nvā: / kyvai / chit' / vak' tui. kui sak' phrat' cā: so' khrań': mha krań' rhoń' ran' asanā: kham cā: akroń'ː," *Hanthawaddy Weekly Review,* June 8, 1901, 598–99.

52. The genre of writing in the voice of animals was used in the cow protection movement as well (Cassie Adcock, Personal Communication, April 2012). A similar appeal appears briefly in Ledi Sayadaw's *Nvā: metta cā:.*

53. "The Animals' Petition to Buddhists," *Times of Burma*, August 29, 1903, 7. The Burmese original first appeared in Mandalay. This English translation of the petition originally appeared in the *Rangoon Gazette* and was reprinted in the *Bangkok Times and Weekly Mail*, August 8, 1903, 7–8.

54. Peter Harvey, *An Introduction to Buddhism: Teachings, History, and Practices* (New York: Cambridge University Press, 1990), 203–4.

55. Ibid.

56. "The Animals' Petition to Buddhists," *Times of Burma*, August 29, 1903, 7.

57. The Burmese movement against meat eating had certain elements in common with European vegetarian movements. There are direct parallels and influences between Burmese Buddhist vegetarianism and the cow protection movement in this period. Leela Gandhi has described the conflict between the utilitarian movement led by the Royal Society for the Prevention of Cruelty to Animals (RSPCA), which sought to punish mainly the working poor for their treatment of animals, and more socialist and anarchist-oriented vegetarian movements, exemplified by the Humanitarian League, which were anti-imperialist. She argues that Mohandas Gandhi's interactions with the latter influenced his ideas of *ahimsa*. Leela Gandhi, *Affective Communities: Anticolonial Thought, Fin-De-Siècle Radicalism, and the Politics of Friendship* (Durham, NC: Duke University Press, 2006), chap. 4. The Buddhist movement in Burma would have interacted with branches of the former and perhaps the latter. They much more strongly resembled the latter in their anticolonial thrust and their focus on individual moral action rather than juridical intervention. The RSPCA had active branches in Burma at the turn of the twentieth century, particularly for legally prosecuting the working poor for the mistreatment of work animals. "S.P.C.A.," *Times of Burma Weekly Summary*, March 24, 1906, 12; "SPCA Rangoon Magistrates Honorary Court," *Burma Echo*, June 8, 1907, 9. There was a Burma Humanitarian League founded in Rangoon in 1923 as well, which was still active as a Buddhist organization in 2005.

58. Hansen, *How to Behave*, 77.

59. Recall the *Anāgata vaṃsa* descriptions of lax monks and monastic practice that precipitated the decline of the *sāsana*, discussed in Chapter 2. On Shwegyin discourse about the decline of the *sāsana* as a rationale for reform and continued strict adherence in performance, see Jason Carbine, *Sons of the Buddha: Continuities and Ruptures in a Burmese Monastic Tradition*, Religion and Society (New York: Walter de Gruyter, 2011).

60. Edward Michael Mendelson, *Sangha and State in Burma: A Study of Monastic Sectarianism and Leadership*, ed. John P. Ferguson (Ithaca, NY: Cornell University Press, 1975), 58–61; Alexey Kirichenko, "The Making of a Culprit: Atula Hsayadaw Shin Yasa and the Politics of Monastic Reform in Eighteenth-Century Burma," *Journal of Burma Studies* 15, no. 2 (2011): 189–229.

61. Mohan Wijayarantna, *Buddhist Monastic Life According to the Texts of the Theravāda Tradition,* trans. Claude Grangier and Steven Collins (New York: Cambridge University Press, 1990), 32, chap. 3.

62. In Ceylon, performance was the central issue in the conflicts over ordination procedures. Kitsiri Malalgoda, *Buddhism in Sinhalese Society, 1750–1900: A Study of Religious Revival and Change* (Berkeley: University of California Press, 1976), 55–57, 68–69, 125–26, 53–58. In Ceylon, the one-shoulder/two-shoulder controversy continued into the late nineteenth century. See Anne M. Blackburn, *Locations of Buddhism: Colonialism and Modernity in Sri Lanka* (Chicago: University of Chicago Press, 2010), 90–103. The formation of the Thammayut sect in Siam highlighted conduct by adopting the Mon manner of wearing robes and carrying bowls. Craig J. Reynolds, "The Buddhist Monkhood in Nineteenth Century Thailand" (PhD diss., Cornell University, 1972).

63. Alexey Kirichenko, *New Spaces for Interaction: Contacts between Burmese and Sinhalese Monks in the Late Nineteenth and Early Twentieth Centuries,* Asia Research Institute Working Paper Series (Singapore: Asia Research Institute, National University of Singapore, 2012).

64. Monks carried on their sectarian debates about performance, and there was a concern about lax, lazy, and political monks among both Burmese and European publics, but these were not given the same emphasis as issues of lay behavior.

65. Laypeople are to abstain from (1) taking life, (2) taking what is not given, (3) sexual impropriety, (4) lying, and (5) the use of intoxicants. On special occasions, they may undertake three further precepts, abstaining from (6) eating after noon, (7) entertainments and adornments, and (8) the use of high and soft seats. For novices, the third precept is a prohibition of all sexual activity, the seventh is divided into two, and a precept is added disallowing the use of money.

66. Harvey, *Introduction to Buddhism,* 199–208.

67. There are numerous reports of bullet-repelling protective tattoos in the nineteenth century. Although none discuss the necessity of keeping a precept, we know from contemporary sources that this was the source of their power. Perhaps the native informants were unwilling to divulge this information to Europeans perceived as potentially threatening. Nicola Beth Tannenbaum, *Who Can Compete against the World? Power-Protection and Buddhism in Shan Worldview* (Ann Arbor, MI: Association for Asian Studies, 1995), 88–89. Shan men in her study often undertook the third precept to refrain from adultery.

68. While Tannenbaum makes a distinction between the use of precepts for this type of power and the notions of morality (men usually seek these tattoos in order to be able to breach other aspects of morality—either as soldiers or thieves), there is a strong parallel in how keeping precepts operated for the individual.

69. "Moulmein," *Burma Echo,* December 7, 1907, 10.

70. "Akyab," *Burma Echo,* January 18, 1908, 10.
71. "Twante," *Burma Echo,* July 6, 1907, 9.
72. "Henzada," *Burma Echo,* May 9, 1908, 9.
73. If the accounts of attendance are correct, Ledi Sayadaw and U Wayama each drew a third of the local Buddhist population to their events; according to the 1911 census, the Buddhist population of Akyab was just over seventeen thousand and Moulmein's Buddhist population was twenty-two thousand. C. Morgan Webb, ed., *Census of India, 1911: Burma,* Part 2—Tables (Rangoon: Superintendent, Government Printing, Burma 1912), 18–19.
74. "Insein," *Burma Echo,* December 7, 1907, 11.
75. Preparations for these events required months of organizing, and the decision to invite a preacher was a matter of some public discussion. Buddhist associations were central to the preparations and played an important role in the event. The women of the Paramattha Thankheip associations escorted Ledi Sayadaw on his arrival and departure, and the boys of the local Anglo-vernacular Boys' School flanked U Dhammaloka.
76. "Bassein," *Burma Echo,* June 22, 1907, 8.
77. Ibid.
78. This Buddhist preaching campaign and others in the prison had the strong support of both the Muslim jailor and the European colonial officials.
79. In the colonies, reformers argued that British policy had precipitated the problem: intoxicants were regulated and a significant source of revenue for the colonial state. The British created an elaborate set of rules about who could and could not purchase alcohol and opium from licensed vendors based on a constructed anthropology of abstaining and nonabstaining races. In practice, however, British regulation brought greater availability and use to the population in Burma. Only those groups that the British understood to have had a tradition of drinking or using opium prior to colonial intervention could legally do so in British territory. However, British control of parts of Lower Burma since 1825 created an exception. This produced a complicated set of regulations in which alcohol could be sold to Chinese, Europeans, and Indians in Upper Burma, but not to Burmese, whereas it was legal to sell alcohol to Burmese in Lower Burma. Opium could be sold only to Chinese in Upper Burma, but was legal for Burmese in Lower Burma. W. R. Winston, *Four Years in Upper Burma* (London: C. H. Kelly, 1892), 88–89, see also chaps. 8 and 9.
80. Brian Howard Harrison, *Drink and the Victorians: The Temperance Question in England, 1815–1872,* 2nd ed. (Staffordshire, UK: Keele University Press, 1994).
81. Ibid., 123–26.
82. Amanda Claybaugh, *The Novel of Purpose: Literature and Social Reform in the Anglo-American World* (Ithaca, NY: Cornell University Press, 2007), 93.
83. Ibid.

84. Harrison, *Drink and the Victorians,* 124.

85. Anne Hansen describes how Ukñā Suttantaprījā Ind used the issue of alcohol and opium as part of his social critique and the creation of modern Buddhist ethics in Cambodia. Hansen, *How to Behave,* 69–72. On Sri Lanka, see A. P. Kannangara, "The Riots of 1915 in Sri Lanka: A Study in the Roots of Communal Violence," *Past and Present* 102 (1984): 130–65; John Rogers, "Cultural Nationalism and Social Reform: The 1904 Temperance Movement in Sri Lanka," *Indian Economic and Social History Review* 23, no. 3 (1989): 319–41.

86. Prohibition—that is, seeking government intervention—was not the focus of any Burmese movement up to 1920. There was one call for government intervention when Arakanese leaders petitioned the chief commissioner in 1864 to curtail the sale of alcohol and opium. Winston, *Four Years in Upper Burma,* 86. On the other hand, Burmese women, and Christian converts in particular, were strong supporters of the Women's Christian Temperance Union's Polyglot Petition, which called for international prohibition. Ian R. Tyrrell, *Woman's World/Woman's Empire: The Woman's Christian Temperance Union in International Perspective, 1800–1930* (Chapel Hill: University of North Carolina Press, 1991), 39–45; Joan W. Swift, *Hattie: A Woman's Mission to Burma* (San Geronimo, CA: Half Meadow Press, 2003), 202–5.

87. "Se rañ' se rak' kui sok' cā pai khran': mha pa pyok' ran' akron':," *Maha-Bodhi News,* June 28, 1902, 74–75; "The Drink Evil," *Burman Buddhist* 1, no. 5 (1908).

88. "Y.M.B.A. Conference," *Burman Buddhist* 5, no. 1 (1911).

89. Kyaw Yan, *Surāmeraya-pakāsanī kyam':* [*Thura meraya pakathani kyan* Treatise on intoxicating liquors], 2nd ed. (Mandalay: Society for Promoting Buddhism Press, 1917). On the Burman Youth's Temperance League, see Rangoon College Buddhist Association, *A Compilation of Lectures* (Rangoon: Sun Press, 1914). The copy I work from here was found at the Universities Central Library, likely an inheritance from the Rangoon College Buddhist Association library. I found it in 2005 with the pages uncut. Perhaps the students of Rangoon College were already so morally pure that its mere presence was sufficient, because it had spent the past century unread. This cannot have been the case for all of the copies because it was reprinted in multiple editions.

90. Alicia Turner, "Narratives of Nation, Questions of Community: Examining Burmese Sources without the Lens of Nation," *Journal of Burma Studies* 15, no. 2 (2011).

91. The text is divided into two sections, "The Benefits of Refraining from Drinking Intoxicants According to the Buddha's *Sāsana*" and "The Consequences of Drinking According to the Observations and Conclusions of Educated Medical Doctors."

92. Kyaw Yan, *Surāmeraya-pakāsanī kyam':* [*Thura meraya pakathani kyan* Treatise on intoxicating liquors], 9–14. My translation. The list form may remind twenty-first-century readers of the contemporary self-help genre, which itself

is the heir of Victorian moralist literature, but it is important to remember that numbered lists are very common in Buddhist literature as a mnemonic and analytic technique.

93. Ibid., 11–14. Following the concerns about the morals of entertainment, they "indulge in festivals and performances" (11–13). The benefits of not drinking, in contrast, include mental health, the ability to avoid dangers, good merit, virtue, and noble thoughts, as well as being decisive, intelligent, and well educated (17–18).

94. Ibid., 20–27.

95. Silacara, *Panca Sila: The Five Precepts* (Rangoon: The Buddhist Theosophical Federation, Burma, 1911), 48.

96. Silacara and Ross, *The Fifth Precept and Social Service,* 43.

97. The sermon was published in *Dhammadethana* magazine: Ledi Sayadaw, "Yac' myui: tarā: to'," *Dhammadesanā tarā: satan': cā* 1, no. 4 (1908): 93–97. The sermon is just one of a number of texts Ledi Sayadaw produced on alcohol. His 1886 letter is also based on the *Vipāka Sutta* verse. See Ledi Sayadaw, "Cuin' pran' se rann' se rak' aettā cā," in *Gambhīra kabyā kyam':* (Yangon: Myat' chu mvan' cā pe thut', 2004 [1886]), 15–18. His more famous treatise on cows, the *Goṇasura dīpanī kyam':,* dealt significantly with issues of alcohol and gambling as well. Portions of the *Goṇasura dīpanī kyam':* are translated in Ledi Sayadaw, *A Talk on Intoxicants and Gambling,* trans. Bhikkhu Pesala (Middlesex, UK: Association for Insight Meditation, 2002). He also wrote a letter on intoxicants from Depayin in 1887: Ledi Sayadaw, "Dīpa ran': se rann' se rak' mettā cā," in *Gambhīra kabyā kyam':* (Yangon: Mrat' chu mvan'cā pe thut', 2004 [1887]), 19–25. My thanks to Erik Braun for bringing these last three sources to my attention.

98. For a discussion of Ledi Sayadaw's preaching tours, see Htay Htay Lwin, "History of the Maha Ledi Sasana" (master's thesis, Mandalay University, 1998), chap. 3.

99. For the recent excellent biography of Ledi Sayadaw, see Erik Braun, *The Birth of Insight: Meditation, Modern Buddhism and the Burmese Monk Ledi Sayadaw,* Buddhism and Modernity (Chicago: University of Chicago Press, 2013).

100. Colston, "Some Recent Social Movements in Burma," 46.

101. Ledi Sayadaw, "Yac' Myui: Tarā: To'," 93. The English is my translation of Ledi Sayadaw's Burmese translation of the Pali.

102. Ibid.

103. Ibid., 94. My translation.

104. Ibid., 93–94.

105. Ibid., 94–95. He specifically identified the Chin, Kachin, and Karen as examples of uncivilized people. The ethnic categorization of "civilization" in the Buddhist literature of the period prefigures a strand of contemporary Buddhist rhetoric on ethnicity and deserves further study.

106. He pointed out that Christians knew these problematic spirits by the names devil, evil spirits, and Satan.
107. Judith L. Richell, *Disease and Demography in Colonial Burma* (Singapore: NUS Press 2006), chap. 5.
108. "Bassein," *Burma Echo*, June 22, 1907, 8.
109. Ledi Sayadaw, "Yac' myui: tarā: to'," 95–97.
110. Ibid., 96. My translation.
111. Ibid.

CHAPTER 5: THE SHOE AND THE *SHIKHO*

1. "Moulmein," *Times of Burma*, August 19, 1899, 7.
2. D., "Boots, Shoes, Slippers and Squatters," *Our Monthly: A Magazine of General Literature* 1, no. 12 (1882): 356–58.
3. "The Wearing of Shoes," 1868, Series 1/1/(A), Accession 1155, File 84, Myanmar National Archives, Yangon, Myanmar; "Native Gentlemen Wearing Shoes at Receptions," 1867, Series 1/1/(A), Accession 1162, File 91(1), Myanmar National Archives, Yangon, Myanmar.
4. "The Wearing of Shoes." Fytche was not alone in his concerns. The decision remained controversial into the twentieth century elsewhere in India. See the concern raised in Gujurat in 1906: "Article in a Gujirate Newspaper Praja Bandhu on Orders Regarding the Wearing of Shoes by Indians on Official Occasions," 1906, BL IOR/L/PJ/6/747, File 505, India Office Records Collection, British Library.
5. Earl H. Pritchard, "The Kotow in the Macartney Embassy to China in 1793," *Far Eastern Quarterly* 2, no. 2 (1943): 163–203; M. K. Gandhi, *An Autobiography: The Story of My Experiments with Truth* (Boston: Beacon Press, 1957).
6. Thongchai Winichakul, "The Quest for 'Siwilai': A Geographical Discourse of Civilizational Thinking in the Late Nineteenth and Early Twentieth-Century Siam," *Journal of Asian Studies* 59, no. 3 (2000): 528–49; Maurizio Peleggi, *Lords of Things: The Fashioning of the Siamese Monarchy's Modern Image* (Honolulu: University of Hawai'i Press, 2002).
7. The suggestion was reported in a tract dedicated to protesting the demeaning requirement that Burmese staff *shikho* (perform a prostrating bow, discussed extensively later in this chapter) their European superiors in places of employment. Its English-educated authors attributed such a symbolic inversion to "misguided and uneducated Burmans." Given the Burmese sense of humor and tradition of comedy in opposition to authority, it seems likely that the interpretation had widespread circulation, even if the elite sought to downplay it in their English-language publication. Burma Social Association, ed., *The Shoe and the Shitko* (Rangoon: Burma Social Association, 1913), viii.

8. E. D. Cuming, *In the Shadow of the Pagoda: Sketches of Burmese Life and Character* (London: W. H. Allen & Co., 1893), 25.

9. Talal Asad, "Religion, Nation-State, Secularism," in *Nation and Religion: Perspectives on Europe and Asia,* ed. Peter van der Veer and Harmut Lehmann (Princeton, NJ: Princeton University Press, 1999), 185.

10. Shwe Waing et al., "The Rangoon Collegiate School," *Times of Burma,* October 3, 1903, 6.

11. "The Strike of School-Masters," *Times of Burma,* September 12, 1903, 5. Given the ambiguities of colonial-era orthography, *shikho* was transliterated variously as "shikho," "shiko," "shikoe," "shickho" and "shitko."

12. "Respect Wanted!," *Times of Burma,* August 15, 1903, 4–5.

13. "Akyab," *Times of Burma,* September 2, 1903, 5; "Prome," *Times of Burma,* August 29, 1903, 5.

14. "Education in Burma: The Shikoing Order," *Times of India,* August 19, 1903, 5.

15. Shwe Waing et al., "The Rangoon Collegiate School," *Times of Burma,* October 3, 1903, 6; "Shikoing: The Last Circular," *Times of Burma,* August 22, 1903, 7.

16. "The Strike of School-Masters," *Times of Burma,* September 12, 1903, 5.

17. "Fabricating 'Respect,'" *Times of Burma,* August 19, 1903, 4–5.

18. "The Strike of School-Masters," *Times of Burma,* September 12, 1903, 5. This article sides strongly with the boys, agreeing that "we do not think that the school-boys will improve their intellectual studies by witnessing the strike of their school masters, unless the Director of Public Instruction intend on converting the Government Collegiate School into a training school for turning out labor agitators, strike organizers, agents for closing industries or the like." However, given the precedent that this strike set for later student strikes, including the 1920 Rangoon University Boycott, it seems likely that this is exactly what the boys gained from the experience.

19. "Advertisement," *Times of Burma,* October 7, 1903, 4.

20. G. C. S. Boys, "Plea of School Boys," *Times of Burma,* August 15, 1903, 3.

21. "Prome," *Times of Burma,* August 29, 1903, 5.

22. When the issue of the *shikho* was raised again in 1912, not in the context of *shikho*ing teachers, but regarding the "official *shikho*" extracted by European and Burmese superiors from their inferiors in government offices and businesses, the *shikho* was not taken as a Buddhist practice. Instead, young urban Burmese agitators argued that the Burmese modernization meant that the *shikho* had ceased to accomplish any demonstration of respect and only degraded the performer. Burma Social Association, *The Shoe and the Shitko.*

23. G. C. S. Boys, "Plea of School Boys," *Times of Burma,* August 15, 1903, 3.

24. Ibid.

25. Ibid.; Taw Sein Ko, "The Origin and Development of the Shiko [1903]," in *Burmese Sketches,* vol. 1 (Rangoon: British Burma Press, 1913); Ananda Metteyya,

"Notes and News: The 'Shikho' in Public Schools," *Buddhism: An Illustrated Quarterly Review* 1, no. 1 (September 1903): 151–53.

26. My thanks to F. K. Lehman for his assistance in understanding the history of this issue.

27. The *Times of Burma* reprinted the comments from the *Rangoon Gazette*. "Respect Wanted," *Times of Burma*, August 15, 1903, 3.

28. "Fabricating 'Respect,'" *Times of Burma*, August 19, 1903, 4–5.

29. Anti Shikoe, "The Mystic 'Shikoe,'" *Times of Burma*, August 22, 1903, 5; Cosmopolite, "Fabricating 'Respect,'" *Times of Burma*, August 19, 1903, 5.

30. Anti Shikoe, "The Mystic 'Shikoe,'" *Times of Burma*, August 22, 1903, 5.

31. "Bhamo (the Heathen Shikho!)," *Times of Burma*, October 7, 1903, 5.

32. "All About a Law-Book," *Times of Burma*, October 21, 1903, 4–5.

33. See, for example, John F. Cady, *A History of Modern Burma* (Ithaca, NY: Cornell University Press, 1958); Tin Phone Nwe, "Vuiṅ' am' bhī 'e [YMBA] kho' buddhakalyāṇayuva asaṅ': ey' lhup' rhā: mhu samuiṅ': 1906–1920" (master's thesis, Rangoon University, 1973).

34. Khin Maung Nyunt, "The 'Shoe Question' (or the Loss and Regaining of Our Independence)," *Guardian* 17, no. 2 (February 1970).

35. He removed his shoes only after he had arrived at the brick wall indicating the *parivena* perimeter and entered.

36. The criticism that gave his sect its name and made him a controversial figure among the laity of Lower Burma was Okpo Sayadaw's insistence on a particular formulation for a recitation used by the laity before taking the precepts. He argued that the correct formulation was not the common "I worship the Buddha, the Dhamma and the Sangha, with the actions (Burmese: *kan*) of my body, with the actions (*kan*) of my mouth and with the actions (*kan*) of my mind." Instead the word *kan* should be replaced with *dwaya*, or means, to highlight that merit is produced not by action, but by the mental intention that preceded action. On this history see: Taṅ' Chve, *Mahādvāranikāya sāsanavaṃsadīpanī* (Rangoon: Ledi Mandain Press, 1974).

37. Ledi Sayadaw, *Sāsanavisodhanī* [*Thathanawithodhani*] (Rangoon: Hanthawaddy, 1954 [1919]), 2:212.

38. "Wearing Shoes in Pagodas," 1919, Series 1/15(D), Accession 1330, File 2P-45, Myanmar National Archives, Yangon, Myanmar.

39. "Shoes at Shwedagon," *Times of Burma*, March 6, 1901, 4–5.

40. "The Shwe Dagon Pagoda," *Times of Burma*, June 15, 1901, 4.

41. "The Shoe Question," *Times of Burma*, May 29, 1901, 4.

42. Alicia Turner, "The Irish Pongyi in Colonial Burma: The Confrontations and Challenges of U Dhammaloka," *Contemporary Buddhism* 11, no. 2 (2010): 149–71; Alicia Turner, Laurence Cox, and Brian Bocking, "Beachcombing, Going Native and Freethinking: Rewriting the History of Early Western Buddhist Monastics," *Contemporary Buddhism* 11, no. 2 (2010): 125–47.

43. "[Concerning the Issue of Europeans Wearing Shoes at the Shwedagon Pagoda],"
Hanthawaddy Weekly Review, May 18, 1901, 570. My thanks to Bo Bo Lasin
for his assistance in locating the articles in the *Hanthawaddy Weekly Review*
for 1901.

44. Later letters to the editor and articles in the *Hanthawaddy Weekly Review*
would return to the terms of the Okpo Sayadaw Zediyingana debates to discuss the canonical injunctions against footwear.

45. "[Concerning the Issue of Europeans Wearing Shoes at the Shwedagon Pa-
goda]," *Hanthawaddy Weekly Review,* May 18, 1901, 570.

46. Ibid.

47. *Times of Burma,* May 29, 1901, 6.

48. "[Arrangements Made Regarding Europeans Wearing Shoes at the Dagon
Sandawshin Pagoda (Shwedagon)]," *Hanthawaddy Weekly Review,* June 1,
1901, 586.

49. While this passage may sound conciliatory, the editor was deeply opposed to
the pagoda trustee's actions. He was cautious not to be too explicitly critical
of the British colonial administration in a time when newspapers were
highly scrutinized for both sedition and incitement. Ibid.; this translation
appeared in "The Shoe Question: The Vernacular Press," *Times of Burma,*
June 5, 1901, 5.

50. "The Shwe Dagon Pagoda," *Times of Burma,* June 15, 1901, 4.

51. Edward Michael Mendelson, *Sangha and State in Burma: A Study of Monastic
Sectarianism and Leadership,* ed. John P. Ferguson (Ithaca, NY: Cornell University Press, 1975), 198.

52. Cady, *A History of Modern Burma,* 189–91. Donald M. Seekins, *State and Society in Modern Rangoon* (New York: Routledge, 2011), 48–52; Juliane Schober,
*Modern Buddhist Conjunctures in Myanmar: Cultural Narratives, Colonial
Legacies, and Civil Society* (Honolulu: University of Hawai'i Press, 2011), 73–
75; Khin Maung Nyunt, "The 'Shoe Question' (or the Loss and Regaining of
Our Independence)"; Michael Charney, *A History of Modern Burma* (Cambridge: Cambridge University Press, 2009), 30–32; Donald Eugene Smith, *Religion and Politics in Burma* (Princeton, NJ: Princeton University Press, 1965),
87–90.

53. Mendelson, *Sangha and State in Burma,* 198.

54. Letter from W. F. Rice to Editors of all Newspapers Published in Burma 28th
May 1918, in "Wearing Shoes in Pagodas," 1919, Myanmar National Archives,
Yangon, Myanmar.

55. Ibid.

56. Letter from Hon'ble W. F. Rice to the Commissioner of Police Rangoon 28th
May 1918, in "Wearing Shoes in Pagodas," 1919.

57. Ibid. The government enforced this censorship. In December of 1919 Maung
Thin, the editor of the Burmese journal *The Knowledge,* was fined 1,000 rupees

for publishing articles on the shoe question. "Burmese Editor Fined: All about the Shoe Question," *Leader* (Allahabad), December 1, 1919, 10.

58. The statement from Siam indicates that the decision about whether one should remove their shoes is based, like the issue of shoes in courts in Burma, on the type of shoes and the presence of socks.

59. "Appointment of Thathanabaing Headship of the Buddhist Church," 1886, Series 1/1/(A), Accession 1778, File 18, Myanmar National Archives, Yangon, Myanmar.

60. Burma Social Association, *The Shoe and the Shitko*. While much of the resolution is a search for a correct Buddhist authority, given the power of pagoda trustees to create local policy, the choice of colonized Ceylon and modernized Siam would have seemed particularly hollow examples to a Burmese readership.

61. Military Department Resolution dated 29 October 1919, in "Wearing Shoes in Pagodas," 1919, 5.

62. Ibid., 6.

63. Ibid., 6.

64. Ibid., 1.

65. Tomoko Masuzawa, *The Invention of World Religions, or, How European Universalism Was Preserved in the Language of Pluralism* (Chicago: University of Chicago Press, 2005), xiv.

66. This was combined with the idea of the nation by 1916.

67. "General News," *Leader* (Allahabad), February 1, 1919, 6.

CHAPTER 6: CONCLUSION

1. Ohn Mar Sein, "The Nationalist Movement Led by the GCBA" (master's thesis, Yangon University, 1999); C. G. Stewart, "The Burma Political Tree: Special Confidential Supplement," *Burma Police Abstract of Intelligence* 36, no. 37 (1932): 1–9.

2. C. P. Khin Maung, *Buddhabhāsā mran'mā asan': ayā: ey' aṭṭhuppatti cā tam':* (Mandalay: Kū bhan': ron': vay: re: cā puṃ nuip' tuik', 1920).

3. It did not reflect a particularly multireligious attitude on the part of nationalists, as one might hope. If anything, nationalist discourse became even more exclusive toward other religions and ethnicities—particularly Indian Muslims.

4. Maung Hla Sein, *The Voice of Young Burma: The Reproductions of the Articles Published by the Publicity Bureau of the University Boycotters* (Rangoon: New Burma Press, 1922).

5. Aye Kyaw, *The Voice of Young Burma*, Southeast Asia Program Series (Ithaca, NY: Southeast Asia Program, Cornell University, 1993), 33.

6. Narratives of the boycott tend to play up the faux monasticism of the strikers, emphasizing that they left their college hostels with very few possessions, many "with only the clothes they were wearing," and pointing out that they "slept on the floor without bedding in the cold night" without complaint. And just as for the monks, the patriotic pious, especially groups of women, soon stepped in with donations to sustain the strikers in their efforts toward liberation. Ibid., 23, 25.

7. Surendra Prasad Singh, *Growth of Nationalism in Burma, 1900–1942* (Calcutta: Firma KLM Private Limited, 1980); Donald Eugene Smith, *Religion and Politics in Burma* (Princeton, NJ: Princeton University Press, 1965); Bruce Matthews, "Buddhism under a Military Regime: The Iron Heel in Burma," *Asian Survey* 33, no. 4 (1993): 408–23.

8. "Lvat' ṅrim': bhvay tarā: ho pvai," *Mran'mā lū myui: myā: lvat' ṅrim': bhvay gyānay* [Freedom journal: For the freedom and welfare of the Burmans] 1, no. 17 (1922).

9. Heinz Bechert, "'To Be Burmese Is to Be Buddhist': Buddhism in Burma," in *The World of Buddhism: Buddhist Monks and Nuns in Society and Culture,* ed. Heinz Bechert and Richard Gombrich (New York: Facts on File Publications, 1984), 147–58.

10. Burma Social Association, ed., *The Shoe and the Shitko* (Rangoon: Burma Social Association, 1913).

11. Ingrid Jordt, *Burma's Mass Lay Meditation Movement: Buddhism and the Cultural Construction of Power* (Athens: Ohio University Press, 2007).

12. Hiroko Kawanami, "U Nu's Liberal Democracy and Buddhist Communalism in Modern Burma" (paper presented at the Buddhism and the Political Process Conference, University of Toronto, Scarborough, April 13–15, 2012).

13. Niklas Foxeus, "The World Emperor's Battle against the Evil Forces," *Journal of Burma Studies* 16, no. 2 (2012): 213–50; Niklas Foxeus, "The Buddhist World Emperor's Mission: Millenarian Buddhism in Postcolonial Burma" (PhD diss., Stockholm University, 2011).

14. See also the recent work by Matthew Walton on the ways in which discussions of morality and a decline in morality as a threat to *sāsana* were developed in the underground publications of monks prior to the protest and in public statements afterward. Matthew J. Walton, "'Democracy Means Acting in Accordance with Truth': The Role of Buddhist Monks in Connecting Morality with Politics in Contemporary Myanmar" (paper presented at the Buddhism and the Political Process Conference, University of Toronto, Scarborough, April 13–15, 2012).

15. Sai Latt, "The Arakan Conflict and Nationalist Threats in Burma," *Asia Sentinel,* July 23, 2012.

16. Benedict R. Anderson, *Imagined Communities: Reflections on the Origin and Spread of Nationalism,* rev. and ext. ed. (London: Verso, 1991).

17. The idea of a Protestant Buddhism too often implies this type of total cultural impact. Richard Gombrich and Gananath Obeyesekere, *Buddhism Transformed: Religious Change in Sri Lanka* (Princeton, NJ: Princeton University Press, 1988).

18. Talal Asad, "Conscripts of Western Civilization," in *Civilization in Crisis: Anthropological Perspectives,* ed. Christine Ward Gailey (Gainesville: University Press of Florida, 1992), 333–34.

19. Ibid., 337.

20. Ibid.

21. Talal Asad, "Religion, Nation-State, Secularism," in *Nation and Religion: Perspectives on Europe and Asia,* ed. Peter van der Veer and Harmut Lehmann (Princeton, NJ: Princeton University Press, 1999), 185.

22. Other local categories like *lokiya* (this worldly)/*lokuttara* (other worldly) had their own sense, different from that of "religion" and "secular," and had to be adjusted to respond to the new landscape.

23. Tomoko Masuzawa, *The Invention of World Religions, or, How European Universalism Was Preserved in the Language of Pluralism* (Chicago: University of Chicago Press, 2005).

24. Partha Chatterjee, *The Nation and Its Fragments: Colonial and Postcolonial Histories,* Princeton Studies in Culture/Power/History (Princeton, NJ: Princeton University Press, 1993).

25. Ibid., 6.

26. Ibid., 237.

27. Jonathan Z. Smith, *Imagining Religion: From Babylon to Jonestown* (Chicago: University of Chicago Press, 1982), xi.

28. There were important relationships between European scholars and Burmese Buddhists in this period, but for the most part they were marginal to the larger Buddhist movements. Correspondences between Shwe Zan Aung, Ledi Sayadaw, Caroline Augusta Foley Rhys Davids, and others helped to shape the study of Buddhism, but had limited impact on the majority of Burmese Buddhists at the time.

29. Jean Comaroff and John L. Comaroff, *Of Revelation and Revolution: Christianity, Colonialism, and Consciousness in South Africa* (Chicago: University of Chicago Press, 1991), 1:29.

BIBLIOGRAPHY

ARCHIVAL SOURCES

India Office Records Collection. British Library. London, England
Myanmar National Archives. Yangon, Myanmar

NEWSPAPERS, BUDDHIST JOURNALS, AND THEIR CONTEMPORARIES

Buddhism: An Illustrated Quarterly Review
Buddhist Review
Burma Echo
Burmah Herald
Burman Buddhist
Chariot of the Dhamma (Burmese)
Dhammadethana (Burmese)
Eclectic Magazine of Foreign Literature
Essence of Buddhism (Burmese)
Freedom Journal: For the Freedom and Welfare of the Burmans (Burmese)
Friend of Burma (Burmese)
Hanthawaddy Weekly Review (Burmese)
Journal of the Burma Research Society
Journal of the Burma Society
Journal of the Maha-Bodhi Society
Leader
Ledi Dhamma Newspaper (Burmese)
Maha-Bodhi News (Burmese)
Mandalay Pariyatti Thathanahita Society Monthly Journal (Burmese)
Myanmar Alin Magazine (Burmese)
Nat Basket
Open Door
Our Monthly: A Magazine of General Literature
Pioneer
Pivot of Buddhism (Burmese)
Rangoon College Magazine
Rangoon Gazette
Rangoon Gazette and Weekly Budget

Thuriya (Sun) (Burmese)
Times of Burma
Times of Burma Weekly Summary
Times of India

COLONIAL REPORTS

Catalogue of Books and Pamphlets Published in Burma. Rangoon: Superintendent, Government Printing, Burma, 1870–1920.
Report on Public Instruction in Burma (RPI). Rangoon: Superintendent, Government Printing, Burma, 1870–1920.
Report on the Administration of Burma (RAB). Rangoon: Superintendent, Government Printing, Burma, 1867–1920.
Report on the Census of British Burma. Rangoon: Government Press, 1875–1881.

BOOKS, TRACTS, AND ARTICLES

Ananda Metteyya. "Buddhist Activities." *Buddhism: An Illustrated Quarterly Review* 1, no. 1 (September 1903): 168–74.
———. "Buddhist Activities." *Buddhism: An Illustrated Quarterly Review* 1, no. 3 (March 1904): 527.
———. "Notes and News: The 'Shikho' in Public Schools." *Buddhism: An Illustrated Quarterly Review* 1, no. 1 (September 1903): 151–53.
———. *On Religious Education in Burma.* Publications of the Buddhasasana Samagama 2. Rangoon: Hanthawaddy, 2446 [1903].
Anderson, Benedict R. *Imagined Communities: Reflections on the Origin and Spread of Nationalism.* Rev. and ext. ed. London: Verso, 1991.
Anderson, Carol. "'For Those Who Are Ignorant': A Study of the *Bauddha Ādahilla.*" In *Consituting Communities: Theravāda Buddhism and the Religious Cultures of South and Southeast Asia,* edited by John Holt and Jacob Kinnard, 171–88. Albany: SUNY Press, 2003.
Asad, Talal. "Conscripts of Western Civilization." In *Civilization in Crisis: Anthropological Perspectives,* edited by Christine Ward Gailey, 333–54. Gainesville: University Press of Florida, 1992.
———. "The Construction of Religion as an Anthropological Category." In *Genealogies of Religion: Discipline and Reasons of Power in Christianity and Islam,* 27–54. Baltimore, MD: Johns Hopkins University Press, 1993.
———. "Religion, Nation-State, Secularism." In *Nation and Religion: Perspectives on Europe and Asia,* edited by Peter van der Veer and Harmut Lehmann, 178–93. Princeton, NJ: Princeton University Press, 1999.

Aye Kyaw. *The Voice of Young Burma.* Southeast Asia Program Series. Ithaca, NY: Southeast Asia Program, Cornell University, 1993.

Bagshawe, Leonard Evans. "A Literature of School Books: A Study of the Burmese Books Approved for Use in Schools by the Education Department in 1885, and of Their Place in the Developing Educational System in British Burma." Master's thesis, School of Oriental and African Studies, University of London, 1976.

————. "The 'Moral and Intellectual Improvement of the People': Western Education in Burma to 1880." In *Études Birmanes: En hommage à Denise Bernot,* edited by Pierre Pichard and François Robinne. Etudes Thématiques, 9. Paris: Ecole Française d'Extrême-Orient, 1998.

Bechert, Heinz. "'To Be Burmese Is to Be Buddhist': Buddhism in Burma." In *The World of Buddhism: Buddhist Monks and Nuns in Society and Culture,* edited by Heinz Bechert and Richard Gombrich, 147–58. New York: Facts on File Publications, 1984.

————. "Über Sanskrit-Bildung und Schulsystem in Birma und Ceylon." *Wiener Zeitschrift für die Kund Süd- und Ostasiens un Archiv für Indiche Philosophie* 7 (1963): 1–12.

Bechert, Heinz, and Heinz Braun, eds. *Pāli Nīti Texts of Burma: Dhammanīti, Lokanīti, Maharahanīti, Rajanīti.* Pali Text Society Publications 171. London: Pali Text Society, 1981.

Bechert, Heinz, Khin Khin Su, Tin Tin Myint, and Heinz Braun. *Burmese Manuscripts.* Verzeichnis der Orientalischen Handschriften in Deutschland Bd. 23. 6 vols. Wiesbaden: Steiner, 1979.

Berkwitz, Stephen. "History and Gratitude in Theravada Buddhism." *Journal of the American Academy of Religion* 71, no. 3 (September 2003): 579–604.

Bha San'. *Yakhan' yakhu mo'lamruin' samuin'.* Moulmein: Ū: Cin' Raṃ aṅ' chan': cā puṃ nhip' tuik', 1949.

Bigandet, Paul. *The Life or Legend of Gaudama, the Buddha of the Burmese, with Annotations.* 4th ed. 2 vols. London: Kegan Paul, Trench, Trübner & Co., 1911 [1858].

Bird, George W. *Wanderings in Burma.* 2nd ed. London: Simpkin, Marshall, Hamilton, Kent and Co., 1897.

Blackburn, Anne M. *Buddhist Learning and Textual Practice in Eighteenth-Century Lankan Monastic Culture.* Princeton, NJ: Princeton University Press, 2001.

————. *Locations of Buddhism: Colonialism and Modernity in Sri Lanka.* Chicago: University of Chicago Press, 2010.

Bode, Mabel Haynes. *The Pali Literature of Burma.* London: Royal Asiatic Society of Great Britain and Ireland, 1909.

————, ed. *Sāsanavaṃsa,* Pali Text Society Publications 121. London: H. Frowde, 1897.

Bopearachchi, Elizabeth. *L'éducation Bouddhique dans la société traditionnelle au Sri Lanka: Les formes de pensée et les formes de socialisation.* Recherches Asiatiques. Paris: Harmattan, 1994.

Borchert, Thomas. "Worry for the Dai Nation: Sipsongpannā Chinese Modernity, and the Problems of Buddhist Modernism." *Journal of Asian Studies* 67, no. 1 (2008): 107–42.

Braun, Erik. *The Birth of Insight: Meditation, Modern Buddhism and the Burmese Monk Ledi Sayadaw.* Buddhism and Modernity. Chicago: University of Chicago Press, 2013.

Brown, George F. R. Grant. *Burma as I Saw It, 1889–1917, with a Chapter on Recent Events.* New York: Frederick A. Stokes Company, 1925.

Brown, Ian. "A Commissioner Calls: Alexander Paterson and Colonial Burma's Prisons." *Journal of Southeast Asian Studies* 38, no. 2 (June 2007): 293–308.

Buddhasasana Samagama. *Revised Prospectus of the Buddhasasana Samagama.* Publications of the Buddhasasana Samagama 1a. Rangoon: Hanthawaddy Press, 1903.

Buddhist Community of Burma. *Buddha Gaya.* Calcutta: Maha Bodhi Society, 1907.

Burchell, Graham, Colin Gordon, and Peter Miller, eds. *The Foucault Effect: Studies in Governmentality.* Chicago: University of Chicago Press, 1991.

Burma Social Association, ed. *The Shoe and the Shitko.* Rangoon: Burma Social Association, 1913.

C. P. Khin Maung. *Buddhabhāsā mran'mā asañ': myā: ey' aṭṭhuppatti cā tam':.* Mandalay: Kū bhan': roṅ': vay: re: cā puṃ nuip' tuik', 1920.

Cady, John F. *A History of Modern Burma.* Ithaca, NY: Cornell University Press, 1958.

Carbine, Jason. "Shwegyin Sāsana: Continuity, Rupture, and Traditionalism in a Buddhist Tradition." In *Historicizing "Tradition" in the Study of Religion,* edited by Steven Engler and Gregory Grieve, 145–74. Berlin: Walter de Gruyter, 2005.

———. *Sons of the Buddha: Continuities and Ruptures in a Burmese Monastic Tradition.* Religion and Society. New York: Walter de Gruyter, 2011.

Charney, Michael. *A History of Modern Burma.* Cambridge: Cambridge University Press, 2009.

———. *Powerful Learning: Buddhist Literati and the Throne in Burma's Last Dynasty.* Ann Arbor: Center for South and Southeast Asian Studies, University of Michigan, 2006.

Chatterjee, Partha. *The Nation and Its Fragments: Colonial and Postcolonial Histories.* Princeton Studies in Culture/Power/History. Princeton, NJ: Princeton University Press, 1993.

Chaṭṭhana Saṅgāyana. CD-ROM. 3rd ed. Dhammagiri: Vipassana Research Institute, 2003.

Chit Tin and William Pruitt. *The Coming Buddha Ariya Metteyya.* 2nd ed. The Wheel Publication No. 381/383. Kandy, Sri Lanka: Buddhist Publication Society, 1992.

Claybaugh, Amanda. *The Novel of Purpose: Literature and Social Reform in the Anglo-American World.* Ithaca, NY: Cornell University Press, 2007.

Co Mum Ñ̇añ':. *Bamā amyui: sa mī:.* Yangon: Sīha puṃ nhip' tuik', 1976.

Cohn, Bernard S. *Colonialism and Its Forms of Knowledge: The British in India.* Princeton, NJ: Princeton University Press, 1996.

Collins, Steven. *Nirvana and Other Buddhist Felicities: Utopias of the Pali Imaginaire.* Cambridge Studies in Religious Traditions 12. Cambridge: Cambridge University Press, 1998.

Colston, F. J. "Some Recent Social Movements in Burma." *Asiatic Quarterly Review* 29, no. 57 (January 1910): 68–87.

———. "Some Recent Social Movements in Burma." *Journal of the Burma Society* 1, no. 1 (April 1910): 35–53.

Comaroff, Jean, and John L. Comaroff. *Of Revelation and Revolution: Christianity, Colonialism, and Consciousness in South Africa,* vol. 1. Chicago: University of Chicago Press, 1991.

———. *Of Revelation and Revolution: The Dialectics of Modernity on a South African Frontier,* vol. 2. Chicago: University of Chicago Press, 1997.

Cowan, Minna G. *The Education of the Women of India.* London: Oliphant, Anderson & Ferrier, 1912.

Crow, John L. "The White Knight in the Yellow Robe: Allan Bennett's Search for Truth." Master's thesis, University of Amsterdam, 2009.

Cuming, E. D. *In the Shadow of the Pagoda: Sketches of Burmese Life and Character.* London: W. H. Allen & Co., 1893.

Deegalle, Mahinda. *Popularizing Buddhism: Preaching as Performance in Sri Lanka.* Albany: SUNY Press, 2006.

Department of Public Instruction. *Report of the Vernacular and Vocational Education Reorganization Committee.* Rangoon: Superintendent, Government Printing and Stationery, Burma, 1936.

———. *Teacher's Handbook on Buddhist Religious Instruction High Department.* Rangoon: Superintendent, Government Printing and Stationery, Burma, 1934.

Dhammasami, Khammai. "Between Idealism and Pragmatism: A Study of Monastic Education in Burma and Thailand from the Seventeenth Century to the Present." PhD diss., University of Oxford, 2004.

Dharmapala, Anagarika. "Moung Hpo Myin, KSM." *Journal of the Maha-Bodhi Society* 3, no. 10–11 (February 1895): 86.

———. *Report of the Maha Bodhi Society, from 1891 to 1915.* Calcutta: Maha Bodhi Society, 1915.

Dirks, Nicholas B. *Castes of Mind: Colonialism and the Making of Modern India.* Princeton, NJ: Princeton University Press, 2001.

Dressler, Markus, and Arvind-Pal S. Mandair. "Introduction: Modernity, Religion-Making and the Postsecular." In *Secularism and Religion-Making,* edited by Markus Dressler and Arvind-Pal S. Mandair, 1–36. New York: Oxford University Press, 2011.

Duara, Prasenjit. *Rescuing History from the Nation: Questioning Narratives of Modern China.* Chicago: University of Chicago Press, 1995.

'E: Krū. *Britishya mran'mā khet' cā kraññ'. tuik' myā: akhre ane 1826–1947.* Yangon: Universities Press, 1979.

Edwards, Penny. "Adventure Capital: Political Enterprise in Colonial Southeast Asia." Paper presented at the Association of Asian Studies, Honolulu, Hawai'i, April 2, 2011.

———. *Cambodge: The Cultivation of a Nation, 1860–1945.* Southeast Asia—Politics, Meaning, Memory. Honolulu: University of Hawai'i Press, 2007.

———. "Relocating the Interlocutor: Taw Sein Ko (1864–1930) and the Itinerancy of Knowledge in British Burma." *South East Asia Research* 12, no. 3 (November 2004): 277–335.

Ferguson, John P. "The Symbolic Dimensions of the Burmese Sangha." PhD diss., Cornell University, 1975.

Ferrars, Max, and Bertha Ferrars. *Burma.* 2nd ed. London: Sampson, Low, Marston and Company, 1901.

Filliozat, Jacqueline. "The Commentaries to the Anāgatavaṃsa in the Pali Manuscripts of the Paris Collections." *Journal of the Pali Text Society* 19 (1993): 43–63.

Forbes, Charles J. F. Smith. *British Burma and Its People: Being Sketches of Native Manners, Customs and Religion.* London: Murray, 1878.

Foucault, Michel. *Discipline and Punish: The Birth of the Prison.* 2nd Vintage Books ed. New York: Vintage Books, 1995.

Foxeus, Niklas. "The Buddhist World Emperor's Mission: Millenarian Buddhism in Postcolonial Burma." PhD diss., Stockholm University, 2011.

———. "The World Emperor's Battle against the Evil Forces." *Journal of Burma Studies* 16, no. 2 (December 2012): 213–50.

Furnivall, John S. *Colonial Policy and Practice: A Comparative Study of Burma and Netherlands India.* New York: New York University Press, 1956.

———. *An Introduction to the Political Economy of Burma.* Rangoon: Burma Book Club Ltd., 1931.

———. "Material for Studying the Social and Economic Evolution of Burma." Unpublished manuscript. Cornell University Library, John M. Echols Collection, n.d.

Fytche, Albert. *Burma Past and Present,* vol. 2. London: C. K. Paul & Co., 1878.

Gandhi, Leela. *Affective Communities: Anticolonial Thought, Fin-De-Siècle Radicalism, and the Politics of Friendship.* Durham, NC: Duke University Press, 2006.

Gandhi, M. K. *An Autobiography: The Story of My Experiments with Truth*. Boston: Beacon Press, 1957.

Gombrich, Richard, and Gananath Obeyesekere. *Buddhism Transformed: Religious Change in Sri Lanka*. Princeton, NJ: Princeton University Press, 1988.

Gouger, Henry. *Two Years Imprisonment in Burma (1824–26)*. Burma Historical Reprint Series. Edited by Guy Lubeigt. Bangkok: White Lotus, 2002 [1860].

Gray, James, ed. *Ancient Proverbs and Maxims from the Burmese Sources: The Niti Literature of Burma*. London: Trubner & Co., 1886.

Hackett, Paul Richmond. "Religious Education of Burman Buddhists." Master's thesis, University of Chicago, 1921.

Hall, H. Fielding. *A People at School*. London: Macmillan and Co., 1906.

———. *The Soul of a People*. 4th ed. London: Macmillan and Co., 1913 [1898].

Hansen, Anne Ruth. *How to Behave: Buddhism and Modernity in Colonial Cambodia, 1860–1930*. Southeast Asia—Politics, Meaning, Memory. Honolulu: University of Hawai'i Press, 2007.

Harmer, Ernest G. "The Transformation of Burma." *London Quarterly Review* 7, no. 1 (January 1902): 53.

Harris, Elizabeth. *Ananda Metteyya: The First British Emissary of Buddhism*. Wheel Publication No. 420/422. Kandy, Sri Lanka: Buddhist Publication Society, 1998.

Harrison, Brian Howard. *Drink and the Victorians: The Temperance Question in England, 1815–1872*. 2nd ed. Staffordshire, UK: Keele University Press, 1994.

Hart, Alice Marion Rowlands. *Picturesque Burma, Past & Present*. London: J. M. Dent & Co., 1897.

Harvey, Peter. *An Introduction to Buddhism: Teachings, History, and Practices*. New York: Cambridge University Press, 1990.

Hordern, Peter. "Buddhist Schools in Burmah." *Fraser's Magazine* 16, no. 95 (November 1877): 626–34.

———. "An Episode in Burmese History: Being a Contribution to the History of Indigenous Oriental Education." *Asiatic Quarterly Review* 4, no. 7 (July 1892): 29–42.

Horner, I. B. "The Buddhist Apocalypse." In *Buddhist Texts through the Ages*, edited by Edward Conze, I. B. Horner, David Snellgrove, and Arthur Waley, 45–50. New York: Harper & Row, 1954.

Htay Htay Lwin. "History of the Maha Ledi Sasana." Master's thesis, Mandalay University, 1998.

Htin Aung, trans. *Burmese Monk's Tales*. New York: Columbia University Press, 1966.

Ikeya, Chie. *Refiguring Women, Colonialism, and Modernity in Burma*. Southeast Asia—Politics, Meaning, Memory. Honolulu: University of Hawai'i Press, 2011.

Jardine, Justice. "University for Burma at Rangoon." *Asiatic Quarterly Review* 7, no. 13 (January 1894): 71–75.

Jordt, Ingrid. *Burma's Mass Lay Meditation Movement: Buddhism and the Cultural Construction of Power.* Athens: Ohio University Press, 2007.

Kannangara, A. P. "The Riots of 1915 in Sri Lanka: A Study in the Roots of Communal Violence." *Past and Present* 102 (February 1984): 130–65.

Kaung. "A Survey of the History of Education in Burma before the British Conquest and After." *Journal of the Burma Research Society* 46, no. 2 (December 1963): 1–125.

Kawanami, Hiroko. "U Nu's Liberal Democracy and Buddhist Communalism in Modern Burma." Paper presented at the Buddhism and the Political Process Conference, University of Toronto, Scarborough, April 13–15, 2012.

Kelly, R. Talbot. *Burma.* 2nd ed. London: A&C Black, Ltd., 1933 [1905].

Khin Maung Nyunt. "The 'Shoe Question' (or the Loss and Regaining of Our Independence)." *Guardian* 17, no. 2 (February 1970): 21–28.

Kirichenko, Alexey. "'The Last of the Mohicans': Taunggwin Hsayadaw and the Transformation of Monastic Hierarchies in Colonial Burma." Paper presented at the Conference on Theravada Buddhism under Colonialism: Adaptation and Response, Narlanda Sriwijaya Centre, Institute for Southeast Asian Studies, Singapore, May 24, 2010.

———. "The Making of a Culprit: Atula Hsayadaw Shin Yasa and the Politics of Monastic Reform in Eighteenth-Century Burma." *Journal of Burma Studies* 15, no. 2 (December 2011): 189–229.

———. *New Spaces for Interaction: Contacts between Burmese and Sinhalese Monks in the Late Nineteenth and Early Twentieth Centuries.* Asia Research Institute Working Paper Series. Singapore: Asia Research Institute, National University of Singapore, 2012.

Krī: Phe. "Saṅ' puṃ krī: mha saṅ' pun': krī: sui. proṅ': sa lo." In *Mran'mā. cvay cum kyam': cā pe bimān' ey' rup' pya bahusuta bhaṇ'.* Yangon: Cā pe bimān' puṃ nhip' tuik', 1973.

Kumada, Naoko. "Rethinking Dana in Burma: The Art of Giving." Paper presented at the Buddhism and the Spirit Cult Revisited Conference, Stanford University, May 22–23, 2004.

Kyaw Dun. *Report of the Committee Appointed to Consider and Report Upon Buddhist Religious Instruction for Buddhist Pupils in Vernacular Lay Schools under Buddhist Management 1928–29.* Rangoon: Superintendent, Government Printing and Stationery, Burma, 1931.

Kyaw Yan. *Mhat' krī: tarā rhac' luṃ:* [One hundred and eight things to remember]. Mandalay: Indian Press, 1903.

———. *Rules of the Kalyanathingaha Society, Myingyan.* Mandalay: Mandalay Times Press, 1897.

———. *Sīla adippāy' laka'svai* [*Thila adeikbe letswe* Handbook on Buddhist precepts]. Mandalay: Irrawaddy Press, 1901.

———. *Surāmeraya-Pakāsanī Kyam'*: [*Thura meraya pakathani kyan* Treatise on itoxicating liquors]. 2nd ed. Mandalay: Society for Promoting Buddhism Press, 1917.

Lawson, John, and Harold Silver. *A Social History of Education in England*. London: Methuen & Co., 1973.

Ledi Sayadaw. "Cuiñ' prañ' se rañ̃' se rak' mettā cā." In *Gambhīra kabyā kyam'*:, 15–18. Yangon: Myat' chu mvan' cā pe thut', 2004 [1886].

———. "Dīpa rañ': se rañ̃' se rak' mettā cā." In *Gambhīra kabyā kyam'*:, 19–25. Yangon: Mrat' chu mvan' cā pe thut', 2004 [1887].

———. *Paramattha samkhip' kyam'*: [*Paramattha thankheip kyan*]. Rangoon: Hanthawaddy, 1956 [1903].

———. *Sāsanavisodhanī* [*Thathanawithodhani*]. 2 vols. Rangoon: Hanthawaddy, 1954 [1919].

———. *A Talk on Intoxicants and Gambling*. Translated by Bhikkhu Pesala. Middlesex, UK: Association for Insight Meditation, 2002.

———. "Yac' myui: tarā: to'." *Dhammadesanā tarā: satañ': cā* [*Dhammadethana*] 1, no. 4 (June 1908): 93–97.

Lewis, Su Lin. "Asian Urbanites and Cosmopolitan Cultures in Bangkok, Penang, and Rangoon 1910–1940." PhD diss., University of Cambridge, 2010.

Lieberman, Victor. *Strange Parallels: Southeast Asia in Global Context c. 800–1830*, vol. 1: *Integration on the Mainland*. New York: Cambridge University Press, 2003.

Loos, Tamara Lynn. *Subject Siam: Family, Law, and Colonial Modernity in Thailand*. Ithaca, NY: Cornell University Press, 2006.

Maddegama, Udaya, and John Holt. *Anāgatavamsa Desana: The Sermon of the Chronicle-to-Be*. Buddhist Tradition Series. Delhi: Motilal Banarsidass Publishers, 1993.

Mahādhamma saṅkram. *Sāsanālaṅkara cā tam'*: [*Thathanalankara sadan*]. Rangoon: Hanthawaddy, 1956.

Mahāvisuddhārum charā to' burā: krī:. *Goṇamātikā ovādakathā kyām'*:. Rangoon: Amyui: sā: cā puṃ nhip' tuik', 1907.

Malalgoda, Kitsiri. *Buddhism in Sinhalese Society, 1750–1900: A Study of Religious Revival and Change*. Berkeley: University of California Press, 1976.

Malcom, Howard. *Travels in the Burman Empire*. Edinburgh: William and Robert Chambers, 1840.

Mandalay Malunze Rice Donating Society. *Mantale: mrui. ma lvan' jhe: chan' lhū asañ': krī: nhac'-100-prañ̃'. cā coñ'*. Mandalay: Ma lvan' jhe: chan' lhū asañ':, 1996.

Mandalay Pariyatti Thathanahita. *Nhac' tac' rā prañ̃'. samuiñ'*:. Mandalay: Sukhavatīpiṭaka, 1998.

Masuzawa, Tomoko. *The Invention of World Religions, or, How European Universalism Was Preserved in the Language of Pluralism*. Chicago: University of Chicago Press, 2005.

Matthews, Bruce. "Buddhism under a Military Regime: The Iron Heel in Burma." *Asian Survey* 33, no. 4 (April 1993): 408–23.

Maung Hla Sein. *The Voice of Young Burma: The Reproductions of the Articles Published by the Publicity Bureau of the University Boycotters*. Rangoon: New Burma Press, 1922.

Maung Maung Pye. *Burma in the Crucible*. Rangoon: Khittaya Publishing House, 1952.

May Oung, and John S. Furnivall. "The Dawn of Nationalism in Burma: The Modern Burman." *Journal of the Burma Research Society* 33, no. 1 (April 1950): 1–7.

McCann, Phillip. "Popular Education, Socialization and Social Control: Spitalfields 1812–1824." In *Popular Education and Socialization in the Nineteenth Century*, edited by Phillip McCann, 1–40. London: Methuen & Co., 1977.

McDaniel, Justin. *Gathering Leaves and Lifting Words*. Seattle: University of Washington Press, 2008.

Mendelson, Edward Michael. *Sangha and State in Burma: A Study of Monastic Sectarianism and Leadership*. Edited by John P. Ferguson. Ithaca, NY: Cornell University Press, 1975.

Minayeff, Ivan Pavlovich. "Anāgata-Vaṃsa." *Journal of the Pali Text Society* (1886): 33–53.

———. *Travels in and Diaries of India and Burma*. Translated by Hirendranath Sanyal. Calcutta: Eastern Trading Co., 1956.

Minekhine Sayadaw. "Lokāyatādivinicchaya." In *Lokāyatādivinicchaya*, edited by Bhurā: Phrū Charā to'. Rangoon: Dī: dut' sataṅ': cā puṃ nhip' tuik', 1929 [1913].

Minus, John. "The Bernard Free Library." In *Annual Report of the Burma Educational Syndicate for the Year 1914–1915*, 5–6. Rangoon: Office of the Superintendent, Government Printing, Burma, 1915.

Mon. *Buddhabhāsāmūla akhre pra kyam': cā*. 4th ed. Rangoon: British Burma Press, 1915.

Moṅ' Jeyyā. *Mran'mā lū kyo' 100*, vol. 1. Rangoon: Unity, 2010.

Myo Myint. "The Politics of Survival in Burma: Diplomacy and Statecraft in the Reign of King Mindon 1853–1871." PhD diss., Cornell University, 1987.

Nattier, Jan. *Once Upon a Future Time: Studies in a Buddhist Prophecy of Decline*. Berkeley, CA: Asian Humanities Press, 1991.

Nethersole, F. R., President Pegu Municipality. "Translation of Entries for the Week Ending 15th August 1902 Made in the Register of Preaching in the Municipal Anglo-Vernacular School at Pegu and Copy of Deputy Commissioner's Remarks Thereon, Dated the 18th August 1902, Forwarded for Information with the Suggestion That Identical or Similar Arrangements Might Be Made

Throughout Burma in Similar Schools." In *On Religious Education in Burma*, 18–25, edited by Ananda Metteyya. Publications of the Buddhasasana Samagama 2. Rangoon: Hanthawaddy, 1902.

Ngwe Thein, ed. *A Guide to the Pagodas on Moulmein Ridge with Notes on Buddhism and References about Moulmein, Burma*. Moulmein: Mingala Sa Pone Hnep Taik, 1961.

Nisbet, John. *Burma under British Rule—and Before*. Westminster: A. Constable, 1901.

Norman, K. R. "The Anāgatavaṃsa Revisited." *Journal of the Pali Text Society* 28 (2006): 1–37.

Ohn Mar Sein. "The Nationalist Movement Led by the GCBA." Master's thesis, Yangon University, 1999.

Olcott, Henry Steele. *Buddhabhāsā ame: aphra kyam':*. Rangoon: Maung Po O, 1886.

———. *Old Diary Leaves: The History of the Theosophical Society*, vol. 4: *1887–92*. Adyar: Theosophical Publishing House, 1910.

'Oṅ' Sin':, ed. *Haṃsāvatī chuṃ ma cā poṅ': khyup'*. Rangoon: Haṃsāvatī puṃ nhip' tuik', 1960.

Peleggi, Maurizio. *Lords of Things: The Fashioning of the Siamese Monarchy's Modern Image*. Honolulu: University of Hawai'i Press, 2002.

———. "Refashioning Civilization: Dress and Bodily Practice in Thai Nation-Building." In *The Politics of Dress in Asia and America*, edited by Mina Roces and Louise Edwards, 65–80. Brighton, UK: Sussex Academic Press, 2009.

Phayre, Lt. Col. Arthur Purves, Chief Commissioner of British Burma to Officiating Secretary to the Government of India Hon. R. N. Cust. "Home Department: Education," Rangoon, 1864. Reprinted in Kaung, "A Survey of the History of Education in Burma," *Journal of the Burma Research Society* 46, no. 2 (December 1963): 83–86.

Poovey, Mary. *Making a Social Body: British Cultural Formation, 1830–1864*. Chicago: University of Chicago Press, 1995.

Pranke, Patrick. "'Bodawpaya's Madness': Monastic Accounts of King Bodawpaya's Conflict with the Burmese Sangha." *Journal of Burma Studies* 12 (2008): 1–28.

———. "History and Eschatology in Burmese Buddhist Chronicles." Paper presented at the Association of Asian Studies, San Diego, CA, March 23, 2013.

———. "The 'Treatise on the Lineage of Elders' (Vaṃsadīpanī): Monastic Reform and the Writing of Buddhist History in Eighteenth-Century Burma." PhD diss., University of Michigan, 2004.

Pritchard, Earl H. "The Kotow in the Macartney Embassy to China in 1793." *Far Eastern Quarterly* 2, no. 2 (February 1943): 163–203.

Prothero, Stephen. "Henry Steel Olcott and 'Protestant Buddhism.'" *Journal of the American Academy of Religion* 63, no. 2 (Summer 1995): 281–302.

Rangoon College Buddhist Association. *A Compilation of Lectures*. Rangoon: Sun Press, 1914.

Reynolds, Craig J. "The Buddhist Monkhood in Nineteenth Century Thailand." PhD diss., Cornell University, 1972.

———. "Thai Manual Knowledge: Theory and Practice." In *Seditious Histories: Contesting Thai and Southeast Asian Pasts*, 214–42. Seattle: University of Washington Press, 2006.

Rhve Kuiṅ': sā. *Anhac' 100 praññ'. Mantale:*. Mandalay: Krī: pvā: re: puṃ nhip' tuik', 1959.

Rhys Davids, T. W., trans. *The Questions of King Milinda*. 2 vols. New York: Dover Publications, 1963.

Richell, Judith L. *Disease and Demography in Colonial Burma*. Singapore: NUS Press, 2006.

Rogers, John. "Cultural Nationalism and Social Reform: The 1904 Temperance Movement in Sri Lanka." *Indian Economic and Social History Review* 23, no. 3 (1989): 319–41.

Ryley, John Horton. *Ralph Fitch, England's Pioneer to India and Burma: His Companions and Contemporaries, with His Remarkable Narrative Told in His Own Words*. London: T. Fisher Unwin, 1899.

Sai Latt. "The Arakan Conflict and Nationalist Threats in Burma." *Asia Sentinel,* July 23, 2012.

Samuels, Jeffrey. "Toward an Action-Oriented Pedagogy: Buddhist Texts and Monastic Education in Contemporary Sri Lanka." *Journal of the American Academy of Religion* 72, no. 4 (2004): 955–71.

San': Thvat'. *Mran'mā nuiṅ' ṅam bhun' to' krī: kyoṅ': paññā re: samuiṅ:*. Yangon: 'Un': paṅ' puṃ nhip' tuik', 1980.

Sangermano, Father. *A Description of the Burmese Empire*. Translated by William Tandy. Rome: Oriental Translation Fund of Great Britain and Ireland, 1833.

Sasaki, Genjun, ed. *Sārasaṅgaha*. Oxford: Pali Text Society, 1992.

Saunders, Kenneth J. *Buddhism in the Modern World*. London: Society for Promoting Christian Knowledge, 1922.

Schober, Juliane. "Colonial Knowledge and Buddhist Education in Burma." In *Buddhism, Power and Political Order,* edited by Ian Charles Harris, 52–70. New York: Routledge, 2007.

———. *Modern Buddhist Conjunctures in Myanmar: Cultural Narratives, Colonial Legacies, and Civil Society*. Honolulu: University of Hawai'i Press, 2011.

Scott, Sir James George. "Buddhists and Buddhism in Burma." *Cornhill Magazine* 42, no. 252 (December 1880): 721–31.

———. *The Burman, His Life and Notions*. New York: Norton & Co., 1963 [1882].

Scott, Sir James George, and J. P. Hardiman, eds. *Gazetteer of Upper Burma and Shan States,* vol. 2 of pt. 1. Rangoon: Superintendent, Government Printing, Burma, 1900.

Seekins, Donald M. *State and Society in Modern Rangoon.* New York: Routledge, 2011.

Silacara. *Panca Sila: The Five Precepts.* Rangoon: The Buddhist Theosophical Federation, Burma, 1911.

Silacara and G. R. T. Ross. *The Fifth Precept and Social Service.* Rangoon College Buddhist Association Publications. Rangoon: Sun Press, 1912.

Sin': Chve Ū:. "Kuiluinī khet' Buddhasāsanā (1885–1938)." Master's thesis, University of Mandalay, 1994.

Singh, Surendra Prasad. *Growth of Nationalism in Burma, 1900–1942.* Calcutta: Firma KLM Private Limited, 1980.

Smith, Donald Eugene. *Religion and Politics in Burma.* Princeton, NJ: Princeton University Press, 1965.

Smith, Jonathan Z. *Imagining Religion: From Babylon to Jonestown.* Chicago: University of Chicago Press, 1982.

Stephens, W. B. *Education in Britain, 1750–1914.* New York: St. Martin's Press, 1998.

Stewart, C. G. "The Burma Political Tree: Special Confidential Supplement." *Burma Police Abstract of Intelligence* 36, no. 37 (September 17, 1932): 1–9.

Strong, John. *Relics of the Buddha.* Princeton, NJ: Princeton University Press, 2004.

Swift, Joan W. *Hattie: A Woman's Mission to Burma.* San Geronimo, CA: Half Meadow Press, 2003.

Symes, Michael. *An Account of an Embassy to the Kingdom of Ava: Sent by the Governor-General of India, in the Year 1795.* London: W. Bulmer and Co., 1800.

Tainturier, Francois. "The Foundation of Mandalay by King Mindon." PhD diss., School of Oriental and African Studies, University of London, 2010.

Tannenbaum, Nicola Beth. *Who Can Compete against the World? Power-Protection and Buddhism in Shan Worldview.* Ann Arbor, MI: Association for Asian Studies, 1995.

Taw Sein Ko, ed. *Burmese Sketches*, vol. 1. Rangoon: British Burma Press, 1913.

———, ed. *Burmese Sketches*, vol. 2. Rangoon: British Burma Press, 1920.

———, ed. *The Kalyani Inscriptions Erected by King Dhammaceti at Pegu in 1476 AD, Text and Translation.* Rangoon: Superintendent, Government Printing, Burma, 1892.

Taw Sein Ko [Rambler, pseud.]. "Education in Burma: From a Native Point of View." *Our Monthly: A Magazine of General Literature* 2, no. 5 (May 1883): 167–69.

———. "My Visit to the Kyoungs on the Day of the Thadingyoot Festival." *Our Monthly: A Magazine of General Literature* 2, no. 11 (1883).

Thongchai Winichakul. "The Quest for 'Siwilai': A Geographical Discourse of Civilizational Thinking in the Late Nineteenth and Early Twentieth-Century Siam." *Journal of Asian Studies* 59, no. 3 (August 2000): 528–49.

———. *Siam Mapped: A History of the Geo-Body of a Nation*. Honolulu: University of Hawai'i Press, 1994.

Tilawka. *Buddhasāsanānuggahanaya cā tam'*:. Mandalay: Mran'mā. tā rā satań': cā puṃ nuip' tuik', 1901.

Tin Phone Nwe. "Vuiń' am' bhī 'e [YMBA] kho' buddhakalyānayuva asań': ey' lhup' rhā: mhu samuiń': 1906–1920." Master's thesis, Rangoon University, 1973.

Toro, Ono. "The Development of Education in Burma." *East Asian Cultural Studies* 20, no. 1–4 (1981): 107–33.

Trenckner, V., Dines Anderson, and Helmer Smith, eds. *A Critical Pāli Dictionary*. Copenhagen: A. F. Høst and Søn, 1924–.

Turner, Alicia. "The Irish Pongyi in Colonial Burma: The Confrontations and Challenges of U Dhammaloka." *Contemporary Buddhism* 11, no. 2 (November 2010): 149–71.

———. "Narratives of Nation, Questions of Community: Examining Burmese Sources without the Lens of Nation." *Journal of Burma Studies* 15, no. 2 (December 2011): 263–82.

———. "Religion Making and Its Failures: Turning Monasteries into Schools and Buddhism into a Religion in Colonial Burma." In *Secularism and Religion-Making*, edited by Markus Dressler and Arvind-Pal S. Mandair, 226–42. New York: Oxford University Press, 2011.

Turner, Alicia, Laurence Cox, and Brian Bocking. "Beachcombing, Going Native and Freethinking: Rewriting the History of Early Western Buddhist Monastics." *Contemporary Buddhism* 11, no. 2 (November 2010): 125–47.

Twomey, D. H. R. "Thathanabaing, Head of Burmese Monks in Burma." *Asiatic Quarterly Review* 17, no. 34 (April 1904): 326.

Tyrrell, Ian R. *Woman's World/Woman's Empire: The Woman's Christian Temperance Union in International Perspective, 1800–1930*. Chapel Hill: University of North Carolina Press, 1991.

Union Buddha Sasana Council. *Report on the Situation of Buddhism in Burma*. Rangoon: Union Buddha Sasana Council, 2498 [1954].

Veidlinger, Daniel M. *Spreading the Dhamma: Writing, Orality, and Textual Transmission in Buddhist Northern Thailand*. Southeast Asia—Politics, Meaning, Memory. Honolulu: University of Hawai'i Press, 2006.

Viswanathan, Gauri. *Masks of Conquest: Literary Study and British Rule in India*. New York: Columbia University Press, 1989.

Wa. *Buddhabhāsā sań' khaṇ': cā dutiya tan': mha catuttha tan'*:. Rangoon: Superintendent, Government Printing and Stationery, Burma, 1939.

Walton, Matthew J. "'Democracy Means Acting in Accordance with Truth': The Role of Buddhist Monks in Connecting Morality with Politics in Contemporary Myanmar." Paper presented at the Buddhism and the Political Process Conference, University of Toronto, Scarborough, April 13–15, 2012.

Ward, K. M. "Right Conduct." In *A Compilation of Lectures,* edited by the Rangoon College Buddhist Association. Rangoon: Sun Press, 1914.

Webb, C. Morgan, ed. *Census of India, 1911: Burma.* Part 2—*Tables.* Rangoon: Superintendent, Government Printing, Burma, 1912.

Weber, Max. *The Protestant Ethic and the Spirit of Capitalism.* 2nd ed. New York: Scribner, 1976.

Whitbread, Kenneth. *Catalogue of Burmese Printed Books in the India Office Library.* London: Her Majesty's Stationery Office, 1969.

White, Sir Herbert Thirkell. *A Civil Servant in Burma.* London: Edward Arnold, 1913.

Who's Who in Burma, under the Distinquished Patronage of H. E. Sir Harcourt Butler, Governor of Burma: A Biographical Record of Prominent Residents of Burma with Photographs & Illustrations. Calcutta and Rangoon: Indo-Burma Publishing Agency, 1927.

Wijayarantna, Mohan. *Buddhist Monastic Life According to the Texts of the Theravāda Tradition.* Translated by Claude Grangier and Steven Collins. New York: Cambridge University Press, 1990.

Win Mar. "The Role of the Malunze Rice Offering Society in Propagating the Buddha Sasana." Master's thesis, Mandalay University, 1996.

Winston, W. R. *Four Years in Upper Burma.* London: C. H. Kelly, 1892.

Wyatt, David K. *The Politics of Reform in Thailand: Education in the Reign of King Chulalongkorn.* Yale Southeast Asia Studies. New Haven, CT: Yale University Press, 1969.

INDEX

Abhidhamma Piṭaka, 33, 34, 42–43, 106
Abhidhammatthasaṅgaha, 41
ācariya, 118
adhammic royalty, 34
adhigama (attaining insight), 27, 31, 162n17
"adopt but adapt," 71, 73, 112–113, 137, 189n7
agārava (disrespect), 125
Akyab (Sittwe): associations in, 76, 78, 180n17;
    Buddhist population census in, 186n73;
    preaching campaigns in, 97–98; school strike
    in, 116
alcohol: abstention from, precepts, 101–102;
    letters to the newspaper, 84, 85; pledges to, 97,
    100; subject of moral tracts, 102–103; subject
    of preaching, 97–98, 103–107. *See also*
    temperance and moral reform
Anāgata vaṃsa, 29, 30–34, 35–37, 162nn21–22,
    164n35, 164n37, 184n59
Anagatawin kyan, 31, 164n31, 164n35
Ananda Metteyya, 18, 67, 69, 178n115
Anderson, Benedict R., 7, 77, 144
Anglo-vernacular schools: Buddhist, 66–71, 73,
    102, 176n93, 177n113, 178n114, 179n129;
    government and missionary, 56, 63, 65, 86;
    schoolboys of, 63–64, 86–88, 115–120, 175n83
animals' appeal for vegetarianism, 92–93,
    183n52, 184n53. *See also* vegetarianism and
    moral reform
antaradhānas, 27, 31, 162n17, 164n35
Arakanese, ethnic group, 76, 161n42, 187n86
Arakan Jubilee Club, 76
Arya Samaj in colonial Burma, 18
Asad, Talal, 9, 113, 148–149, 150, 151, 152
asceticism: concerns for insufficient monastic,
    24–26, 27, 94–95, 121–122; lay practices of
    pseudo–, 95, 96, 139. *See also specific practices*
Asoka, 15, 25
atheism in colonial Burma, 18, 127
attire customs and norms, 94, 110–112, 185n62,
    193n58. *See also* footwear and colonialism

Bagshawe, L. E., 57, 170n27
Bassein: associations in, 78, 79; prison sermon by
    Ledi Sayadaw, 99
Bauddha ādahilla, 90

Bechert, Heinz, 52
beef eating. *See* cow protection movement;
    vegetarianism and moral reform
behavior and moral reform, 88–96, 97, 102, 103,
    108–109, 183n50, 185n62
Berkwitz, Stephen, 8–9, 81
Bernard Free Library, 30, 38, 165n55
Bhamo, *shikho* controversy in, 119
bhāvanā (mental cultivation), 88–89, 140–141
Bigandet, Paul, 48, 168n14
Blackburn, Anne M., 6, 24, 27, 52
Bodawpaya, King, 28, 35, 37, 52
Bodh Gaya, 30, 32
Borchert, Thomas, 7
boys: at Anglo-vernacular schools, 63–64,
    86–88, 102, 115, 175n83; monastery education
    of, 42, 45–51, 169n21
Braun, Erik, 21, 166n70, 188n97, 188n99
British colonial administration: ambivalence
    and divergence within, 14–15, 49, 55–56,
    56–57, 70, 115, 146, 147–148; and category of
    religion, 14–15, 58–59, 70, 113, 116–119,
    130–133; census and, 47–48, 83, 142, 168n11,
    168n13, 181n26; chief commissioners of, 30, 53,
    111; educational goals of, 48–49, 56–59;
    ethical pledges and, 99, 186n78; footwear
    debate and, 111, 120–125, 128–131, 192n57;
    judges, 16, 64, 110–112; of Lower Burma, 13,
    159n20; monastery education and, 45–51,
    53–59, 172n50, 172n52, 173n54; monastic
    community resistance to, 60–62; noninterfer-
    ence in religious affairs, 10–13, 15, 70, 120, 126,
    130–135; as patron of Buddhism, 14–16, 38,
    126; on print media, 192n49; recognition of
    Thathanabaing, 11, 14–17, 38, 61, 173n52,
    180n16; state *vs.* religious authority under,
    10–17, 146–154, 158n15; temperance and, 100,
    186n79; transition from Burmese to, 1, 23–25;
    viceroy, 14, 30, 128. *See also* education
Brown, George E. R. Grant, 49
Brown, Ian, 182n32
Buddhabatha Thathana Pyu Association
    (Society for Promoting Buddhism), 69, 79
Buddhaghosa, 27. *See also* Shin Buddhaghosa
    School

OTHER VOLUMES IN THE SERIES